BADD NEWZ

THE UNTOLD STORY OF THE
MICHAEL VICK

DOG FIGHTING CASE

Copyright © 2009 Dog Fighting Investigation Publications LLC. All Rights Reserved.

BADD NEWZ

THE UNTOLD STORY OF THE MICHAEL VICK DOG FIGHTING CASE

KATHY STROUSE
with DOG ANGEL

TABLE OF CONTENTS

INTRODUCTION
CAST OF CHARACTERS
1 THE KILLING FIELDS
2 TOUCHDOWN
3 THE PIT GAME
4 THE SEARCH
5 THE PLOT THICKENS
6 DOG ANGEL
7 THE PIT BULL TERRIER
8 THE VICTIMS
9 CLIMBING ABOARD THE ROLLERCOASTER
10 THE ROAD LESS TRAVELED
11 A MEDIA FEEDING FRENZY
PICTURES
12 LIKE A BAD MOVIE
13 THE RISE OF BADD NEWZ KENNELS
14 MICHAEL DWAYNE VICK
15 THE CASE COMES TOGETHER
16 CRASH
17 VICK TAKES A PLEA
18 VICK FUMBLES
19 THE SENTENCE
20 THE DOGS GO TO NEW HOMES
21 AFTERMATH
EPILOGUE
ACKNOWLEDGEMENTS
GLOSSARY OF TERMS
BIBLIOGRAPHY

INTRODUCTION

Criminal behavior by wealthy and spoiled professional athletes is nothing new. DUIs, illegal drugs and gambling, assaults, night club shootings-even murders for hire-have often been little more than footnotes in the national media. No one was prepared for the way the Michael Vick dog fighting case would capture the hearts of the American public.

Prior to this case, dog fighting was something most people never even imagined. If they had heard of it at all, they believed only lowest and most ignorant members of society engaged in such behavior. Michael Vick put an entirely new face to animal cruelty and to dog fighting. Admired and wealthy beyond most people's dreams, the public was shocked and appalled, demanding to know, "Why?"

Never before did ordinary people take to the streets demanding the ouster of a professional athlete. The visceral response to the cruelty and the brutal slayings of the dogs from Vick's fighting kennel caught even seasoned and cynical journalists by surprise. The investigation became the top story for virtually every major news outlet in the country.

This book is the story of how the Michael Vick case was made, and the challenges investigators faced at every turn. Those who love animals will learn about the tremendous courage and determination of those who dared to pit themselves against a man of fame and fortune. It was the right thing to do—because cruelty to animals and dog fighting are despicable and brutal crimes no matter who commits them. One particular and poetic irony stands out in this case. It was a drug sniffing dog that "hit on" the car driven by Michael Vick's cousin, Davon Boddie, in Hampton, Virginia on April 20, 2007. That very night the dominos began to fall in the Badd Newz Kennels' brutal exploitation of innocent animals because of a dog!

For the first time, the reader will go behind the scenes to share in the undercover investigation; the struggles, betrayals, plots, schemes and strategies that finally led to justice for the perpetrators and for their innocent victims. The majority of the material contained in these pages has never before been made public.

The stakes in this case were extremely high. The combined efforts of Assistant U.S. Attorney Mike Gill, USDA Office of the Inspector General (OIG) Special Agent Jim Knorr, Surry County Deputy Bill Brinkman, the Virginia State Police Drug Task Force, many Animal Control Officers, the Virginia Animal Fighting Task Force (VAFTF), the Humane Society of the United States (HSUS), undercover operative Dog Angel, the Virginia Animal Control Association (VACA) and many others were required. One of the driving forces for all of us was the knowledge that if Vick and his crew walked, all of the dogs would be returned to their life of torture and cruelty. Badd Newz Kennels would go back to business as usual. And, our failure would send a clear message to the youth of America who admired, looked up to and emulated the Falcons Quarterback. "If Mike can do it, it must be cool."

The Vick case ultimately had a profoundly positive effect on dog fighting. Before Michael Vick, law enforcement was often reluctant to act in these cases, even though HSUS estimates that in 80% of dog fighting arrests, other crimes such as illegal drugs and guns are found. Ironically, the drug dealers who take elaborate steps to insulate their illicit trade are often more vulnerable through their dog fighting activity.

This is the story of the most infamous dog fighting investigation in American history.

CAST OF CHARACTERS

Virginia O: Old school dog fighter, breeder and referee; set up matches for Badd Newz Kennels, acted as an advisor to the Badd Newz crew, and served as referee for dog fights

Badd Newz Kennels: Dog fighting kennel owned by Michael Vick in partnership with Purnell Peace, Quanis Phillips, and Tony Taylor; kennel allegedly named after the nickname for Newport News where Vick and Phillips grew up

Blank, Arthur: Atlanta Falcons Football Team owner

Boddie, Davon: Cousin to Michael Vick; his drug arrest in Hampton, Virginia in April of 2007 led authorities to the dog fighting operation known as Badd Newz Kennels

Brinkman, Bill: Surry County, Virginia Deputy Sheriff and member of the Virginia State Police Drug Task Force; chief investigator for the Badd Newz Kennels case

Brown, Harold: Surry County, Virginia Sheriff

Butts, Benjamin: AKA "Benny"; owner of Hardcore Kennels in Surry County; long time dog fighter who became an associate of Badd Newz Kennels, moving dogs and training equipment to the Badd Newz location; trained and conditioned dogs for Badd Newz Kennels; ousted in 2006 after a falling out with Vick

Cheynoweth, Ann: Director of the Animal Cruelty and Fighting Campaign HSUS

Dinkins, Beth: USDA Office of the Inspector General (OIG) Special Agent

Dog Angel: Alias of undercover dog fighting investigator responsible for 100's of convictions for illegal dog fighting in the United States since the late 1970s. Ongoing cases include those in the US and Europe

Dohrman, George: Reported for *Sports Illustrated* magazine and author of the article "The House on Moonlight Road"

Gianotto, Allison: Web administrator for Pet-Abuse.com

Gill, Michael: Assistant US Attorney for the Eastern District of the United States; assigned to prosecute the federal Badd Newz Kennels case

Goodell, Roger: National Football League Commissioner

Goodwin, John: Manager Animal Fighting Issues the Humane Society of the United States (HSUS)

Hudson, Henry: Judge for the US District Court for the Eastern District of Virginia

Huss, Rebecca: Animal-law expert and professor from Valparaiso University School of Law assigned as guardian to the 53 seized pit bulls

Kilgore, Kevin: Animal Control Supervisor from Hanover, Virginia and president of the Virginia Animal Control Association (VACA)

Knorr, Jim: USDA Office of the Inspector General (OIG) Special Agent; chief investigator for the federal case against Badd Newz Kennels

Kumpf, Mark: President National Animal Control Association (NACA)

Merck, DVM, Melinda: Forensic Veterinarian employed by the American Society for the Prevention of Cruelty to Animals (ASPCA) and pioneer in the use of forensics in the prosecution of animal abuse and animal fighting cases

Mims, Carl: Owner of the Bona Fide Kennel Registry for pit bull dogs, and unwitting source of information about owners of fighting dogs

Peace, Purnell: AKA "P-Funk"; owner of Too Bad Kennels and Badd Newz Kennels partner; cousin of Tony Taylor

Phillips, Quanis: AKA "Q"; childhood friend of Michael Vick and Badd Newz Kennels partner

Poindexter, Gerald: Surry County, Virginia Commonwealth Attorney (Prosecutor)

Rattay, Nicole: Representative of Bay Area Doglovers Responsible About Pitbulls (Bad Rap) sent to Virginia to work with the seized Vick pit bulls

Reynolds, Phillip: AKA "Fat Bill"; Convicted on federal charges relating to dog fighting; his unwitting intelligence led arrests and convictions for a number of other dog fighters

Samuels, Richard: President Virginia Animal Fighting Task Force (VAFTF)

Strouse, Kathy: Animal Control Superintendent Chesapeake, Virginia; legislative liaison Virginia Animal Control Association (VACA) and member Board of Directors Virginia Animal Fighting Task Force (VAFTF)

Taylor, Tony: AKA "T" or "Chief"; Badd Newz Kennels partner ousted in 2004; cousin of Purnell Peace

Vick, Michael Dwayne: AKA "Ookie"; former Atlanta Falcons Quarterback; chief owner and administrator of Badd Newz Kennels

Virginia Animal Fighting Task Force: (VAFTF) Made up of law enforcement, animal control officers, prosecutors, members of HSUS and veterinarians, this group provides assistance to jurisdictions throughout Virginia in the investigation and prosecution of animal fighters

Welch, Michelle: Member Board of Directors Virginia Animal Fighting Task Force (VAFTF); former Deputy Commonwealth Attorney for Richmond, Virginia

Wright, Kelvin: Chesapeake Police Department Major and eventual Chief of Police

CHAPTER 1 THE KILLING FIELDS

It was warm for April. An unusually mild Virginia winter had eased almost imperceptibly into a balmy spring. There were sounds of young men playing a game of hoops on the court behind the opulent white house on the winding country road at 1915 Moonlight Road. The small church across the street was deserted. There were no services that evening. The laughter from the young men drifted beyond the court to the "yard" where four other men were engaged in more serious work.

    P-Funk, Q, and Ookie were disgusted. The three, who preferred to be known by their nicknames, had been "rolling" or testing dogs to evaluate their potential as money generating fighters. Two by two, they dragged the eight prospects up the ladder to the second floor of the black painted building behind the large, graceful white mansion. The entire upstairs room was a pit—a place where dogs are fought, sometimes to the death. The interior of this room was also painted black, but the smears and stains of blood could still be seen and told a chilling story. There was a boom box in one corner and several folding chairs. Two by two P-Funk and Q forced the dogs to face each other holding them nose to nose. They shoved them towards their opponent, preventing their escape until the dogs had no choice but to defend themselves. Virginia O was on hand to supervise and give expert advice. From the old school of "dogmen", as fighters call themselves, Virginia O was in his 60's and was well known and respected in dog fighting circles. It was he who arranged or "hooked up" men with a good dog looking for a cash fight or "match." The other three men were much younger.

    The tests were disappointing. None of the eight dogs sparked any real excitement in the men. The ones that fought at all did so for only a few minutes before giving up. A couple refused to fight at all. Virginia O shrugged and dragged one of the dogs down the ladder to the ground floor once again. Grabbing a garden hose, he began to rinse the blood and saliva off of the dog, remembering as he worked many better fighting dogs. Dogs like Striper, P-Funk, Q and Virginia O had taken him to a fight in North Carolina earlier that year. P-Funk had driven that cold night-bitterly cold for such a mild winter. The men had turned off Route 258 and traveled down a long dirt road. Finally they had come to a house where a crowd of people milled about. Behind a high wooden fence was a "yard" of pit bulls. Inside the small house was equipment used to train fighting dogs. From here, the three men had joined another group and had driven further down the dirt road to a house on the right hand side. At the rear of the back yard, a clearing among the trees served as the "pit" for the fight. It had been a good battle. Striper had fought well, refusing to quit, proving that he was "game". P-Funk, Q and Virginia O had been elated by Striper's win. They had not had to report to Ookie that his stake money had been lost. Instead, they had taken home the purse.

Virginia O placed the wet dog in one of the kennels to the right of the black "pit" building. The other kennels were occupied by Rottweiler's, beagles, Presa Canarios, and pit bulls, including the ones that had been tested this evening. The basketball game was still going on. He turned as he heard P-Funk approach. P-Funk asked him if to help out by hosing down the dog kennels to remove the urine and feces. He had some other work to do. When he finished, he said, he would be back to "feed up".

Virginia O washed down the kennels and then strolled back into the woods where 30 more pit bulls were restrained by heavy chains attached to car axles buried deep in the ground. He usually visited the Moonlight Road property about once a month. At one time his visits had been weekly, but he had become frustrated. These young guys not only did not know what they were doing when it came to grooming fighting dogs, they refused to listen to someone who did.

P-Funk returned to the black pit building where Q and Ookie waited impatiently. The men had already made their decision. Only good fighting dogs were worth the food it took to keep them. A good fighting dog was one that had the drive and determination to fight to the death, whether it was his own or his opponent's. The eight prospects this night had all failed the test, so they had to go. Together the men drowned two of the dogs in a five gallon bucket of water. They hanged all but one of the others. The men made a noose from a nylon rope and looped it around the neck of each of the dogs, one by one. The other end of the rope was attached to a board that had been nailed to one of the trees that grew in the yard behind the pit building near the kennels. The kenneled dogs were forced to watch the brutal executions. They had no escape. The strangling dogs panicked, kicking and flailing as they fought against the noose that tightened cutting off their air. Their eyes bulged. They lost control of their bladders and bowels.

One witness would later tell investigators that a red pit bull continued struggling against the noose that night, valiantly refusing to die. Ookie became annoyed. This was taking too long. He grabbed the dog up and jerked off the nylon rope. Q would later admit that he grabbed one end of the dog; Ookie the other. Together they slammed the dog onto the ground several times with such force they fractured its skull, neck and several ribs.

Unaware of what was happening at the kennels, Virginia O wandered among the 30 pit bulls, checking their chains. Often he found collars that were too tight, or dogs that actually had raw spots from where the collars had irritated their necks. He bent down to adjust a collar. The dog refused to be still. Grateful for even this small attention, the animal's entire rear end wagged while he nudged the man with his head and panted excitedly. Virginia O glanced up at the sound of the engine from the "4 X 4". Two young men were driving the small vehicle towards the woods. He knew one of them. He started to call out to him, but suddenly stopped, his gaze frozen on the back of the "4 X 4". There were the eight dogs. Their limp bodies were splayed on top of each other. Tongues were hanging out; eyes were bulging. Virginia O was stunned. He could still hear the laughter and shouts floating towards the woods from the basketball court as if everything were normal.

    He felt as if there was a great weight on his chest, a heaviness pressing him down. He could not believe things had come to this. Like some old school mafia bosses, old school dog fighters like Virginia O had a code of ethics despite their illegal activities. These young men had no such code. They showed no mercy or compassion for any of the dogs they used and abused.

    Virginia O believed that good dogs needed patience and training. Game fighters had to be nurtured and developed. Game is the term used for a dog that has the tenacity, will, and drive to stay in the pit and to fight beyond its own endurance, exhaustion, and sometimes even its own survival. This quality is prized beyond all others by dogmen. But Virginia O knew even game dogs did not win all of the time. He remembered a "show" featuring several "matches", or fights, that these same young men had hosted here at Moonlight Road in 2002. Ookie had been present. One fight was between Junior Mafia's Floyd and Virginia O's Shorty. Floyd had prevailed over Shorty in 42 minutes. In spite of this, Shorty was named "gamest dog in show", because although he was severely wounded, he continued to fight on.

    The best dog Ookie ever had was one that Virginia O had sold to P-Funk's cousin, a man who went by the nickname of "Chief". Originally called Blaze, Chief changed the dog's name to Jane. Jane later became a champion, winning three fights.

    Apparently unwilling to be guided even by the man who provided this champion dog, Ookie bought dogs Virginia O could see at once were "no good". Ookie had recently paid $5,000 to a man named Carl Mims in North Carolina for a "pure red boy" dog. Mims was well known as a pit bull breeder, and his dogs figure prominently in the pedigrees of many champion fighting pit bulls. Mims also administers the Bona Fide Kennel Club pit bull registry, one of the most popular registries on the east coast for fighting dogs. Maybe this new Mims dog would turn out to be something, but Virginia O doubted it. Mims would be a fool to sell a really good prospect to these guys.

    "These guys were like the gang that couldn't shoot straight," Virginia O would one day explain. "If you told them, see this cup here. It is for cold only. Don't put anything hot in this cup. It'll crack. They would go right ahead and put hot in it." Ookie and his friends were not serious enough about the pit dog game. They would rather hang out and smoke dope. That was one reason, Virginia O said, he started staying away from the property. Another was "too many crack heads".

    Virginia O had fought dogs for many years. But what he saw in Ookie and his friends that night turned his stomach. Virginia O left Moonlight Road never to return.

CHAPTER 2 TOUCHDOWN

I expected Wednesday, April 25, 2007 to be a quiet day; even though we hesitate to use that word at Chesapeake Animal Control. We usually call it the "Q" word. We are careful not to actually say the word out loud, because we don't want to jinx ourselves. So, I was hoping for a "Q" day. We are closed on Wednesdays, and I use the day to catch up on paperwork and projects. My name is Kathy Strouse, and I am the Animal Control Superintendent for the Chesapeake Police Department in Virginia.

We had just finished our weekly staff meeting, and I strolled back up front to my office ready to tackle my day. Animal Control was out of money, and it was only April. The Police Department had agreed to transfer enough money to our budget to get us through to June 30, the end of the fiscal year. My job this day was to dive into the fascinating world of budget calculations, and compute just how much this would take.

In an effort to postpone the inevitable, I decided to check my e-mail first. There was a message from Kevin Kilgore, the president of the Virginia Animal Control Association (VACA). VACA is the organization that represents Virginia animal control officers (ACOs). Our mission is to improve the profession of animal control—working conditions, compensation, training and status. I was a board member myself, serving as the legislative liaison, so it was not unusual to hear from Kevin or other board members. I could not know that this message would change everything and pitch me headlong into the biggest case of my life.

Kevin's message read that he had received a call from a very new ACO in Surry County, Virginia. ACO James Smith was asking for assistance on a possible dog fighting case. Kevin did not know if things were at the activation point yet, but urged anyone who could help to give the ACO a call. By activation point, Kevin meant bringing in the newly formed Virginia Animal Fighting Task Force (VAFTF). The task force had been formed to combat rampant animal fighting in Virginia.

There had already been a number of successful prosecutions in our state. In Richmond, 40 year old Stacey Miller had just been convicted of felony dog fighting, two counts of felony animal cruelty, multiple counts of misdemeanor cruelty, and possession of steroids. He had been sentenced to four years in prison, fined $20,000 and prohibited from owning companion (pet) animals. I had recently testified for the first time as an expert witness in the case of Alfred Charles Taylor in Chesapeake Circuit Court. Taylor had been convicted of dog fighting, possession of marijuana, and possession with intent to distribute cocaine. He was awaiting sentencing. His girlfriend, Lisa Washington would later be convicted of the same charges.

Suddenly the budget crisis was the last thing on my mind. As fast as my fingers could move, I typed a reply to Kevin promising to call Surry ACO James Smith. My intuition told me that dog fighting in Surry County, Virginia could only mean two people, Hardcore Benny Butts or Michael Vick.

Back in 2000, Surry County Deputy Sheriff Bill Brinkman conducted a search of Butts' property. Members of the State Drug Task Force had been doing routine flyovers of rural areas, as part of the Marijuana Eradication Program. The officers observed what they believed to be marijuana plants growing on the property of one Benny Butts. A visit to the property confirmed the presence of a healthy marijuana crop. On the property, the officers also found approximately 30 pit bulls on heavy tow chains and assorted fighting paraphernalia.

ACOs, including some from Chesapeake, were called in to assist with the execution of a search warrant for dog fighting. They found a huge dog fighting operation that included dogs, equipment, paraphernalia, publications, drugs and weapons. It was a classically beautiful textbook dog fighting case.

The ACOs had no way of knowing while they were collecting the dogs and fight paraphernalia that this case was doomed. Deputies had not waited for the initial drug search warrant before entering the property and removing marijuana plants. Deputy Brinkman always maintained that Butts had arrived home that day and given his consent for the search of the property. As the officers searched, they had found the dogs and the training equipment. They then secured a search warrant for dog fighting. Butts had even confessed to dog fighting in a written statement to Brinkman.

"I, Ben Butts, give this statement to Deputy W. Brinkman at the Surry County Sheriff Department concerning dog charges. Mainly the 33 dogs located at my resident (sic) which were either involved in dog fighting or being raised for dog fighting. Not all these dogs belong to myself, I do bored (sic) pit bulls for other people, I do have knowledge of other people, places and activity."

According to Brinkman, the local prosecutor, Gerald Poindexter, refused to defend the search when the defense challenged it. Poindexter, he said, stated he did not believe in consent searches. The charges were dismissed; the dogs and all of the evidence were returned to Butts. He was never again questioned about any of the information at which he had hinted. Hardcore Kennels went back to business as usual.

I remembered all too well the 2000 case and its outcome. It had left a rancid taste in my mouth at the time, and I had real concerns about involving our department with Surry County again. I was thinking of all of this as I dialed the number for Surry County ACO James Smith. He was a new officer who had just completed his basic training at a regional animal control academy. He told me he thought he was about to embark on a very big dog fighting case. He said he was glad to hear from me, because he needed someone knowledgeable about dog fighting. Would I help him? I would know what to do and how to do it right. I had been one of his instructors at the animal control academy. ACO Smith asked me if I could mobilize a team and prepare to respond if he needed us. I would check with my bosses, I replied.

I called Major Kelvin Wright. The epitome of a gentleman and a renaissance man, Wright is fortyish with a hearty laugh and a mega watt smile. About 5 feet 10, with a moustache, and just beginning to gray, Major Wright always looks like he just stepped off the pages of GQ. He is soft spoken, caring, thoughtful, articulate, dedicated and brilliant. I told the Major what was happening, and how anxious I was to participate. He asked if I knew who the suspect was. I told him I had an idea, but did not know for sure. I asked for permission to take some of my officers with me to assist if we got the call. He did not hesitate for a moment; he just said, "go".

I promised to let the Major know the moment I got a call, and we hung up. The rest of the day passed without a word from ACO Smith. My mind was a million miles away. I was on pins and needles jumping every time the telephone rang. This state of hyper alertness was exhausting. I struggled to keep my mind on the columns of numbers churning from my calculator. They insisted on fading into visions of what might be happening in Surry. Who was it? Could it possibly be.....? No, I could not even allow the name to fully form in my thoughts. How many dogs would be there? Would they be wounded? What if the press showed up? What else would we find? Would the outcome be the same as the 2000 case?

Finally I forced myself to finish the budget transfer request. Still the call did not come. There was nothing more I could do. I gave up and headed for home. I had just finished feeding my own two dogs when the phone rang at 5:45 p.m. It was ACO Smith. Would we come? I told him I would call my people and be on the way. I asked him who it was. Smith said he would tell me when I got there. I had to be satisfied with that. We were to meet him at the BP gas station at the corner of routes 258 and 10 in Surry. There was no need to change clothes. I was still in my uniform, superstitiously willing the call to come. I alerted the other officers, Melanie Tobin, Tracy Stevens and brand new Kathleen Perry. I then called Major Wright and told him it was a "go". We were off to Surry County.

From the BP station, we followed ACO Smith down route 10 until we came to Moonlight Drive on the left just past the bridge. The country road twisted and turned. Finally, I could see a huge many faceted white house in the distance on the left hand side of the road. Across the street was a small church. Smith turned into the driveway. My stomach lurched. This was a mansion, and it certainly did not belong to Benny Butts. I had seen this house before. It belonged to Michael Vick.

We turned into the driveway at 1915 Moonlight Road behind Smith. We could see several police officers already on scene. There were State Police Officers, ACOs from Isle of Wight and Southampton Counties, and local sheriff deputy, Bill Brinkman, who was still assigned to the State Police Drug Task Force. I recognized Brinkman from the Butts case seven years earlier. He was in plain clothes wearing a red polo shirt and khakis. His unruly sandy was hair was brushed back from his forehead, and his mouth was set under a bushy moustache. Brinkman is the definition of a "good ole boy", but without the slow southern drawl. Instead words tumble from his mouth in rush as if they can barely keep pace with is thoughts.

I stood for a moment at the side of the road, remembering the last time I had seen this house. Two years earlier, in 2005, I had stood in exactly this same spot. I had been visiting a friend, local business man, Rex Riley. Rex knew about my obsession with tracking dog fighters. He told me that football player Michael Vick had built a house in Surry. We discussed the rumors that were rife both in the animal welfare community and in Surry County that Vick was a dog fighter. Rex believed them. According to him, it was an open secret in Surry that Vick was fighting dogs. Rex told me that neighbors on Moonlight Road had talked to him about the dog fights that were held on Vick's property. He also said he had recently been to the Surry Hardware Store where Vick was leaving after purchasing $600 worth of dog food. I asked Rex how Vick got away with it. Rex laughed and shrugged his shoulders. I took this to mean that if Vick was fighting dogs, he must know he had nothing to fear from local authorities. I remembered Rex asked me if I wanted to see the house. Of course I did! That fall day we took a ride down Moonlight Road.

Now I stood there again, remembering the first time I had seen the huge white house with its several facets and wings behind the white faux wrought iron fence. I remembered craning my neck looking at the black buildings beyond the house—the same black buildings I was looking at now. At the time I had yearned to get a better look at the property, to see any dogs that might be there. But it was impossible. I was out of my jurisdiction, and there was absolutely no probable cause to enter the property. Two years ago there had been nothing to do but climb back into the car.

Tonight I had come full circle.

CHAPTER 3 THE PIT GAME

Dog fighters almost never use the word fight. They talk about the "game", "show", "match", "roll", or "bump". Because stake money can be many thousands of dollars, sanctioned fights often include written contracts. The contracts stipulate the date of the match, the names, sexes and weights of the two dogs to be fought. Males are fought with males and females with females. Contracts will also specify the stake money, forfeiture terms, the name of the referee, and the rules by which the dogs will be fought. Although dog fighting rules can vary slightly, most follow a traditional structure based on the infamous Cajun Rules written by one time Lafayette Louisiana Police Chief Gaboon Trahan.

One piece of information usually omitted from a contract is the actual location of the fight. Fueled both by the knowledge that their actions are illegal and by their own paranoia, fighters will arrange to meet at a neutral location. The promoter or person hosting the fight will lead the group to the actual location, once he is certain that they have not been followed and are safe from detection by law enforcement.

The period of preparation for a dog fight is called the "keep". Usually about six weeks in length, it is designed to strengthen the dog and increase his stamina and endurance. Dietary supplements, vitamins, hormones, and even steroids may be used as part of the program. Exercise, using equipment such as treadmills and cat mills or jennies is also a key component. The goal is to deliver a well conditioned dog at the agreed upon weight by the day of the fight. The owner of a dog who is overweight on the day of the fight will have to pay a penalty to his opponent known as a forfeit. One of the most well known keep programs was developed over 30 years ago by a man named Ben Colopy, AKA "Barney Fife", an infamous dog fighter. This keep has been published many times in various dog fighting publications and can still be downloaded from the internet. Using his alias, Barney Fife he also wrote a number of "educational" articles for underground publications that provided instruction on the ins and outs of the game.

I actually met Ben Colopy in the 1980's when I was a young shelter director for an SPCA. One of our investigators had been working with local animal control on a case that involved the seizure of two pit bulls. Colopy came to our shelter and introduced himself to me as a veterinary technician from Maryland. He warned me about people who would misuse this wonderful breed, and deplored the crime of dog fighting. He even gave an interview for a local television station. I was so naïve that I had absolutely no idea who he was. I had barely begun to delve into the morbidly fascinating world of the degenerates who called this brutal pastime a sport. Once I realized who he was, it was too late. I never saw Colopy again.

In Virginia, where Ben Colopy set up his dog fighting operation, he became good friends with a variety of dogmen who were impressed by his knowledge and ability with the dogs. By then his entire life centered around two addictions-dog fighting and drugs. He was so committed to the dog game that he even took a job as a weights and measures inspector so that he could to travel throughout Virginia and visit the various fighting kennels that operated in the state. Even his choice of a girlfriend was dictated by dog fighting. She was a veterinarian. Unfortunately for Colopy, as soon as she found out about his favorite pastime, she ended the relationship.

Dog fighters do not typically take their injured dogs to a veterinarian for fear of being reported. Horribly mangled dogs are frequently returned to their chains or kennels without any treatment even if they were winners. They go into shock from the terrible blood loss and organ damage. A West Virginia dog fighter used a backhoe to dig huge holes around his property into which injured dogs that were still breathing would be unceremoniously dumped and buried alive. Another example was a dog fighter, known as Big Thicket. After his Grand Champion Ajax defeated Champion Noriega in a fight that lasted an hour and 10 minutes, Big Thicket simply stuffed Ajax into a kennel and shipped him home from New York City on an overnight commercial flight. Ajax died two days later.

Other dog fighters are slightly less callous, and they try to provide some type of care for their dogs after fights. Once upon a time they sought out men like Ben Colopy. Colopy was not only known for his infamous *Barney Fife's Keep*, he was also considered an excellent triage specialist. Over the years, Colopy had so honed his skills that dogmen swore there was no one like him for ability to bring an injured dog back from the brink of death. Colopy warmed injured dogs with electric blankets, administered IV fluids and injected them with antibiotics other drugs. Had Colopy chosen another path, he might have been a veterinarian, a nurse or a teacher. Instead, Colopy's life ended when he died of a drug overdose in 1998.

Although dog fighters come and go, the game continues, and the fights follow the same general rules and procedures. Upon arrival at a dog fight, dogs are weighed. Forfeits, if any are paid. The purse for a fight usually equals the stake money minus some fees. These include a fee for the promoter, who sets up, arranges and often hosts the fight, and the fee for the referee. Entrance fees for spectators and side bets between them generate more money. After the weigh in, the dogs are both washed. The purpose of the bath is to remove any caustic substance that a crooked owner may have put on his dog to discourage his opponent from biting. Each man washes his opponent's dog, usually while a friend of the opponent watches this process, again to prevent any foul play. The dogs are then returned to their owners.

Today, dog fighting has become a favorite pastime among drug dealers. They have the means to bet staggering amounts of money. Add the "street bling" that comes with earning a title of top game dog, and there is an irresistible temptation to cheat. In the dog world, the use of drugs and performance enhancing steroids is not considered cheating, and is quite common. Many a high end dogman uses steroids. The dosage and keep instructions are found on the internet and discussed openly. But a number of other practices are considered cheating. The most common of these is a known as a rub.

One such rub is made by boiling down chewing tobacco, drying out the thick paste, and grinding it to a fine powder. The result is Nicotine Sulfate, a very potent drug. A variety of shampoos are specifically designed to remove any rubs, so, a sly dogman will keep the Nicotine Sulfate powder hidden until after the washing and the dogs are placed in the pit. Then he applies the rub to selected areas. The opposing dog will not want to bite him, even in a fight for his life. There are risks to this tactic because the second way Nicotine Sulfate works is that when absorbed through the skin, it causes the heart to begin racing and can lead to severe overheating or even a heart attack.

A dog fighter who often used rubs, according to an undercover investigator, was Phillip AKA Fat Bill Reynolds. Fat Bill was disdained by many dog fighters who claimed he would go to any lengths to disparage a man's reputation behind his back. At one time he was the publisher of an underground magazine called *The American Game Dog Times*. In most issues Fat Bill wrote an editorial column in which he shared gossip from the dog game. On one occasion he wrote about a dog fighter's wife claiming that when a dogman brought a dog to a certain kennel for breeding, he would get more than a stud service for the dog. The wife, Fat Bill claimed, provided sexual favors to the visitors.

Fat Bill would often instruct one of his yard boys to put Nicotine Sulfate in between the foot pads of their opponents' dogs as he was removed from the wash. He would apply Vaseline to his yard boy's hands to make sure he did not absorb the powder himself. About 10 minutes into the fight, the opposing dog would begin to overheat, and Fat Bill's dog would win.

A rub that can remain undetected is highly prized because of the huge sums of cash often on the line. One time Super Kennels had three dogs matched against Latin Force Kennels and Cuban Missing Link. Over $250,000 was on the line. Super Kennels had lost before to both kennels and wanted revenge, so they hired the number one chemical expert in the dog game at that time, a Virginia drug dealer known as Bones from Vietnam Kennels. Super Kennels paid Bones $25,000 to develop a rub that would ensure victory. Bones did his job superbly, and all three of the Super Kennels dogs won. During the celebration after the fights, one of the Super Kennels guys called the home of the Latin Force Kennels owner, and the wife answered. The man reminded her that they had met at the fight earlier. The only problem was the wife had not been at the fight. The woman the man had seen was her husband's girl friend. Enraged, the wife promptly removed a couple of floorboards in her home, picked up her husband's $2 million in cash, tipped off the local police to her husband's activities, packed up her children and left.

Another common way to cheat is to sharpen the dogs' teeth. Using a dremel tool, the shaft of the tooth is sharpened. Since cheating is expected, most dogmen will check the tips of the teeth on their opponent's dog, but not the side. Once a dog with sharpened teeth bites and breaks the skin of the other dog, he begins to shake allowing the sharpened teeth to do maximum damage. Fat Bill also used the teeth sharpening method. His former yard boys likened Fat Bill to a Nazi concentration camp officer who conducted experiments using a variety of methods and drugs on his live victims. In 2001, Fat Bill was convicted on federal cruelty charges stemming from the sale of video tapes depicting dog fights. When sentencing him, Federal Judge Samuel Wilson said he was shocked by Reynolds' "insensitivity to life." Reynolds served 30 months in federal prison and was required to pay a fine of $10,000 plus costs of the case.

Finally, when all the preparations and cheating are completed, the dogs are placed into the pit. A dog fighting pit is usually an area approximately 16 X 20 feet. Pits can be a room, a clearing in the woods, a sunken automotive bay, an empty swimming pool, an enclosure formed by hay bales, or sections of plywood that hinge together for easy set up and take down. Across opposite corners of the pit, there may be painted, taped or drawn scratch lines, behind which, the owner or handler holds his dog between his knees, as both face the corner. Outside of each corner will be the handler's "corner man", or assistant, and a man from his opponent's team to watch over things. Only the two handlers and the referee are allowed in the pit.

At the referee's command, both handlers will turn and "face" their dogs from behind the scratch lines. The referee's next command will be to release the dogs. Both dogs must charge across the pit and attack their opponent. Handlers will often be on their hands and knees with their own faces inches away from the battling dogs. They may hoot, holler, clap hands and otherwise encourage their own dog, but neither handler may touch a dog until ordered to do so by the referee. The need to be so close to the dogs during a fight illustrates clearly why "man biters" have historically been ruthlessly "culled" from breeding programs and destroyed.

The fight continues until there is a "turn", which means one dog turns its head and shoulders away from its opponent without trying to reinitiate the attack. If a turn is called, the dogs will be sent to their corners and rested for approximately 20-30 seconds. The handlers will sponge off blood and saliva. At the referee's command, the dogs will be faced. The dog that turned is released first; it is his job to race across the pit and to attack his opponent. This is called a "scratch". The opposing handler will carefully watch the approach to determine the most strategic time to release his own dog; too soon and he will not have determined that the opposing dog is coming the full distance; too late and his dog may be at a disadvantage. From this point on when things slow down, or the dogs are "out of holds", they will take turns scratching. Referees will also call a "handle" for the dogs if one is fanged, or has caught his lip on his tooth. It is possible for fights to last for hours, leaving the dogs heaving, so exhausted and out of breath that they can no longer advance the carnage, but only hold on to their opponents. The longest reported fight was six hours. If it becomes necessary to forcibly separate the dogs, "break sticks" are used to pry their jaws apart in order to release their hold on their opponent. The fight ends when one dog is counted out for failing to scratch, a dog dies, or a handler picks up his dog conceding the fight.

A handler picking up a dog can follow proper etiquette and offer his opponent a scratch to win. This allows the winner to show that his dog is ready to fight on. In turn, a handler who decides to pick up his dog may be offered a courtesy scratch. This allows him to show that, although he is conceding the match, his dog is still "game" and willing to continue.

A dog becomes a champion when he or she wins three sanctioned matches. A grand champion is a dog that wins five consecutive matches. A grand champion cannot have a loss in his record, and would revert to champion status if such a thing occurred. Becoming a champion or a grand champion increases a dog's value for breeding. Puppies of champions command high prices. Another important designation is ROM, or Register of Merit. ROM is conferred on a male that has produced five champions or a female that has produced four champions. Puppies from dogs that are ROM command high prices, because of the perceived likelihood that they too will be good fighters.

A common trait among dog fighters is the tendency to talk as if they had been in the pit instead of their dogs. A Maryland dog fighter and drug dealer, who did not have an ounce of his dog's athletic ability, used to describe his matches, "Yeah, he got on my nose but I didn't holler, I worked my way into his mouth and did my dental work on his lower teeth; then I went into his back end, where he started hollering. I knew I had him". Dogmen will often liken these battles, in which they force man's best friend to participate, to football games and boxing matches. They ignore the obvious fact that boxers and ball players are not tearing their opponents apart with razor sharp teeth, snapping bones, disemboweling their opponents, and even tearing off faces. The real truth about the carnage can often be gleaned from the underground magazines themselves.

The poorly punctuated and barely grammatical story of the first fight of "Fat Bill's Two Eyes" could be found on the internet as late as 2008. His owner cared nothing for the fact that this dog could barely see his opponent.

"Two eye was sired by mountain mans bandit bred to ch bolero. He was the runt of the litter born blind in one eye and cloudy eye in the right eye. he got the name two eyes because my son said that was the only thing he would never have. He was a normal pup though he never let fact he was blind make him look or act like any other good dog."

"At 18 months he was schooled as he started young and was talented and needed little practice to know what he was bred for, the pit. First show was into over the hill's kennel cowboy, he was a two time winner. At the start of the match two eyes didn't start. I knew why I had bred him back secretly to his mother 2 times the week before the show, cowboy ran over and two eyes thought it was more sex, wrong and he got his ass kicked for 15 minutes. Soon he got his act together and by the hour mark he was way out front and over the hill's Keith asked if I would scratch to win. I agreed and we separated the dogs with sticks. The referee an inexperienced boy by the name of Brian debow was holding the stick and standing about 10 feet to my right. I am holding two eyes preparing to let go on release. The one "side" rule when we matched two eyes that was made was complete silence when he scratched as he was blind. Well the ref told us to face the dogs and I did, as I the ref drops the sticks on the floor and two eyes runs to the sticks I grab him back over the line and the crowd goes wild yelling "FOUL". Well it wasn't a foul the referee dropped the sticks. So at that point I just let him go he ran over to the other dog and the fight starts back up. Over the Hill's whines oh that's a foul , I said "fuck you, if you want to continue this by scratch and turn and watch your dog die, fine, if you want to pick up your dog fine, other wise sit back and watch the execution." They offered me another scratch to win, I knew he would go, I took the offer, made the ref set the sticks down on the floor outside the box before the scratch and two eyes flew across the box to win number 1. "

Another story attributed to Krazyside Kennels may be found on the internet describing a match between Champion Krazyside Kennels Nino and Champion Brickhouse Benny Blanco. Krazyside Kennels was the kennel of former professional football player LeShon Johnson, who was convicted of dog fighting in 2005. In that case 200 dogs were seized, and 20 people were convicted. Johnson himself received a five year deferred sentence. Oklahoma Bureau of Narcotics and Dangerous Drugs Agent Jim Ward worked undercover on that case and witnessed Johnson participating in dog fights. In the article, the author refers to himself as Eljaye. His pride in the fighting ability of his dog is as apparent as the lack of any concern for the horrific injury suffered by his dog.

"The day came and Nino was feeling good. Another 45 minute drive to the location and we entered the spot where both dogs were weighed and washed. Blanco was dead on at 46 and Nino as expected at 45. We released both dogs and before Nino really got out of the corner, Blanco got him by the front leg, shook and popped a serious bleeder. Within the first 30 seconds Blanco snapped Nino's ankle. I must admit, I began to worry a little and Nino began to peel him off by the nose. Nino and I both knew he had to keep Blanco off him or he could be seriously hurt. It was even for the first 40 minutes, however Nino showing to be the stronger dog. At 45 a turn is called on Nino, with Nino making a hard three legged scratch. By the hour mark we made a handle, and Blanco makes a hard scratch. Nino starts to take control of the match as he was biting hard on the head. At the 1:30 mark Nino began to make Blanco sing. I really began to cheer Nino on after 4 scratches each. At 1:48 Blanco is picked up and makes a slow courtesy scratch. Champion Nino is declared the winner. Ch. Nino has proven to us his ability to finish a dog quickly, his intelligence to adapt to his opponent, and his gameness in staying in it for the long haul without the use of Steroids."

A pedigree for Nino was posted on line in April of 2001. It included the notation, "Nino is a 4XW [4 time winner] in four states and a 1X B.O.S. [1 time Best of Show] He is 1 of only 5 AGDT [American Game Dog Times] Champions to date. He's an EXTREMELY strong, rough and intelligent bulldog. He is our definition of a TRUE game bulldog. He has proven himself game and has nerves of steel."

The author announces at the end of the article that Nino is being retired, and thanks "My brother/partner, Teddy, my brother-in-law E-Love, Vietnam Kennels, Black and Blue Kennels, Eric, (my yard man) and most of all my wife and the Lord for making this possible".

A fight description in one underground publication described a match between Grace's Champion Elmo and O Steven's Virgil, who would go on to be a grand champion.

"Virgil met Elmo in the corner and Elmo popped an artery in Virgil's muzzle and another one in his shoulder. By eight minutes Elmo had Virgil down. But Virgil was deep into the chest from the bottom. When under pressure Virgil seemed to lose his temper and sure showed it this day! For at the eight minute mark, he came off the bottom with Elmo's chest in his mouth and he pressed Elmo over his head. Elmo's front legs fell over Virgil's back while his legs were suspended in mid air. Virgil then threw Elmo into the pit wall. He made a flurry into the throat for a couple of minutes and switched to a belly and kidney hold. Virgil had unusually long fangs and he buried them up to the gum lines in his kidneys. Virgil let loose and then repeated this procedure two more times. After that Elmo was not fighting back. His owner gave up the fight at thirty minutes. But his dog died a short time later."

Another report not only illustrates how dogs are killed in fights, but also how easy it is to conduct fights—in a living room no less!

Chinaman was a dog that belonged to Tom Garner of North Carolina, a name well known in both the fight game and in law enforcement. Garner was convicted of attending a dog fight in 1983. Although the name Garner can frequently be found in the pedigrees of fighting dogs, he claims to be simply a breeder of pit bulls. If those to whom he sells dogs use them for illegal purposes, he is not responsible.

"Chinaman's next roll was into Doc, a highly respected wrecker. If he could hang with Doc for even 10 minutes, Chinaman would be worth a bet. Doc came out hard and slammed Chinaman into the corner and tried to trade with Chinaman. Big mistake! Chinaman hit the gut and killed the Doctor in his own living room in 17 minutes! It was clear Chinaman was something special."

Chinaman would go on to be both a champion and ROM. Southern Kennels Mayday would also become a grand champion and ROM.

"It was Mayday's easiest fight. He used Big Red like a punching bag. He mopped the floor with him. People watching wanted to change his name to PAYDAY...Others were calling him KILLING MACHINE... It ended with Mayday SCREAMING in the corner. He was just getting started. He wanted another hour..."

The Sporting Dog Journal, or *SDJ*, is arguably the most infamous of the underground dog fighting magazines. In its heyday, *SDJ* reported as many as 2000 fights a year. Dog fighters would submit reports of fights that had taken place and request certificates of championship. In addition to these, the magazine featured the championship announcements, dogs, puppies, and equipment for sale. It also featured articles and forums all devoted to the sport dog fighting. *SDJ* was not a publication one could pick up at Barnes and Noble or PetsMart. In order to subscribe, one needed a current subscriber to be a sponsor. In spite of the restriction, the magazine at its height had a subscription list of approximately 6,000 names. Former publishers of the magazine, James Fricchione and Jack Kelly were arrested in 2004, and *SDJ* ceased publication for a time. It resurfaced briefly for one issue only to die again in 2007. Fricchione and Kelly were convicted in Pennsylvania of conspiracy and promoting animal cruelty. Fricchione had already been sentenced in New York in 2004 to 2-7 years for one count of dog fighting and four counts of animal cruelty. He and Kelly received probation for the Pennsylvania charges.

When Jack Kelly alone published *SDJ* he set up an A and B section of the magazine. The A section contained fight reports involving participants and referees that he knew personally. The reports in this section were the ones he felt were the most reliable. The B section contained reports that he could not validate to know if the people submitting them really fought the dogs. Kelly had no idea how helpful he was to law enforcement.

In one of Fricchione's last issues, he published a statement, "As dog people we should take heed and make changes to insure (sic) our safety. Remember, the Humane Society has been raiding people's homes since the '70s and will continue their witch hunt for as long as the (pit bull) remains in existence."

The Fricchione convictions turned out to be a bittersweet victory. The demise of *SDJ* meant the end of one of the best vehicles for investigators to link the published fight reports to the people who participated. To understand the type of valuable information with which *SDJ* was filled, below is a typical fight report. These were traditionally terse and written in a thinly disguised code. In 2001, the 1116th fight reported was between Hell on Earth and Proset's Cock Diesel and Comin' Hard Kennel's Kennel Bother's Rutkus. This report read,

> 11/12/2001
> Hell on Earth and Proset's Cock Diesel + M48.5 Comin' Hard Kennel's Kennel Bother's Rutkus. Rutkus 2XW is Eli breeding. CD 2XW off GR CH Mayday/Proset's CH Sugar. CD behind and after 2 each Rutkus won't go at 1:15
> Winner: Hell on Earth and Proset's Cock Diesel

Decoding this report, one understands that this was a fight between two male dogs, Cock Diesel (CD) and Rutkus. Both dogs weighed 48 and ½ pounds, and both dogs had won two previous fights. CD was the son of Grand Champion Mayday and a champion mother named Sugar. The parents of Rutkus are not listed. The report states merely that he is from Eli breeding. Eli was a famous fighting dog that belonged to Floyd Boudreaux, often called the "godfather" of dog fighting. Boudreaux was arrested in Louisiana on dog fighting charges in 2005, but acquitted in 2008. Both dogs completed 2 scratches, but Rutkus would not continue the fight after one hour and 15 minutes. CD was declared the winner, thus making him a Champion.

Dog Fighting has always been about money. Huge amounts of money are at stake in these matches. In addition, a high quality fighting dog can be one of the most expensive dogs in the world. In 2003, a group known as Latin Force Kennels had a dog called Barracuda. He was a grand champion who had won nine fights and made over $750,000 for his owners. He was bred 65 times for a $1,500 stud fee each time. At age seven, Barracuda sold for $80,000.

Disagreements surrounding the sales of dogs are also common. An unwitting informant once told an investigator about two members of the Bloods gang who drove to North Carolina, where they made an offer of $50,000 for a four time winning dog and $40,000 for a three time winner. Though the owner claimed to be unable to even make the payment on his trailer, he refused to sell. The disappointed Bloods appealed to the man's wife, even offering to pay her $10,000 to convince her husband to sell. The husband remained adamant, and the couple separated over the incident.

Puppies bred from the successful fighting dogs sell for $1,500 up to $2,500. Southern Kennels, the home of Grand Champion Mayday sold an average of 30 puppies a month for over five years, each one going for anywhere from $1,000 to $1,500. It was a good day for law enforcement when laws were passed to make it illegal to buy, sell or possess dogs for fighting. Prior to this time, law enforcement had to catch people in the act of fighting. Today, undercover buys of fighting dogs, similar to undercover drug buys, are just another tool the good guys can use to catch dog fighters.

Cash is not the only currency for the sale of fighting dogs. Fat Bill was known to offer almost anything he owned for the right puppy or dog. According to one investigator, a number of dogmen swore that Fat Bill thought nothing of offering a weekend of "around the world" sex with his young girl friend in exchange for a puppy.

In recent years, new players have entered the fight game. These are street gangs. Some argue that gangs are pushing the old time dog fighters out. Fueled by huge sums of cash from the distribution of illegal drugs and weapons, gangs are able to bet serious money on dog fights. One such fight was held in Spartanburg, South Carolina. Jamaican Joe's dog TK beat a feared and much favored nine time winner called Firecracker.

The fight between Firecracker and TK was brutal. TK bit the other dog so savagely that Firecracker's face was destroyed. The skin was actually ripped from his muzzle, and his lungs filled with blood. Unfazed by his gruesome appearance, the crowd roared in approval. Unable to breathe and with his muzzle crushed, Firecracker suffered a cruel death. Even when his owners realized his condition they refused to pick him up. Instead they hoped that TK would not keep fighting a down and out dog. TK did not stop, however, and in the end Firecracker lost his life as a dead game dog. The crowd gave him a standing ovation.

When the fight was over, Jamaican Joe and his crew took off with nearly a million dollars in winnings. Behind them were three cars filled with rival gang members bent on stealing the money. In front of them were two more cars of gang members intent on an ambush. Jamaican Joe and his crew managed to elude them all, and made it safely back to Joe's run down trailer in Florida. One sure way for a criminal and non taxpayer to attract attention is to live in a big house and drive an expensive car. Joe knew that a rundown looking trailer was the perfect front to hide his true earnings. He was confident that no police officer on a preliminary drive by would be tempted to look deeper. But although Joe managed to make it home, his trailer would later be invaded and ransacked by the rival gang members looking for the huge sum of cash from the fight. When they did not find the money, the gang burned the trailer to the ground.

In the early days of dog fighting such things did not happen. Things are different today. A regular working person does not usually have access to a million dollars in cash. Banks require customers to complete paperwork for any deposit or withdrawal over $10,000. These transactions are also reported to the FDIC and IRS. Access to over a million dollars in cash requires a non-taxpaying line of work.

Dog fighting is still legal in some parts of the world such as Japan and parts of Russia. Matches attract huge crowds of spectators. In America, most investigators agree that the internet has increased the popularity of dog fighting, allowing criminals to find others like themselves. It has also helped America to become the number one exporter of fighting dogs in the world. American dog fighters can now reach out to their counterparts in Germany, Russia, Italy,

Mexico, and other countries. The internet has spawned a new breed of novice dog fighters eager to advance their name and reap the huge potential profits over the blood of their dogs.

Some of those new to the game are more intent on turning quick profits than concentrating on the serious breeding programs that demand gameness as well as non aggression towards humans. They do not discriminate against the man biters. And while the media often rushes to call any dog that attacks a human being a pit bull, regardless of its actual breed, it is true that attacks by pit bulls have increased, and that this increase has included fatalities. However, it should be noted that the rise in popularity of breeding, selling and fighting dogs has meant a huge increase in their numbers compared to other breeds. Shelters are overrun with unwanted pit bulls. They are often unwanted because they are NOT aggressive. In many areas of the country, 20-25% of the dogs received at shelters are discarded pit bulls.

Some law enforcement agencies continue to insist that dog fighting is an issue for humane societies and animal controls. Though committed to stamping out this scourge, humane society representatives generally lack law enforcement powers. In many states, ACOs do as well! When law enforcement does make an arrest, they hope that it will serve as a deterrent to others. As long as this cruel blood sport continues, Americans can expect to see more injuries and fatalities from powerful animals in the worst possible hands. ACOs, law enforcement officers, HSUS and other animal welfare professionals are determined to make dog fighting nothing more than a grizzly memory of the history of the breed.

CHAPTER 4 THE SEARCH

It all really began when a man named Davon Boddie was arrested in Hampton, Virginia on April 20, 2007, after a police dog tracked a scent of marijuana coming from his parked car. When Boddie was patted down, police found marijuana on him and later in the trunk of his car. He was charged with distribution of marijuana and possession of a controlled substance with intent to distribute. When asked, Boddie gave police 1915 Moonlight Road in Surry County, Virginia as his home address.

According to an undercover operative, Vick soon learned of the arrest, and he was furious. He flew home to Virginia and summoned Boddie. Later, news sources would write a story about Michael Vick having been a no-show at a DC Capitol breakfast, where he was to have been presented with an award for his work to help youth. His mother attended in his place.

Vick had to deal with his cousin. The rest of the Vick crew was equally livid with the young man. Boddie was ordered to surrender the keys and car that Vick had given him. Vick told Boddie he was out. There would be no more house, no more car, no more walking around cash, nothing. This reaction would come back to haunt Vick and his crew.

But it was too late to stop the chain of events Boddie's arrest set in motion. As a result of his statement about his address, officers from the multi-jurisdictional State Drug Task Force secured a warrant to search for drugs at 1915 Moonlight Road in Surry County. Officers executed the warrant on Wednesday, April 25, 2007. Deputy Bill Brinkman was familiar with this address. He knew that there were dogs on the property, and he took along the local ACO, James Smith. It was during the execution of this warrant that officers saw suspicious looking equipment and scarred and wounded dogs. ACO Smith made the call to Chesapeake.

I was still staring at the house when Brinkman, Smith and a couple of the State police officers approached. Chesapeake ACOs Tobin, Stevens and Perry stood beside me. Brinkman and a couple of officers escorted us towards the back of the property past the huge white house, the basketball court and the above ground pool. I could immediately see the black outbuildings on either side of a winding dirt path leading back towards woods at the rear of the property. Along the way, we encountered two young men. One was a scowling Purnell Peace. The second was Quanis Phillips, dressed from head to toe, including his shoes, in bright yellow. He looks like a canary, I thought.

On the right side of the path was a two story black building; beyond it a smaller single story one. Against the two story building were stacks of wooden boxes that looked like dog houses. They were sun bleached and coated with dust, leaves and pine needles.

There were two more black buildings on our left, and as we approached, we saw a long row of kennels containing dogs off to the right. On either side of the path, dotted here and there were other single chain link kennels. Tall pine trees rose majestically providing shade from the sun. Nailed to one of these was a piece of two by four approximately three feet in length.

The officers escorted me into the first outbuilding on the left. Inside were treadmills— three of them--and a carpet mill. Both of these devices are used to exercise and condition pit bulls for a fight. A carpet mill is a round flat carpet covered disk approximately six to eight feet in diameter. This disk is mounted on a shaft. A dog is tethered to a ceiling beam above the disk, and as he walks, the disk rotates under his feet. There were two chains suspended from the beam. On one of the beams was written "TBK". Over this, the letters "BNK" had been written.

As we exited, we observed a stationary vertical pole rising out of the ground. It was the center shaft portion of a cat jenny. Resembling a small horse walker, this device is used to exercise pit bulls in preparation for a fight. A large metal beam assembly is mounted and turns on top of the vertical pole. A dog is secured by a leash to one end of this beam. Just out of reach, the trainer will hang something to bait the dog, like a strip of animal hide or a cage containing a live animal. At the other end of the beam, there is a counter balance usually with weights added. The dog chases the bait as the beam turns on the shaft. Later that night, we would find the upper beam portion of the jenny in the tall grass behind this building.

The next building we entered was also on the left. Inside we could see medicines and dietary supplements on a counter to the right of the door. To the left of the door was a bank of four stainless steel cages. Sitting on top of these was a bottle of injectible diuretic. I was familiar with this kind of drug. It is sometimes given to a dog before a fight, so that he will empty himself out allowing him to make weight. After a fight, a dog suffering from multiple severe wounds might be given it as well. Often these dogs will go into shock and the kidneys can shut down. They are given IV or subcutaneous fluids, and a diuretic to stimulate urination.

We turned next to the buildings on our right. The first building we entered looked like a garage. As we entered we saw several rolls of beige colored carpet on the left against the wall. Each roll had a slit cut in it. At the end of the roll, the carpet was sliced to create tab that was tucked into the slit keeping the roll in place. Also to the left was a scale hanging from the ceiling. It was typical of the ones we had seen many times and equipped with a hook on the bottom. Because most dogs are fought at an agreed upon weight, there is an actual weighing in before each fight. Dogs are picked up and hung by their collars or perhaps a harness and suspended in the air from the scale to determine the weight.

Straight ahead was an electric human treadmill that had been modified by affixing plywood sides to it. It was also equipped with a chain and a clasp for a collar. On top of the treadmill were some syringes, some used and some unused. There was a refrigerator to the right of the treadmill. On top of it was a box of new syringes.

On the floor to the right of the doorway was a box of collars, some fairly new looking, others worn and old. The rancid stench of old leather collars took my breath away. Right in the middle of the room was a device known as a breeding stand, or as it is called in the dog fighters' vernacular, a rape stand. A female dog is strapped down and secured to this device so that she cannot bite a male dog during breeding.

On a workbench against the wall on the far right were several automotive products, as well as canine fungal treatments, de-wormers, and various products for wound treatment, sealing, and dressing.

In the upper left corner of this building, next to the stacks and stacks of bagged Gold Professional Dog Food, was a ladder leading to the second floor. I climbed towards the opening that gave way to the second level, where I came face to face with a large drip of what appeared to be dried blood. Continuing upward, I finally stood and surveyed the room. Brinkman, Smith and a couple of other officers followed. The entire room was painted black. Despite the black paint, we could see spatters and smears of more blood on the walls. In the center of the floor was a clean rectangular pattern. It appeared that this was where the carpet had been laid to provide traction for the fighting dogs and to absorb the blood. Around the edges of this clean pattern were more blood spatters, stains and smears. Next to a folding chair on the right of the access opening, was a plastic bucket and lid. On top of this was a tooth. It looked like a canine tooth from a dog. There was a boom box on the floor and a blood streaked sweatshirt jacket hung from the air conditioner. None of us spoke. A pall of agony still hung in the air. We could almost hear the cries of the dogs that had suffered here. This room told us that Michael Vick was absolutely committed to dog fighting. I was used to seeing makeshift and temporary set ups to fight or train dogs, but this property appeared to have been designed from the ground up to be a dog fighting, training and breeding empire. Silently, we each descended the ladder and walked outside into the light towards the next building on the right.

This one was small and very dark inside. It appeared to be some kind of isolation building. The odor of urine and feces in the building was overpowering. The ammonia fumes burned our nostrils and throats as we tried to breathe. On each side of the center aisle inside were 4 runways. In the second runway on the right was a buckskin or tan colored pit bull.

Outside to the right of this building was a set of kennels containing pit bulls, two Presa Canarios, two Rottweilers, and a number of beagles. Several of the pit bulls were scarred. Two of the pit bulls had fresh wounds and lacerations over top of old scarring. The second dog also had a deformed left front leg. We thought this might be the result of a bad break that had healed improperly due to lack of treatment. In the individual kennels scattered about the yard were more dogs. Some of these had what looked like fungal infections of the skin, cherry eye cysts, and old scars. None of the dogs had adequate water. Most had none at all, and the ones that did had only dirty water in bowls that were coated with green slime. Virginia law requires that dogs be provided clean water is clean receptacles. These dogs that were forced to fight and die for the entertainment of men were made to drink filth.

In my experience, I have found two types of dog fighters. One will spend every penny on the set up for the dogs, while their families live in dirty, mice infested shacks or trailers. The other type lived in luxury themselves while begrudging their animals even life's most basic needs—clean water. In every dog fighting case, it is always heartbreaking to see the dogs. That green slime water would stay with me.

We found a second jenny towards the back of the property where 30 more pit bull dogs were chained in the woods. All of them were restrained with heavy chains attached to car axles buried deep into the ground next to dilapidated dog houses. Each chain provided just enough length to allow a dog to agitate and be agitated by the others, while preventing any actual contact.

ACO Smith accompanied me on this brief tour of the property. My job was to confirm what the other officers already suspected. We were looking at a large scale dog fighting operation. I conferred with Deputy Brinkman and a couple of the State police officers. We decided that the next step should be to have ACO Smith apply for a search warrant for dog fighting evidence. We felt it was highly likely that there would be much more evidence than what had been in plain view upon execution of the drug warrant. Brinkman handed me a diskette. The warrant, he said, was already done for the most part. He had already prepared it. Our eyes met. So, he had expected to find evidence of dog fighting. He suggested that I accompany ACO Smith to the Sheriff's Office. Surry was not my jurisdiction, so I could only assist Smith in securing his warrant from the magistrate. One of my officers, Melanie Tobin, went with us.

The warrant should have been done in no time at all, but things never go as planned. First, we found that the disk was corrupted. Whatever Brinkman had typed on the affidavit as the probable cause for the search was gone. It was simply not there. In order to issue a search warrant in Virginia, a magistrate or judge must approve an officer's statement that probable cause exists to justify a search. ACO Smith looked stricken. He had no idea how to write an affidavit. There was nothing else to be done. I sat down to write it from scratch. I was terrified. This was going to be a BIG case. What if I blew it? I forced myself to concentrate on the task at hand. I could do this. I had written search warrants before. I just had to focus. I conferred with Smith and ACO Tobin as I wrote, making certain that they had both seen each item I was listing. Finally, it was done and we were ready to print. Unfortunately, our troubles had just begun. The document would not print. We found ourselves moving from computer to computer with our disk trying in vain to print our affidavit and warrant. No one working at the office lifted a finger to help us or mentioned that the actual problem was that the printer would not pick up the sheets of paper from the tray. Finally, and by the merest chance, we figured out that we had to feed each sheet individually. It seemed we were on a roll. We printed the affidavit, and then the disk suddenly crashed completely. The kindly magistrate, Mr. Ellis, retyped the search warrant for us after he satisfied himself that our affidavit justified the warrant.

His review of the affidavit was entertaining after the stress of trying to get the documents printed. He read a portion out loud, and then asked, "Well, what makes you think this is dog fighting?"

I responded, "Read on." He continued reading and occasionally stopping.

"Well what about….well how…well what does?" Each time I responded, "Keep reading." When he finally got to the end, his questions had been answered. He turned to his own computer and typed the warrant. The magistrate told ACO Smith to raise his hand. Smith had seen everything I had typed. He raised his hand and swore to it. With the signed warrant in hand we were off.

It was 10:40 p.m. by the time we finally returned to Moonlight Road. We were getting a late start and all of us were tired. It was hot and muggy, and very dark. We started with the house. In the upstairs television room we found copies of veterinary bills. We found more vet bills downstairs that had credit card receipts stapled to them. From these, we hoped to be able to tell who was paying the bills for the dogs.

In every room were bullets and empty shell casings, but no weapons. The deputies called out to us. They found a stack of registrations and pedigrees, but being unfamiliar with fighting bloodlines, the deputies could not interpret them. They handed the papers to me. My heart skipped. The dogs named in these documents had come from bloodlines of dog fighting royalty. I recognized names such as Tant, Crenshaw, Boudreaux, Carver, Garner, Chavis, Loposay, Mims, Hollingsworth, Patrick, Finley, Colby, and--as the breath caught in my throat—Hardcore! Hardcore was none other than Benny Butts. The pedigrees included such famous fighters as Hardcore's Champion Mystic, Tant's Grand Champion Yellow, Tant's Miss Jocko, Hollingsworth Champion May Day, Loposay's Champion Shogun, S.T.P.'s Champion Black Pazmanian, J. Crenshaw's Champions Jeep and Honeybunch, Boudreaux' Eli, and Walling's Bullyson.

The stack included registrations for Big Boy, Lil Chong, and a dog that had been purchased from Carl Mims of Bona Fide Kennel Club. This dog was a chocolate and white named Too Bad Kennel's Rusty. We would learn much more about Too Bad Kennels and these three dogs later. What struck us immediately was the name of Rusty's owner on the registration, signed by Mims. It was Michael Dwayne Vick.

We bagged the evidence from the house and moved outside to begin a full inventory of each building. On the way, we met attorney Larry Woodward, who had apparently just arrived. Woodard represented Michael Vick. A couple of the police officers stopped to speak with him while the rest of us proceeded towards the black buildings. We had not opened any containers or cabinets during our initial walk through, merely observing items in plain view. Now we could do a thorough search. In the building with the stainless steel cages, we found more drugs and supplements. We also found a break stick, a device used to pry the jaws of fighting dogs apart when attempting to separate them. Inside a cookie tin—one of the kind that contain the Danish butter cookies typically given at Christmas—was a plastic grocery bag that held a bottle of dexamethazone, an injectible anti inflammatory medication. This drug is used to combat swelling for wounded dogs. We noted that the floors of the two stainless steel cages on the right were covered with blood.

We moved next to the isolation building on the right. The little female buckskin pit bull inside seemed so lethargic. The terrible fumes inside-- the overpowering odor of urine and feces—had to be affecting her sensitive nose. We moved her outside to one of the empty runs in the row of kennels to the right of the building. She seemed to perk up almost immediately.

While we were working, Assistant County Supervisor for Surry County John Edwards arrived. He asked me if it was going to be necessary to confiscate all of the dogs. By this time, a rough count indicated that we had at least 60 dogs. I explained that the dogs were evidence and, as in any criminal case, it was vital to secure that evidence. He turned from me and asked one of my officers, Tracy Stevens, if she did not think this was just a badly run kennel. Her response was an emphatic and succinct No! I explained to Mr. Edwards that ACO Smith, as the officer on the warrant, could seize all of the dogs but continue to maintain them on site. However, this would mean that arrangements would need to be made for round the clock security, or dogs would simply disappear. I explained that the authority for the seizure of the dogs came from a Virginia State Code that allowed an ACO to seize any animal found abandoned, neglected, or cruelly treated, and from the dog fighting statute that directed the officers to seize any dogs used for or intended for use in fighting. Aside from the fact that dog fighting was inherently cruel, animals here were in filth, without water, and a number of them needed medical care.

Realizing that a small county like Surry would not be likely to have the space in their shelter for so many animals, I offered to start making calls to surrounding animal controls and other shelters. I was certain that other agencies would be willing to provide housing. Edwards declined this offer. A feeling of déjà vu overwhelmed me. Would this be a repeat of the 2000 Benny Butts case? Brinkman must have had his own doubts. He would later tell me he had already called his old friend, USDA Office of the Inspector General (OIG) Special Agent Jim Knorr to alert him.

Eventually exhaustion and darkness overtook us. We had to make a decision about what to do. I told Brinkman that we needed a forensics unit to process the pit. A phone call later, he reported that it would be at least two hours before a forensics team would be able to respond. We decided to call it a night. We would return in the morning to finish processing the scene. ACO Smith prepared to remove the five dogs in need of immediate medical care—the two with fresh wounds, three more with skin infections and cherry eye cysts—so that they could be transported to a veterinary hospital.

One officer remained on the property to establish that we had not released the scene, and that we could lawfully return. Before leaving, my officers and I insisted that all of the remaining dogs be fed and watered. There was no water supply back in the woods where the 30 pit bulls were chained, so water had to be trucked to the back of the property. The dogs were hungry, thirsty and delighted to have anyone pay some attention to them. By 1:30 a.m. in the morning, we were hot, dirty, exhausted, and finally finished. It was an hour's drive home, where I peeled off my clothes and fell into bed a little after 3 a.m. too exhausted to even shower.

CHAPTER 5 THE PLOT THICKENS

After a mere three hours of sleep, I dragged myself out of bed later that morning. It was Thursday, April 26, 2007. A shower and coffee helped force my eyes to open and my brain to function. I was on auto pilot the entire drive to the office. After checking messages and putting out some minor fires, I was once again on my way to Moonlight Road. ACOs Tobin and Perry were following in another vehicle. ACO Stevens was not available, so her place was taken by petite Sharon Pesar, another new officer.

At Moonlight Road we resumed the overwhelming task of cataloging and collecting evidence. Surry County had deployed a truck with a large trailer so that we could load the treadmills, jennies, carpet mills, cages and other bulky items. We carefully numbered, tagged, cataloged, and photographed every item we collected. The State Police Forensic team was already on scene. Officer Tim Brown was upstairs processing the pit. Throughout the morning, Brown collected samples everywhere we found blood. He collected blood from inside one of the runways in the isolation building. Was this where injured dogs were placed after a fight? As Brown collected blood from the treadmills, we noticed a section of wall above the carpet mill. Written on the wall were the names of dogs, and beside each name were numbers such as 1:10 and 1:20. One of the names on the wall was Cleo. Was this the record of the times that these dogs spent on the treadmills or carpet mills? We decided to take this with us. One of the other State police officers carefully cut out the wall section, which was promptly bagged and numbered.

Officers photographed the beam above the carpet mill which bore the letters, "TBK", and over those "BNK". Brinkman pointed to one of the treadmills and asked me if I recognized it. This particular treadmill had metal side rails that were painted bright yellow. I wasn't sure. Brinkman said he believed this was the same treadmill he and my officers had seized in 2000 from the home of Benny Butts.

"Well, I still have the photographs from that case," I said. I would later go through those pictures and find that Brinkman's memory was excellent. There was the yellow treadmill, the black treadmill, and the old carpet mill. After the Butts case was thrown out, all of these pieces had been returned to him. Now, seven years later, here they were on Michael Vick's property in another dog fighting investigation. Brinkman told me he had information that Butts had been coming to Moonlight Road for a while to help Vick condition the dogs for fighting. I asked him where Butts was now, and Brinkman responded tersely, "He gave himself a 'hot shot'", meaning Butts had died of a drug overdose.

In the middle of cataloging and photographing the medicines and dietary supplements, I heard Brinkman call my name. I turned to see him approaching accompanied by someone I had not seen before. He was approximately 50 years old, African American, medium height, stocky, with bushy gray hair and a mustache. He was dressed casually in a shirt with a floral pattern. Brinkman introduced me to Surry County Commonwealth Attorney Gerald Poindexter. I shook his hand as he asked what I thought we had here. I responded that I had no doubt that this was a large dog fighting operation, including a pit. One of the other officers took Mr. Poindexter off to look at the pit, and I returned to the task at hand.

Finally, I had to tear myself away. The others would have to finish processing the scene. I hated to leave, but I had a meeting in Richmond that day for the VAFTF. As I walked to my truck, I saw vans from the local television stations parked across the street in the church yard. Reporters were milling around. A few were shooting stand ups. When they saw me the reporters began clamoring and shouting questions. I answered a few of them, while avoiding any mention of the one person uppermost in all of our minds.

I was late for my meeting. I slipped quietly into the room and slid into the closest chair, trying not to interrupt. The VAFTF was in its infancy. We had not even finished drafting our bylaws and constitution, and now suddenly we were in the middle of what might be the biggest dog fighting case any of us had ever seen. As soon as there was a break, the other members turned excitedly to me, demanding to know what was happening in Surry. By now they already knew a search had been carried out at the home of Michael Vick. They were eager to hear the latest and to offer help.

It was a tremendous relief to know that some impressive players were ready to play for the home team on this case. Michelle Welch was a former Deputy Commonwealth Attorney from Richmond, Virginia, who now worked for the Virginia Attorney General's Office. She had plenty of experience prosecuting cruelty and dog fighting cases. John Goodwin, Director of Animal Fighting Operations for the Humane Society of the United States (HSUS) was an expert in this area. Richard Samuels was the president of the Task Force. Medium height with dark hair and a swarthy complexion, Richard has the lazy drawl of a good ole county boy. He is a living, breathing textbook of animal fighting knowledge with a passion for bringing cock fighters and dog fighters to justice. Samuels has been instrumental in taking down a number of Virginia dog fighters. He is known for excellent research and background work ups on his bad guys.

In the midst of this spirited dialog, one man sat quietly. Seemingly immune to the excitement, he serenely pecked away at his lap top. He was the type of man who always seems to pass unnoticed in any crowd. His appearance is non-descript. I had met this man before, but he looked completely different today. I did not even recognize him until Goodwin directed my attention to him. Goodwin is relentless in his pursuit of animal fighters, and he had invited this man to help with the Surry case.

Known as Dog Angel, this undercover operative would eventually put together intelligence on Vick's entire operation. Now Dog Angel calmly closed his lap top, unfolded his limbs and rose from his chair. Smiling he greeted me with an outstretched hand, which I took. Well, it looks like you're having a pretty exciting time", he said, "and this is only the beginning." Dog Angel said he had a lot to tell me.

At our first meeting over a month ago, I had been extremely wary and distrustful of him. I had managed to find out his real name, and I knew he had been a dog fighter himself from the late 60's to the late 70's. He knew the game inside and out, having stood pit side with the likes of Maurice Carver, Jack Kelly, Billy Stepp, James Crenshaw and Fletcher Chavis, all of whom were dog fighting legends. I had questioned Goodwin about him. "How do you know we can trust him? Why is he doing this? How do we know he's not working for the other side?" Dog Angel, Goodwin had calmly replied, had actively worked with HSUS on their list of the twenty most wanted dog fighters and had been involved with HSUS since the late 70's. His work had resulted in a 90 % conviction rate for those dog fighters targeted by law enforcement. Goodwin had gone on to say that Dog Angel's information and ability to infiltrate the underbelly of the dog fighting world was second to none. He could get inside a dog fighter's entire operation, often by creating a variety of fake identities. In one case Dog Angel had actually taken a job as the yard boy for a major dog fighting operation.

I trusted John Goodwin, so I felt I would have to trust Dog Angel, at least until he gave me a reason not to. Little did I dream that this inauspicious beginning would be the start a collaboration that would change both our lives. Dog Angel already knew plenty about Vick's operation and would soon work his way to the inner circle of Vick's friends, teammates and fellow dog fighters. I would be amazed at how effectively he would do this, and how trusting of him those close to Vick would be.

Goodwin was right. Dog Angel has helped to make many busts over the years both in the dog fighting world and the world of organized crime. He has been involved in helping authorities put together major cases in the booming drug trade, but busting dog fighters is still Dog Angel's favorite activity. One such is a man who lives in Chesapeake, Virginia, Clarence Ernie Swain. Once known as Dirty Ernie, Swain was arrested at a dog fight in Georgia in the 1980's where Dog Angel was working undercover. Swain's dog, Black Smoke, was a winner, and Swain was offered $3,000 for the dog, but turned it down. At that point Dog Angel signaled law enforcement, who were waiting to raid the fight. He followed the case to Swain's conviction for dog fighting. The dog fighters did not know the true identity of the undercover operative causing them so much trouble, but they agreed "Dog Angel is no joke".

At the time of the Vick raid, Dog Angel was working on a case involving a big time game dog breeder in North Carolina. He abandoned this plan when news of the Moonlight Road search reached him. As a matter of fact, Michael Vick had been on Dog Angel's list for some time, and he had already begun to gather intelligence from some of his valuable but unwitting sources. Using one of his many fake identities, Dog Angel learned plenty from Bona Fide Kennel Club's Carl Mims. Dog Angel said Mims loved to gossip, and when it came to other dogmen, nothing was secret. According to Dog Angel, he was not the only investigator to use Mims as a source of information. Mims, he laughed, had no idea he was so helpful to law enforcement.

Now Dog Angel told me that Michael Vick had bought dogs from Carl Mims. One of the dogs was a pure red boy dog that had cost somewhere between $5,000 and $10,000, he said. He went on to explain that he had heard Michael Vick had been buying dogs from Hell on Earth Kennels in Maryland, allegedly run by White Mike Stewart. Dog Angel said that Stewart frequently traveled to Vick's property to help with the conditioning and the keep of the dogs.

He said he thought that Vick's kennel name might be Too Bad Kennels. I said nothing, remembering the registration I had seen the night before for Vick's dog, Too Bad Kennel's Rusty, who had been bred and sold by Carl Mims. He thought Benny Butts, of Hardcore Kennels, was now using the kennel name B.N.K. He had no idea what the letters stood for.

Dog Angel recommended that the authorities follow the money. According to Dog Angel, Vick had approximately seven businesses that he had set up as a way to move and launder money. He went on to say that Vick's practice was to set up a friend or relative in one of these small businesses. These guys drove Escalades and other high end vehicles while throwing around substantial sums of money. Nonetheless, Dog Angel said he heard there was resentment brewing among some of the crew. Some were growing weary of what they called Vick's stinginess, and felt that they were not being paid their share.

Dog Angel told me that a guy named Q did a lot of the work with the dogs and handled them at fights. Vick, he said, did not actually handle the dogs in the pit. He would just show up and bet. I believed Q might be Quanis Phillips, who had been at the house the night before.

Vick, Dog Angel said, was close to a certain professional athlete who allegedly had ties to Crip gang members. In fact, he said, Vick had used this man's "enforcer" after a dispute with one of his own crew members, a man named Tony Taylor. The enforcer had been recruited to throw Taylor off of the property at Moonlight Road. He also strongly recommended that we obtain the services of a forensics accountant to investigate Vick's finances. Dog Angle said everyone of Vick's crew knew exactly what was going on in terms of the money, that no taxes were being paid, and that they were each part of an elaborate scheme to launder and hide gambling proceeds from dog fights.

Next, Dog Angel said we should look for an older African American man from Newport News. Known as Virginia O, this man was a prolific dog fighter who traveled across Virginia and other states including Mississippi, Alabama and the Carolinas. It was Virginia O who actually set up the fights for Vick. This was designed to keep Vick's name out of any arrangements. Dog Angel did not know his real name. Dog Angel advised me to tell the investigators to look for Virginia O and Tony Taylor. They would be able to tell them plenty about Vick and his operation.

Finally, Dog Angel warned that he had already heard Vick's cousin, Davon Boddie, was slated to take the fall for the dog fighting. "Could that really happen?" I asked. Dog Angel smiled and quipped that with Vick's money it was definitely possible. It might not be Boddie, but he had no doubt that someone would be willing if the price were right.

While Dog Angel and I were talking, one of my officers, Melanie Tobin, called to tell me she was having a problem with the local officials in Surry. She and my other two officers were still in the process of photographing and cataloging the dogs, but the locals were insisting that she wrap things up and get out. ACO Tobin is a very methodical and thorough officer. She wanted to make certain she and the other two officers did everything right and did not in any way compromise the case. I wondered if this was an omen. I remembered how hard we had worked on the Butts case only to have it thrown out. I asked her to find the officer in charge and tell him Surry County asked for our help. They asked us to bring a team, because they knew we would know what we were doing and would do it right. So, we were going to do just that. We were going to do it right for as long as it took. If that was not acceptable, then we WOULD leave. We would not come back or assist any further. If that message was not clear, I asked Tobin to have him call me directly. I did not get a call. They must have gotten the message.

I left the meeting for the long drive home. My mind was in turmoil. Dog Angel had given me plenty to think about. At about 4:45 p.m., I called ACO Tobin from the road for an update. She said she and the other officers from Chesapeake had six dogs with them that they were taking back to our shelter. More dogs were being sent to other area shelters. I thanked her and asked her to pass on my thanks to the others. I told Tobin I would see her the following morning.

I decided to call Surry County Commonwealth Attorney Gerald Poindexter. When the secretary answered, I identified myself, but she said Poindexter had just left. I asked to leave a message, and reiterated that I had met him on the scene of the search at Moonlight Road. She asked me to wait and a moment later he was on the line. I tried to repress a smile.

Poindexter told me he was only a part time prosecutor, and that this case was going to require a lot of resources that he did not have. I did my best to reassure him by telling him HSUS was already poised to offer legal assistance in the person of Ethan Eddy, an attorney for the VAFTF. They were also prepared to provide financial assistance for the care of the dogs. I wanted to get that statement on the table, because I remembered during the Butts case, Surry County had refused both legal and veterinary assistance from HSUS. One of the female dogs seized from Butts' home died at the Surry County pound. I had always wondered if she might have been saved had she been given medical care. Next I told Poindexter about VAFTF member and attorney Michelle Welch. She had experience trying dog fighting cases, I said, and had offered to help if she was needed.

I assured him of my assistance in any capacity that I was able to fulfill. I shared with him the information that Dog Angel had given me. Poindexter told me that he expected to rely heavily on me and that he would be in touch. He asked me to put everything that we had discussed, along with contact information for the various individuals, in an e-mail and send it to him the next day. I assured him that I would. I hung up and tried to convince myself things would be okay. Still, for some reason, our conversation had left me unsettled.

CHAPTER 6 DOG ANGEL

How does a person become enmeshed as an undercover operative in the dangerous and sordid world of illegal dog fighting? Where is that passion and drive born? What kind of catalyst inspires someone to first place his feet on this rocky and often discouraging road? Is it a single event, or a culmination?

One man embarked on his journey at the early age of only 12. As a child, Dog Angel was the butt of jokes and teasing, a perfect target for neighborhood bullies. His father was an insurance salesman who rarely stayed with any job for longer than one or two years, frequently uprooting the family to move to a new town. Dog Angel always felt like the new kid on the block. He describes his childhood as hell. By the time he was 12 years old, Dog Angel was still only 5'3" and weighed a mere 84 pounds dripping wet.

Dog Angel turned to dogs for the friendship he craved. His first dog was a mixed bred standard poodle, named Dino. Ironically it was through Dino that Dog Angel would first enter the world of professional dog fighting.

A Louisiana man, who was installing a fence in the family back yard at the time, taught Dino to do tricks and fashioned a braided leash for the dog. He was an authentic Cajun, who also seemed to know a lot about dogs. Young Dog Angel came to regard the Cajun as a longed for father figure. When the fence was finally finished, the young boy cried at the thought of losing his friend. The Cajun reassured him promising to bring him a custom dog house for Dino that he was building out of left over material.

One day a new family moved into the neighborhood, the Tomics, from Albany, New York.* Dog Angel's parents were the neighborhood welcome wagon, but he hated to be dragged along on these visits. His paralyzing shyness prevented him from saying a word though he secretly prayed each visit might bring the longed for friend. On a hot summer Sunday, Dog Angel and his family drove over to meet the Tomics, where they were greeted by a bear of dog. At 130 pounds, and sporting both attitude and a spiked collar, Buck seemed to be a larger than life black and tan monster. Not only did he have a deep resounding bark, but he bore facial and leg scars to indicate he had been in some type of fight with another animal.

Mr. Tomic came outside and put the dog inside the fence. Dog Angel could not take his eyes off of this mountain of a man. A strange and uncomfortable feeling formed in the pit of his stomach. Watching the man's eyes dart and the way he carried himself Dog Angel thought Tomic was unlike anyone he had ever met. An imposing six feet tall and about 240 pounds, Tomic was a stark contrast to Dog Angel's father who was slightly built with an unimposing manner. Looking from the dog to Mr. Tomic, Dog Angel wanted nothing more than to get out of there and go home. Surprisingly, the mountain man was engaging and friendly. At first this disarmed the young boy, but without warning the feeling of distrust came rushing back.

Maybe Tomic sensed this. He put his arm around the boy as if to reassure him. The boy could smell the man's fetid breath, and his stomach rebelled. Later he would learn that this was the breath of a man that had been really drunk the night before. Tomic told the boy he should meet his son, Jeff, and pointed to the front door of the house. Like his father, Jeff was physically imposing. At only 12, he was a mature 5'9" and about 180 pounds. Dog Angel's instincts told him that this family was trouble, but he forced these apprehensions to the back of his mind.

Dog Angel learned that Jeff Tomic's dog, Buck, was a Rottweiler. Jeff often came to Dog Angel's house to play with Dino. He repeatedly asked Dog Angel to bring Dino to his house to play with Buck, and one day the boy agreed. As the two boys approached the Tomic's yard, the usually outgoing and confident Dino became nervous, perhaps sensing danger. Jeff repeatedly tried to sooth Dog Angel, saying, "It's okay; he will be fine". Little did Dog Angel know that "fine" was the furthest thing from the way this visit would turn out.

As the two boys entered the Tomic's back yard, Dino trembled and strained at his leash trying to pull away. Jeff went into his house and brought Buck outside, immediately releasing his hold on the animal. Buck charged across the yard and took hold of Dino shaking him like a rag doll. Dino howled in pain so loudly that the noise brought Mr. Tomic outside grinning from ear to ear. Neither father nor son made any move to stop the fight. Dog Angel watched both Tomics. The man and his son looked high, as if under the effect of a drug. Years later Dog Angel would see this same look on the faces of countless dog fighters. They love the sight of dogs fighting one another, but the greatest rush comes from seeing one of their dogs kill another dog.

In little more than 30 seconds, Dog Angel's beloved Dino lay dead. In shock, he picked up the limp body and ran towards home. To his astonishment, Jeff followed him. As he entered his own yard, his mother watched him in shock. She saw Dino dead in her son's arms, and broke down. Through her tears, she asked her son what had happened. Before Dog Angel could respond, Jeff blurted that Dino had snapped at his dog, Buck and then tried to bite him. He claimed that Buck had defended himself and had killed Dino. As he wove this lie, Jeff stared hard at the boy cradling his dead pet. Dog Angel had seen this look many times on the faces of other bullies. The look was enough to terrify him into silence.

Dog Angel buried Dino in the back yard that day. He was tortured by guilt and impotent rage. Why had he not trusted his own instincts? Dog Angel swore he would have his

*The name and the city that this family came from have been changed.

revenge. Jeff had killed Dog Angel's one good friend, Dino, for fun, and then lied about it. The looks on the faces of both Tomics as they savored Dino's cruel death haunted him.

When the Cajun returned with the dog house he had built, Dog Angel told him what had happened to Dino. In his thick accent, the Cajun said he wanted to give the boy a new dog. The Cajun drove to Louisiana and returned with a muscular little 35 pound pit bull named Lavern. Lavern was full of energy and smart as a whip. He had some scars that reminded Dog Angel of the ones he had seen on Buck, but this little dog did not have the attitude of the big bad Rottweiler. Suddenly Dog Angel remembered Dino, and he told the Cajun he could not keep Lavern; he was afraid the Tomic's dog would kill him, too. To the boy's surprise, the Cajun merely smiled and said not to worry; Lavern would handle the big dog with ease. "No way," the boy thought. This little dog was surely no match for the 130 pound Buck. The Cajun promised to show the boy what he meant first hand.

Dog Angel avoided the Tomics, but surreptitiously watched the activities at their home. He did not realize it, but it was here that his investigative skills were born. It seemed Mr. Tomic was motorcycle mechanic and a member of one of the wannabe Hell's Angels type of gangs that had sprung up around the area.

The rage that Dog Angel felt towards Jeff and his family continued to boil. So when the Cajun came to him one day with his idea, the boy jumped at it. The Cajun told the boy he had discovered that George and his gang regularly fought dogs, but the ones they used were what the Cajun called "curs". Young Dog Angel had never heard this term, but he would learn that it was the most degrading description that could be applied to a fighting dog. The Cajun told the boy he was going to put the Tomics and Buck in their place and avenge Dino.

The Cajun set up a fight between Lavern and Buck. At the age of 12, Dog Angel was about to attend his first dog fight. The Cajun said they had four weeks to prepare. He instructed the boy to play fetch with Lavern. Little did Dog Angel realize that he was conditioning a dog to fight. During this four week period, the Cajun brought Lavern raw meat and chicken. He kept an eye on the boy and Lavern, repeatedly asking the boy if he was up to what was being planned. Dog Angel swore that he was. He could barely sleep at night. Could the vengeance he sought for Dino's death be within reach?

One day Dog Angel asked what the fight was going to be like. The Cajun replied that the fight would take place at George Tomic's motorcycle shop, and that they would be the last "show". There were a total of four fights planned. Dog Angel asked if other kids would be attending. The Cajun responded that there would indeed be kids, including the boy's old nemesis, Jeff. The Tomics, he said, were dog fighters from New York, where people fought all sorts of dogs from Bandogs to Rottweilers to Akita's, and it seemed George was schooling his son to follow in his footsteps. The two of them had casually used Dino as practice for Buck. The Rottweiler, the Cajun said, had already defeated four non pit bulls in other fights. The Cajun explained to the boy that in the south people fought dogs like Lavern. He was a pure bred American Pit Bull Terrier. The Cajun went on to say that dog fighting was something that either the boy would never want to see again, or it would be something that would rule his heart and mind for the rest of his life. Dog Angel asked the Cajun which way he thought he would go. The Cajun laughed and replied, "You will be hooked".

On fight night, the Cajun and Dog Angel told the boy's parents they were going to see a movie. The fights were to start at 6 p.m. In those days, fights were scheduled early in the evening because children and wives regularly attended. On the way to the motorcycle shop, the Cajun explained what was going to happen. Each fight would be timed, and a referee would judge the fight to make sure the rules were followed. When the two arrived, Dog Angel was surprised to find the atmosphere charged with the same type of energy as at some of his little league games. There was a stand selling hotdogs. He noticed a couple of local policemen who had recently visited his school to talk to the kids about staying out of trouble. There were several men in business suits, a host of guys sporting GMC Service patches on their overalls and a mix of African Americans who lived in the area. What struck Dog Angel forcibly was that everyone seemed to be equal. Even at his young age, he knew that this was not what he observed in his everyday life; people were judged based on their job, the amount of money they made, and the color of their skin, among other things.

That night, the first three fights contained none of the destruction that Dog Angel had seen with Buck and Dino. The Tomics only arrived after they were over. They laughed when they saw Dog Angel. The Cajun had walked away to the concession stand to get some food and drinks for the two of them. The boy had never felt so alone. The Tomics approached him and demanded to know what he was doing there. Dog Angel gathered every ounce of courage and confronted the elder Tomic, deliberately using the man's first name as he responded that he was here for the fight. Tomic's face was purple with rage, at the audacity of a 12 year kid calling him George. Just at that moment, the Cajun returned, and handed the food and drink to the boy. Dog Angel had never felt less like eating, but took it nonetheless. The Cajun asked George if he wanted to raise the bet. George said, "Sure". The Tomics asked what the boy was doing there, and the Cajun replied that he would be fighting the boy's dog, Lavern. The Tomics took one look at the little pit bull, and promptly quadrupled the bet.

It was time. There was no weighing in; the referee simple shouted, "Pit your dogs". Dog Angel's heart was pumping and his mouth was suddenly dry. Jeff and his father laughed at the small Lavern. The Cajun turned to the boy from his corner of the pit. "Relax my friend. It will be over soon." Suddenly they heard the referee shout, "Release your dogs." Lavern flew across the pit and grabbed Buck by the nose shaking like crazy. The big Rottie fought hard trying to get the little dog off of him, but at about the five minute mark, he started howling. Dog Angel found himself feeling sorry for Buck, but then he glanced over at Jeff and George Tomic. Both wore the dumbfounded expression of an unintelligent man who cannot understand what he is seeing. At that point the Cajun called out, "Turn", meaning that the Rottie had turned away from the fight. The boy had no idea what had happened, but cheered anyway.

After the turn, the Cajun got down beside little Lavern and started calling to him. He pointed to where he wanted Lavern to go. Lavern looked at the Cajun, then at the boy, and went to the throat of the big Rottie. The fight had now been raging for almost 12 minutes. By this time, Buck was on his back, howling, unable to free himself from Lavern. Jeff was crying and begging his father to stop the fight. Suddenly the Rottie made it to his feet. Seeing this,

Jeff raised his head sneering at the other boy. He thought Buck was rallying for a win. Suddenly his face crumbled. The same look was mirrored on the face of his father. Buck was not rallying; instead the savagely injured animal was trying to jump out of the pit. He had taken enough from this 35 pound terror. At that point, George Tomic conceded the fight. At 14 minutes, the referee announced that Lavern was the winner.

Dog Angel jumped for joy. Never had he felt such a grand feeling. The adrenalin rush was like a drug--a drug that has proven to be more addictive than heroin for many a dog fighter. He looked at his nemesis, Jeff. Could this be the bully who had so intimidated him? This tearful boy whose father had to support him to even keep him on his feet?

The Cajun had been right. Dog Angel was hooked. In the days that followed he relived the moments of Lavern's triumph over and over again. Dog Angel began to carry himself with new confidence, not because of anything he had done, but because of his pride in this little dog. Somehow Lavern's courage and ability translated to the boy. The days of being bullied were over.

The fight at the motorcycle shop changed Dog Angel's life forever, and he began his descent into the underground world of professional dog fighters. In just one day, he had learned the rules of the game, tasted the culture, seen how self worth for dogmen is forever linked to the ability of their dogs to fight and win, observed the diverse cross section of people involved, and set his foot on the path tread by every dog fighter-the never ending quest for the ultimate fighting dog. Dog Angel became a dog fighting junkie, feverishly pursuing his addiction. It would prove stronger than any of the drugs with which he would experiment.

I once asked Dog Angel what had made him to change from dog fighter to investigator. At first I thought he was not going to answer me. Then he looked up and explained, "One day I made a decision to leave every sin I had committed behind." He told me the story of the event that changed his life forever.

By the age of 21, Dog Angel had been fighting dogs for nine years and had seen over 200 dog fights. To his amazement, he found he was no longer enjoying these battles and had even begun to feel a vague disgust about them. In a turn of events more surprising to him than anyone else, an event happened that convinced Dog Angel to switch sides.

The moment of truth came at a fight in New York. One of the dogs in the pit had its bottom jaw partially torn off. It hung useless and bloody. In Dog Angel's circle, if a dog was losing and had no chance of winning, the owner would pick it up and concede the fight. But here in New York, the owner made no move to pick up his dog. The poor dog could do nothing to defend himself, and he was protesting and crying in pain. When the other dog grabbed him by the tongue, he actually screamed. Still no pick up. The referee called a handle, or a pause to the fight, and both dogs were taken to their corners. The dog with the broken jaw lay exhausted in horrible pain, looking up at his owner, and then wagged his tail. At the owner's urging, the critically injured animal tried to scratch, or return to the fight, but within minutes collapsed unable to continue. When the other dog began to attack his genitals, he screamed in pure agony. It was a horror show at this point. The owner of the critically injured dog finally conceded the fight. He was so affronted that his dog had quit, he dug a shallow grave, tossed his dog in and left him to die a slow death from his injuries.

The cruel carnage of that fight was the end for Dog Angel. For months he was tormented by the memory of what he had seen. At first, he tried to think of a suitable revenge against the people responsible, but then an idea came to him. Dog Angel said he was touched by an angel that night, who told him he had to change his life completely. He had to abandon drugs, alcohol and the dogs. "I had never been an angel before, but I could be one from this day forward. God would forgive me for the mistakes I had made if I put my past behind me and followed a new path for my life."

Dog Angel made a call to HSUS and spoke with a man named Frantz Dantzler, the director of Field Services and Investigations. Dantzler served in this capacity for nearly four decades, during which time he investigated animal fighting, cruelty cases that included the killing of baby seals by clubbing them to death, puppy mills, wild horse roundups, animal auctions, and the abusive exotic bird trade. Dantzler testified before a congressional committee in 1976, urging Congress to provide for enforcement of the animal fighting prohibitions in the Animal Welfare Act. Dantzler helped to make the HSUS the foremost authority on the nationwide network of illegal animal fighting enterprises. Dog Angel told Dantzler his story, and made a promise to work with him to target dog fighters and bring them to justice. It was Dantzler who would give him the name Dog Angel. They made an interesting team. Dantzler was a bear of a man who stood over 6'5". He was the complete opposite of the much smaller Dog Angel, but together they would wreak havoc on dog fighters and their operations across the United States.

From that point on, Dog Angel began to seek out well known dog fighters. He witnessed the top dogs of all time in some of their most famous fights, and met an incredibly diverse cast of characters. With the same addictive drive with which he had pursued the fight game, Dog Angel now honed his skills for the other side. Later, when technology exploded, he became an expert in internet usage, including the art of tracking and placing spyware on computers. Each year he adds new skills to his portfolio. He has used over 22 separate identities to delve deeply into the underground world of professional dog fighters. He has provided the kind of valuable information to law enforcement that they might otherwise never have been able to obtain.

Dog Angel has an everyman appearance that helps him to be unremarkable. Facial hair and a few days in the tanning booth, he can pass as Hispanic. A shave and a quick clean up can transform him to a Russian. A shaved his head and carb binge allow him to revel in the role of classic southern red neck. He practices his chameleon like skills on unsuspecting friends and business associates, clearly enjoying himself immensely when they fail to recognize him. Dog Angel knows the dog game--the lingo, the famous bloodlines, the players and the attitude. He lurks on the message boards, in chat rooms, and hacks his way in to the computers of unsuspecting dog fighters. His work has led to busts in Georgia, North Carolina, Florida, California, New York, South Carolina, Virginia, Tennessee, Oklahoma, Illinois and Mississippi. Single and shunning the ties of normal family life, he moves throughout the inner dog fighting circles like a ghost.

As soon as news of the Moonlight Road raid was broadcast, John Goodwin from HSUS called Dog Angel and asked him to go to work on this case. In his turn, Dog Angel asked who his contact would be. The name he heard was familiar. Goodwin said he should work with Kathy Strouse out of Chesapeake, and a VAFTF board member. Dog Angel knew the name. He recalled meeting me at a recent Task Force meeting. His initial impression, he later told me, was of a woman who was a rare combination of big picture thinking and attention to detail with a "dead game" attitude (borrowing a term from the dog fighting world meaning will not quit).

Though Dog Angel took great pride in his record for bringing down dog fighters, he realized that everything he had learned was about to be put to the test. In spite of having spent 35 years hunting dog fighters, when the Michael Vick case exploded, Dog Angel was not optimistic. Here was a man with unlimited resources. Many people believed that there was no way to win this case. Dog Angel was determined to prove them wrong. He already knew way too much about Michael Vick's activities in the dog fighting world to indulge in the fantasy of his supposed innocence. The home team would need irrefutable evidence. Any case against Michael Vick would need to be airtight. He had a lot to lose, and he would not go down without a fight. Dog Angel had heard allegations that Vick had ties to gangs and other groups capable of violence. Those who sought to bring him to justice might face real danger.

On the other hand, a victory in a case of this magnitude might just strike the most important blow against dog fighters in the history of this cruel blood sport. That could make the last 35 years worth it all. Dog Angel decided he was in. He told John he would see him at the Task Force meeting, and he would talk with Kathy.

CHAPTER 7 THE PIT BULL TERRIER

The American Pit Bull Terrier, as we know it today is the product of evolution. It has its origins in the dogs that were used for bull baiting, a common form of entertainment up until the early 1800's. A bull was staked to the ground and dogs were released upon it. Crowds cheered as dogs were gored before the successful members of the pack succeeded in bringing down the enraged bull and killing it. This form of sport was outlawed in Great Britain, and its proponents began to out cross their bull dogs with smaller terrier type dogs to create the pit bull terrier. It was too difficult to conduct clandestine bull baiting events, so the sport of pit matches between two dogs grew popular.

The pit bull came to America around the time of the Civil War, and with him the blood sport of dog fighting. Fighters consistently bred dogs to enhance their aggression towards other dogs. They engineered dogs that did not respond to their own pain and suffering, often ignoring their own self preservation. They bred dogs that not only often failed to give normal canine warning signals such as growling, but also failed to respond to classic signs of canine submission. Instead these dogs would continue attacking. Their entire program of breeding, diet and exercise was designed to create a powerful, well muscled, hard biting fighting machine.

Other Americans saw what they believed was the true heart of this breed. During the Civil War, a small stray dog wandered into the camp of the 11th Pennsylvania Infantry. She was quickly adopted by one of the young soldiers, who named her Sallie. In 1863, Sallie marched with her regiment from Virginia to Pennsylvania. During the battle of Gettysburg on July first of that year, the Union Army was forced to retreat and regroup at Cemetery Hill. Among the many missing was Sallie. When the soldiers made their way back to the scene of the retreat at Oak Ridge several days later, they found Sallie very much alive. She was lying beside the body of her fallen master, faithful to him even in death. The soldiers took Sallie with them, and she became their official mascot until she was killed at the Battle of Hatcher's Run in Virginia the following year. Today at the site of the Battle of Gettysburg stands a monument to the 11th Pennsylvania Infantry. At the base of the full size bronze statue of a Union soldier sleeps a bronze statuette of what appears to be a pit bull. The veterans of the 11th Pennsylvania had wanted to honor Sallie, who had not only brought so much happiness to the soldiers, but remained a symbol of loyalty during the horror of war.

By the dawn of the 1900's, the pit bull terrier had become America's dog. He was depicted on a patriotic poster along with an English bulldog, a German dachshund, a French bulldog and a Russian wolfhound by an artist named Wallace Robinson in 1914. All of the dogs were dressed in military uniforms. The pit bull was in the center of the poster. The caption read, "I'm neutral, BUT- Not Afraid of any of them".

Stubby, a young pit bull terrier born in 1917 became the most decorated dog in American military history. His young marine owner, Corporal John Conroy, smuggled him aboard a troop transport in World War I. The tenacious little dog saved his unit from both a gas attack and discovery by German forces. He roused the men by barking when he smelled the gas, so that they were able to put on their masks in time, saving hundreds of lives. Later he alerted the men to the presence of a German spy who had discovered their location and was attempting to crawl away to alert the enemy, until Stubby captured him by the seat of his pants. Stubby was given his own gas mask fashioned by the men he saved. He was wounded twice, but he survived the war to return home with his master.

Stubby was honored for his bravery by receipt of a number of medals and the honorary award of the rank of Sergeant. He led a number of parades and met Presidents Wilson, Coolidge and Harding. He stayed with his beloved owner, John, until the little dog died in 1926. Today, Stubby is on display with his military coat and medals at the Smithsonian's National Museum of American History.

The pit bull became one of the most popular choices for a family pet—good with children, fiercely loyal, eager to please and devoted to his owner. He was Petey in the Little Rascals series, and Tige, the dog inside the Buster Brown shoe. Sadly, the very qualities that made him such a perfect family protector also made it easy to exploit him for more sinister purposes.

Massachusetts was the first state to ban the barbaric sport of dog fighting in 1835. Other states followed. Today dog fighting is a felony in all 50 states. Idaho and Wyoming were the last states to enact the felony language in 2008. Even possession of fighting dogs is illegal. Violation is a felony everywhere except New York, Texas, and West Virginia where it is a misdemeanor. Attending a dog fight as a spectator is also illegal in every state except Hawaii and Montana.

Dog Fighting knows no racial, social or economic boundaries. Participants are rich and poor, ignorant and educated. They have included judges, police officers, sheriffs, probation officers, animal control officers, teachers, lawyers, veterinarians, and sports figures. The infamous Cajun Rules of dog fighting were written by Lafayette, Louisiana Police Chief Gaboon Trahan. Trahan hosted fights that attracted competitors from all over the South. The Cajun Rules can still be downloaded from the internet today.

With the advent of the internet, dog fighters suddenly found that they were able to reach to each other in ways that have never before been possible. In private chat rooms and on membership only message boards, they brag about past fights, set up new ones, offer puppies and dogs for sale and at stud. They trash suspected snitches, law enforcement, animal welfare workers, and each other. Underground and online publications hawk products and equipment, provide blow by blow accounts of fights, offer keep instructions to prepare dogs for fights and after the match instructions to self treat severely injured dogs. Authors of articles often state emphatically that all accounts are fictional. Hundreds of web sites for dog fighting kennels and breeders proclaim that no dogs are bought or sold for illegal purposes; "No violations of the Federal Animal Welfare Act." It is a laughable smokescreen.

Proponents claim that the dogs love to fight, that they have been bred for it and they choose to be in the box. They ignore the fact that animals confronted with a perceived threat usually have two options—fight or flight. Trapped in a pit facing another dog, these animals no longer have the option of flight. Their injuries are frequently horrific and even fatal.

Dogmen often proclaim that they love their dogs. Yet except for fights, the vast majority of these dogs live their entire lives on heavy chains attached to dilapidated dog houses set on barren patches of earth. Frequently, the grass has been worn completely away by the constant and lonely pacing by an animal denied the companionship of the humans he prefers even to his own kind. The dog fighters defend their actions with a religious zeal. Many say the pit game is not a hobby that a man takes up, but a passion a man is born to. The investigators that pursue these criminals believe that part of the attraction lies in the fact that this grisly sport allows the dogmen to align themselves with qualities they will never have themselves. Though sickened by the fighting, many people cannot help admiring the heart, loyalty and courage of these dogs. Having no loyalty of their own, the dogmen say that a dog who quits is not worth the food it takes to feed him or the space it takes to keep him chained. These cowards think nothing of killing dogs that perform poorly. These animals have been shot, stabbed, beaten, hanged, bludgeoned, electrocuted, drowned, duck taped, set on fire, and simply left on a chain to starve to death.

Many people in today's society are calling for a ban on and annihilation of the American pit bull terrier. Around the country they have had some successes. Pit bulls are banned in Denver, Colorado, Prince George County, Maryland, and other cities across American. More localities are considering similar bans, and in some areas, their keeping is already strictly regulated. Defenders of the pit bull believe that laws should punish the deed, not the breed. They maintain that if the pit bull is banned, criminals will simply move on to another breed of fighting dog, and there are plenty to choose from-Argentine Dogo, Fila Brasileiro, Alano Espanol, Presa Canario, Cane Corso, Cordoba Fighting Dog and more. Defenders often see their mission as rescue of the pit bull, so that he might reclaim his former status as one of America's most popular family pets. As a result of their efforts, pit bulls are finding their way into public service as law dogs, search and rescue dogs, and even therapy dogs.

Across the country ACOs struggle with what to do with dogs seized from fighting operations. In most cases the dogs are euthanized. Few of these departments have the resources to evaluate, retrain and carefully screen future homes for these dogs. Whether people advocate rescue or the sad alternative of euthanasia, most would agree that the pit bull remains the most consistently exploited and abused breed of dog in our country today.

CHAPTER 8 THE VICTIMS

The 66 dogs from Moonlight Drive were being cared for by a number of shelters in southeast Virginia. The beagles, Rottweilers, Presa Canarios and several pit bulls went to Virginia Beach Animal Control. Surry County kept 10 pit bulls in their own shelter. On behalf of the City of Chesapeake, I agreed to assist Surry County by sheltering 10 of the pit bulls until their fate could be decided. My officers picked up six pit bulls the day of the Task Force meeting, and four more the next day, which was Thursday. It was not until Friday, April 29, 2007 that I first met the dogs that would be under our care for the next seven months.

Each dog was examined by our veterinarian. Their overall health seemed to be surprisingly good. Each one was vaccinated for kennel cough, tested for heartworms, wormed for intestinal parasites, and treated for fleas.

Several of the dogs seemed to want to play, but we found ourselves challenged to provide toys that they could not destroy. We knew that we needed to provide some sort of enrichment to keep them stimulated and prevent a syndrome shelter people often call "kennel crazy". It is extremely stressful for social creatures such as dogs to be kenneled for long periods. They can begin to act out by developing aggressive behaviors, spinning in their kennel, self mutilating, or conversely, becoming depressed and withdrawn. Someone laughingly suggested bowling balls as indestructible toys, so we contacted a local bowling alley and explained what we were looking for and why. The people there were happy to donate the bowling balls we needed. In the end, all of the dogs did well for as long as they were with us. While kennel life is certainly not an ideal situation, for these dogs, it was probably better than anything they had ever known before. That thought somehow made us even sadder.

We had no idea what any of their names were so we chose new ones. ACO Tracy Stevens and Shelter Attendant, Billy Cartwright gave each of them the names we would call them throughout their stay. The first dog was in run 86. He was a blackish brown, or seal colored, male who loved to play and was sweet and loving to all of us. He was the hardest of all of the dogs to name. For days the shelter attendants struggled to come up with something suitable. In the meantime they settled for calling him by his kennel number. Finally they decided to permanently call him 86 like one of the spy characters in the old television program *Get Smart*. 86 loved the bowling balls and the Kong toys filled with peanut butter and treats.

Tessa was the name given to the female black and white pit bull in run 88. She was really excited about toys, even though they seemed unfamiliar to her and she did little but watch them at first. We realized she had probably never had a toy. Cookies, as we called biscuits and treats, sent her over the edge! Seeing her excitement over something as simple as dog biscuits made our hearts constrict each time we watched her.

Run 90 was Buster, a male black and white pit bull. Low to the ground with a huge head, he absolutely loved our shelter attendant, Billy, and Billy loved him. Buster could have cared less about toys. He just wanted someone's undivided attention and a hand constantly stroking him. He loved to lie in Billy's lap with his tongue lolling, his tail beating the ground, and a huge grin on his face.

We had a hard time keeping weight on Bonita in run 113. She was a heavily scarred black pit bull with a small spot of white on her chest. All of Bonita's canine teeth had been ground or filed down to stumps. At first, we suspected that she may have been used as a bait dog for training others to fight. She had also been heavily bred, and we learned later that her teeth had been ground down to prevent her from lashing out at the stud dogs. Bonita loved toys and loved attention from people, but was highly dog aggressive. Within about a week, she developed an upper respiratory infection that, despite treatment and medication, only became worse. She developed pneumonia and had to be hospitalized where she was placed on strong antibiotics and oxygen before finally making a full recovery.

Little Red was extremely shy. She was a heavily scarred red female in run 116. Billy worked overtime to earn her trust. Gradually she learned that he and ACO Stevens were the keepers of the cookies. She decided that she loved them both, but continued to be afraid of everyone else, especially men. Little Red was missing all of her canine teeth. We could only wonder if she had been a bait dog, or maybe she was a seasoned fighter whose teeth were removed later in life. She had also been heavily bred.

Miss Petey was named after the dog from The Little Rascals. She was a white female with black spots who loved people, toys, and cookies. She was the most trusting of all of the dogs, completely happy go lucky all of the time. Miss Petey was in run 118.

In 119 was Shadow, an older seal and white colored male. The shelter attendants gave him his name because he was so very timid. He was always sweet, and soon became known for the way he wrinkled his lips into a smile that showed his front teeth each time he was touched. He was clueless about what to do with toys, and would only pick up his cookie to eat it when he thought no one was watching.

Next door was Big Fella in run 120. He was a tan and white male, who expressed a dignified enjoyment for the bowling balls, Kongs and cookies. The shelter attendants found him to be the calmest and most laid back of all the dogs.

Socks was a red and white female who was extremely fearful. She would cower and shrink, not even daring to look at people when approached. She had an odd head tilt, and we were concerned that she might suffer from some sort of neurological problem. Still our veterinarian found nothing wrong with her. It would take many months before she trusted the shelter attendants, who talked to her and fed her every day. Eventually she would come to trust Billy and ACO Stevens. Socks also became very fond of her bowling ball and cookies. She was in run 121.

The last dog was a male black and white tuxedo style in run 92. At first, the shelter attendants did not trust him. He seemed to be moody, and would charge the kennel door as soon as shelter attendants turned their backs to walk away. He would hide behind the cinder block frame of the doorway that separated the backside of his run from the front and peek at people passing. He was dubbed Sneaky Eyes. To our surprise, we soon learned that Sneaky Eyes was really just a big, frightened baby! When shelter attendants took him outside he froze, crouching low to the ground and trembling. Coaxed to move, he would only creep, keeping his tail tucked so far that it touched his belly. We believed he had spent his whole life chained, and just had no idea what to do without that heavy weight on his neck. Deb, one of our office assistants, adored him, and soon we would all come to share her love for this little dog. Out of all of the dogs, Sneaky Eyes would make the most amazing transformation.

We often wondered as the case unfolded what our dogs had been forced to witness at the hell that was Moonlight Road. The thought made us sick, but at the same time we marveled at the resilience and the forgiveness of these animals.

When we began, we had no idea that we would have these dogs for many months. This situation was hardest on the shelter attendants. They had no illusions about the typical fate of fighting dogs. They understood the reasons, so they tried their best to avoid becoming emotionally attached to any of them. Of course, it could not work, and it did not work. It was impossible to care for these creatures every day and remain immune to their big brown eyes, and the personalities that were blossoming as the dogs slowly came out of their shells.

One day ACO Stevens and Billy came to me to ask that, if and when the time came to euthanize these dogs, they be excused from participating. Euthanasia is an unpleasant, but regular part of their duties, but I completely understood and respected their feelings in the case of these dogs. Stevens especially became very attached to all of them. Every day she was on duty, she visited each of them and handed out cookies. Supervisor Lynn Roberson and I agreed that if the time came, we would carry out the sad duty.

In spite of what we believed would be the fate of the ten pit bulls in our shelter, we continued to hope that somehow there might be a happier future in store for them. With that in mind, I tried to urge Poindexter to set a date for a custody hearing on the dogs. Up to that point, no one had come forward to claim ownership of any of them. The ACO from Surry County had the authority to petition the general district court for custody of all of the dogs. This would allow Surry to make a decision on what would be done with them. Should any individual appear in court to contest the custody award, Poindexter would be able to identify that person as an owner and a potential defendant for the dog fighting case. Poindexter's response to me was that the dog fighting statute did not require him to hold a hearing. I agreed that the statute only required the ACO to seize dogs used for dog fighting, but suggested that he look at another statute that allowed animal control to petition for custody of animals. Otherwise, I said, these animals would be in limbo, and we would have to hold onto them indefinitely.

Poindexter would never set a hearing for custody of the dogs.

CHAPTER 9 CLIMBING ABOARD THE ROLLERCOASTER

On Friday morning, April 27, I spoke with my friend Mark Kumpf. Mark was the former president of VACA and would soon be elected president of the National Animal Control Association (NACA). He had recently relocated to Ohio as the Montgomery County Animal Services Manager. He was very interested in the Surry dog fighting case and promised to help in any way he could.

The media was clamoring for details, so the VAFTF sent out a press release. Unfortunately, the press release identified me as the lead investigator from the task force. The media took that phrase and translated it to mean lead investigator on the case, an error that would cause a flood of media inquiries both at work and at home. Unaware of the error, I was stunned when the calls began to pour in that day. I could only be thankful for the ladies at the front desk who ran interference and kept them at bay.

One bright spot was an e-mail that I received from Alison Gianotto, the web administrator for the site, *Pet-Abuse.com*, a national data base of animal cruelty and fighting cases across the country. She is very knowledgeable about fighting dog lines and the human players involved in this despicable pastime. Add to that the fact that she is a computer genius and you have an incredible resource for any investigation. Alison asked what she could do. I was thrilled that she was willing to help. I told her that I could not think of a better person to hunt for Vick's footprint on the web.

Very quickly she began sending me information. Some of the first files she sent were articles from the media coverage of the search at Vick's property on Moonlight Road that had begun to flood the airwaves, newsstands and the net. Vick was categorically denying any involvement in or connection to the dogs from Moonlight Road. Alison and I agreed that it sounded as though Vick was expecting his friends and family to fall on their swords for the greater good—him. She promised to continue to work on gathering information.

Almost immediately, reporters began to refute Vick's claim, airing statements by neighbors who claimed Vick was frequently at the house, and even purchased supplies for the dogs, including needles, syringes and huge quantities of dog food.

A report from a FOX Sports Radio carried an interesting quote from host Chris Landry. Landry said in an interview on Radio 620 WDAE in Tampa, Florida, that Ray Buchanan, a former Atlanta defensive back, had told him Vick had been involved in dog fighting for years. According to Landry, Buchanan said Vick not only knew about the fighting operation, he was behind it and paying for all of it. Buchanan quickly denied making those statements, but Landry responded stubbornly that he stood by his report. Atlanta Falcons owner Arthur Blank told reporters from The Atlanta Journal Constitution that he was obviously concerned. "From the facts so far, he said, it's not a pretty picture. It's clearly an issue, and we'll wait to see what revolves around it."

I received an interesting tip that afternoon. According to Dog Angel, Stacey Miller, the convicted dog fighter from the Richmond area, claimed to have attended fights on Vick's property on Moonlight Road where Vick himself had been present. Perhaps Miller would be willing to talk with investigators. I promised to share this information with Poindexter.

More information continued to come in throughout the day. I received a call from Deputy Bill Brinkman. He asked me to check with Dog Angel and my other contacts to see if anyone might have an Atlanta phone number for Vick. I brought him up to date on what I had found out from Dog Angel thus far. We needed to find Tony Taylor and the man known only as Virginia O. Brinkman asked me to set up a meeting with Dog Angel. I doubted that this would happen, but agreed to pass on the message. I sent an e-mail message for Dog Angel to John Goodwin of HSUS, who responded that there was no way Dog Angel would meet with anyone face to face. He had to be protected. There was a chance, Goodwin said, that the man might agree to a conference call.

A short time later, I was astonished to get a call directly from Dog Angel. We had not spoken since the day of the VAFTF meeting. He had NEVER called me directly before. Other than our two brief meetings, Dog Angel had always communicated through Goodwin. We discussed the proposed meeting, and surprisingly he appeared to consider it, until I told him who the players were. The moment I mentioned the meeting was being requested by a deputy from Surry County, he snapped, "Absolutely not!" Not only would he not meet with them, he would not even participate in a conference call.

"If, you know, if you tell me your guy is straight up, I believe you," he said, "but he's working in a hornet's nest, a snake pit, and I don't trust any of them." Dog Angel insisted that any information he had to pass on would have to go through Goodwin or me.

We then moved on to rather strange topic. Dog Angel said he was aware I had found out his true identity. I said nothing. Goodwin must have told him, I thought. Dog Angel suggested ways that I might have learned who he was. I was not willing to confirm or deny how I knew, so I did not respond. He moved on to say he also suspected that I did not trust him. He assured me that he was one of the good guys, and asked me to give him my word that I would not compromise him. He said if dog fighters found out that he was actually working undercover, they would kill him. He would be dead. I did not trust him, but I gave him my word that I would never reveal to anyone his true identity. The image of the two of us circling each other like a couple of wary dogs flashed in my mind. When I hung up the phone I had no idea that call was the beginning of our long term collaboration on the Michael Vick case.

Saturday, April 28 was supposed to be a day of relaxation, but I could not make the wheels in my head stop turning. I finally could not stand it any longer. I started to pull up more files that Alison had sent me, including Vick's kennel web site, Vick's K-9 Kennels. The address for the kennel was the 1900 block of Moonlight Road. The contact person for the kennel was Quanis Phillips. I was certain by now that the Q Dog Angel had told me about and Quanis Phillips were one in the same person.

Alison sent me a video of a commercial Vick had made in which he was hawking Nike sneakers. The audio was hard to understand. Vick seems to mumble, but he can be heard saying, "I love my dog," and then the video cuts to a picture of a blue pit bull. There had been a blue pit on the property that we had seized.

That same day Vick was in New York for the NFL draft. Football Commissioner Roger Goodell requested a meeting with him at Radio City Music Hall. One report stated that despite repeated questions and pleas from Goodell to be completely honest, Vick continued to deny any involvement in dog fighting. Goodell was hoping for confidential yet full disclosure, so that the Falcons and the organization could deal with the fallout. Vick assured him there was nothing to worry about, and that he was never at the house on Moonlight Road. When Dog Angel heard this, he knew a line had been drawn. Vick would now have to cover his tracks. To borrow a game dog term, he said we were now in for a "long show".

Alison forwarded me an intriguing internet post from one of the many message boards where dog fighters lurked dated January 7, 2006 that read, "I had the baddest female in my opinion....Michael Vick (pro football player for those who don't know) has the money to go out and buy the top dog in the nation... He brought his dog to the ring and it got pieced up [badly injured] on a $40,000 bet..." The writer was claiming that he actually fought a dog against one belonging to Michael Vick! We could hardly contain our excitement.

Next, Alison sent me an article that mentioned fun facts about athletes. It said that Vick's favorite pet was his pit bull, Champagne. Another article mentioned that Vick had been on the internet the other day doing research on another of his interests, breeding pit bulls. His female, the article said, had already produced one litter, and Vick had a budding breeding kennel in the works. I forwarded everything to Deputy Brinkman.

I received a message from Dog Angel that Vick was terrified that his prints would be found all over the pit and the training equipment. I immediately called Brinkman to ask if the State Police had printed anything at the scene. To my disappointment he said they had not.

I decided enough was enough. The rest of the weekend passed in a haze of yard work, housework, and pets—all the most normal of activities, but I could not rid myself of the cloud of suspense that hung over everything.

On Monday morning Brinkman telephoned to say he was going to a meeting about the case with Surry County officials, and that he would call me later to let me know what happened.

He also said that he had an informant who confirmed what Dog Angel had told me about the involvement of Tony Taylor. The informant, known only as "C", also knew Virginia O. He did not know the man's full name, but believed his first name might be Oscar. C had told Brinkman that dogs had been killed and buried on the property.

That afternoon, I talked with Kristin Hamman. She is a special agent with the USDA OIG, and she handles, among other things, dog fighting cases. Hamman urged me to contact John Goodwin at HSUS again. Goodwin, she knew, had a contact at IRS. She suggested I pass on the information contained in the blog about the $40,000 bet lost by Vick. If I could, she said, I should speak with the agent directly. Hamman warned me that any contact with IRS would be one sided. I would give information, and the agent would tell me nothing. That was fine.

Before I left work that day, Mark Kumpf called me. He said WVEC TV 13, the ABC affiliate in our area, was running a story. The reporter said that according to Sheriff Harold Brown and Commonwealth Attorney Gerald Poindexter in Surry County, Vick would not likely face any charges. I stood frozen with the phone in my hand. Poindexter had certainly not said anything like this to me during our conversations. Brinkman had not called me to tell me what had happened at the meeting. This news hit me like a blow. Was this case going the way of the 2000 Benny Butts case? Was another dog fighter going to get a free pass?

Brinkman finally called at around 5:15 that afternoon. He was agitated and upset. They were after his job. In response to my question, he said "they" were his local department—Sheriff Harold Brown and Commonwealth Attorney Gerald Poindexter. Had Dog Angel been right not to trust these people? Brinkman said there had been a roundtable meeting that morning. State Police Officers, Sheriff Brown, Special Agent from the USDA OIG Jim Knorr, and ACO James Smith from Surry had all attended. Brinkman told me that Poindexter and Smith had entered the meeting together. Poindexter asked Smith what he had seen out at Moonlight Road. Smith replied, "Well, I really didn't see nothing wrong out there. A couple of bowls were dirty. And they all had food and some water."

"No they didn't," I practically shouted into the phone. "Oh, we... we gave Smith a list of the things that were wrong! What about the treadmills, jennies, the pit, the blood, the paraphernalia, the scarred and injured dogs?"

"That's why I even called and asked [Officer Tobin]," Brinkman replied in disgust. "I asked her, 'What did Smith tell you as you was walking around? 'Cause when I first talked to him, I said 'James, this is what we got'. And he come walking through there, after I did my initial, he came walking back and said we got this, and this and this. Then all of a sudden this morning at that meeting, nothing?! Everything went north. I said bullshit."

"Bullshit is exactly right," I said. "Because Bill, there was a list, a *laundry* list of problems. We wrote them all down for him."

Brinkman continued, "I wanted to go get another search warrant and go get the dogs, exhume the dogs and everything like that. Okay, fine. The sheriff...Poindexter even asked the sheriff, 'Do you agree?

'Yep, we're going to get a search warrant and go do that.'

"Jim Knorr, us...the state police was there and everything. All right, so we get ready to leave, and Poindexter says, 'Okay, we're all in agreement. Sheriff, you sure you want to go get a search warrant? Why don't you just go up there and ask permission from the owner?'

"I looked at Poindexter and said, 'No. We're getting a warrant. Cause, I had permission on Benny Butts. I had *written* consent. I'm not going down that road again.'"

Brinkman remembered all too well his ill fated search of Benny Butts' property in 2000. He also remembered Poindexter's statement at the time that he did not believe in consent searches! Brinkman went on to say that Poindexter asked him,

"How are we going to prosecute these people, Mr. Brinkman, when we don't have a court house?"

"That's not my fault," he replied. "Crime still goes on, you got a court house or not. They can use the court house in Sussex."

Brinkman said all was not lost. He planned to meet with a federal prosecutor. The case, he said, might be ready to explode.

"Wait a minute," I said. "Are you saying this thing could go federal?"

"I sure hope so," he replied. "Cause otherwise, we're dead in the water."

On Tuesday, May 1st, the rollercoaster ride continued. I called and spoke with my old friend Rex Riley from Surry. We chatted awhile, and then I asked him to tell me the story again about Vick buying dog food at the local hardware store. Rex said he had gone to Surry Hardware one day, where a friend of his asked him, "Do you know who that was?" He pointed to a young man who had been leaving the store as Rex entered.

Rex responded, "No."

His friend said, "That was Michael Vick. He just bought $600 worth of dog food and a fishing reel."

I asked Rex if he knew whether Vick had an account at the store. Had he paid by credit card or cash? When was the last time Vick had been in the store? Had he continued to shop there? Rex was not sure. I asked him if there was anyone else who might be willing to talk with authorities about what had been going on at the Moonlight Road house. Rex gave me the names of several neighbors who, he said, knew about the dog fighting and could place Michael Vick on the property many times. Rex promised to let me know if he came up with any other information.

I hung up and noticed I had a message from Brinkman. He was anxious to talk to me about a story that had aired on WAVY TV 10, the local NBC affiliate. I had watched it myself that morning, and had already asked Alison from *Pet-Abuse.com* to capture it for me as a file. WAVY TV 10 Reporter Mary Kay Maloney featured footage from a 2003 story showing the Moonlight Road house under construction. The film showed the black buildings, dogs, dog houses, and a fenced area enclosing a fully assembled cat jenny! Mary Kay said she had interviewed the builders and construction workers at the time, who claimed they spoke with Vick frequently when he visited the construction site, and they often spoke about the dogs. I told Brinkman I would send him the file of the story. Next I repeated the story Rex had shared about the purchases from Surry Hardware and gave him the names of the two neighbors.

It seemed like only moments later when my phone rang again. "We got him!" Brinkman said excitedly. Brinkman had found the man who had pointed out Vick to Rex that day. Brinkman learned that Vick often bought dog food at Surry Hardware, and always paid cash. This categorically refuted Vick's claim that he had nothing to do with the dogs. Brinkman said he also found out that the Premium Gold Dog Food, bags upon bags of which we had seen in the building that housed the pit, had been purchased by Vick in Suffolk, a neighboring city. Brinkman said he would attempt to track down exactly where.

Brinkman had other news. He and Special Agent Jim Knorr had been to see Assistant US Attorney Mike Gill and had laid out their case before him. Brinkman told Gill, "My case is being pulled out from underneath me and, now I'm not going to get prosecution. I'm going to be used as a pawn. The case will be 'mistried', and then that's going to be my fault." Knorr and Brinkman explained that they believed the Vick case constituted a violation of the Federal Animal Welfare Act, and the federal government should become involved. Gill was non committal, but as the men left they felt hopeful that the Feds would take an interest.

I sent an e-mail out to the VAFTF and a few other friends with a list of people and dog names. I knew many of us had old copies of pedigrees, registrations, and *SDJ*s. I hoped that the members of the task force would go through their paper work and old magazines to look for any names from my list. I recognized how time consuming this would be, but I needed some help. John Goodwin quickly e-mailed me to report that none of the Moonlight Road suspects' names appeared on his copy of the subscriber list for *SDJ*. Although none of our suspects appeared to be subscribers, Goodwin did find numerous references to Virginia O, Hardcore, Too Bad Kennels, Vick and MV Kennels. He sent them all to me, and I forwarded them to Brinkman.

At 1:30 p.m. that afternoon, two State Police Officers from the Drug Task Force arrived at my office unannounced asking to interview me. I went over everything that I had learned and passed on to Brinkman. They had questions regarding the uses of the equipment, drugs and other items that had been recovered. We discussed some of the possible arguments a defense attorney might make. They seemed concerned about whether we actually had enough evidence for a conviction. I felt strongly that we did. We had plenty of equipment, drugs, paraphernalia, scarred dogs, and we had the bloody pit. I promised I would continue to share anything I learned with Brinkman. Their next request took me completely by surprise. They asked to speak with Dog Angel. I told them I doubted that would happen, but I would ask. Dog Angel's reply was a succinct, "Hell no!"

On Wednesday, May 2, 2007, I drove to Charlottesville, Virginia for a VACA Board of Directors meeting. Board meetings usually last for about 4 hours, and it was a 3 hour drive both ways, so it was usually a long day. At the meeting, Board members were eager for information on the progress of the case. Everyone offered to help in any way they could.

During one of our breaks, I spoke to Goodwin by phone. He was concerned about statements he said were coming out of the Sheriff's department in Surry. Did the local authorities in Surry have a good handle on things, he wanted to know. Did they know how to put together a dog fighting case? He also said that as far as he knew, no one from Surry had made any calls or efforts to accept the offers of assistance that had poured in--help that Poindexter had told me he would need.

I knew that Ann Cheynoweth, the Executive Director of Animal Fighting Issues for HSUS had called Poindexter to offer information and assistance. Poindexter, she said, responded with a profanity laced "we don't need your help" message.

As I drove home from the meeting, I received a call from the man himself-Surry Commonwealth Attorney Gerald Poindexter. I was extremely wary as we talked about the case so far. He asked me about the significance of various pieces of the evidence that we had recovered. Taken separately, I said, no one single piece was irrefutable evidence of dog fighting. Each was a piece of the puzzle that when put together led to no rational conclusion other than dog fighting. He seemed satisfied with this. He shared with me the fact that he had received hate mail when the Butts case had fallen apart, and the dogs and equipment had been returned to Butts. Butts, of course, had continued his dog fighting activities until his death. I suggested, as I had in our previous conversation, that he speak with some of the many people who were ready to offer assistance in this case—attorneys, dog fighting experts, and members of nationally recognized animal organizations such as HSUS and the ASPCA. I reminded him that Michelle Welch who had experience trying dog fighting cases was willing to help if called upon. Forensic veterinarian, Dr. Melinda Merck, had also offered her assistance. Dr. Merck was the author of a much respected book titled *Veterinary Forensic Investigation of Animal Cruelty: A Guide for Veterinarians and Law Enforcement*. Dr. Merck had testified as an expert witness in a number of animal cruelty and fighting cases. I told Poindexter I would send him contact numbers the following day, and we ended our conversation.

By then my cell phone was nearly dead, which was fine. I was tired of talking. I would send the information to Poindexter the next day via email. I hoped that the doubts voiced by Goodwin, Ann Chynoweth, Brinkman and Dog Angel would prove to be unfounded.

That evening, Goodwin called me again. He told me he had heard there was a video tape of a dogfight that showed Michael Vick in attendance. I knew nothing about this, and Goodwin admitted he had no idea where the tape might be if it in fact existed. The phone rang again. This time it was Brinkman. He spoke about trying to set up a meeting the following Monday. He told me that he had found another informant, who claimed to have attended a fight at Moonlight Road where Vick had been present. He had also talked to the builders of Vick's house who would confirm that the dogs and paraphernalia were already there when construction began on the house. I was surprised Brinkman did not seem happier about these latest developments. The reason, he said, was that Poindexter had been screaming at Sheriff Brown to fire him. He hoped things might improve when he presented his new information. A meeting was scheduled for the following Monday morning at 10:00 a.m. at Poindexter's office to review the evidence.

I could not help wishing that Amy James were trying this case. James is an Assistant Commonwealth Attorney for Chesapeake. She handles cruelty cases and dog fighting cases for Animal Control in Chesapeake with total commitment and precision. In the early days of our acquaintance, I remember her telling me she did not really know a lot about dog fighting. I sent her a DVD, a kind of training aid, called *Off the Chain*. She called me to say she did not want to watch it; she was not sure she could stand it. I begged her; she could fast forward through the fighting scenes, I said. I wanted her to see the appalling rationalization and justification of the dog fighters in their own words, as they appeared on the tape. Reluctantly, she agreed, and later reported that the tape was very helpful. James now has five dog fighting convictions under her belt.

I contacted the members of the VAFTF to discuss the concerns we were all having about the case thus far. We agreed that Brinkman needed federal help. Michelle Welch and Richard Samuels both placed calls to the Feds. After hearing how Poindexter had responded to Ann Cheynoweth from HSUS, Goodwin called some of his own federal contacts.

Friday, May 4, I received a couple of calls from reporters who wanted to know what was happening with the dogs; was there going to be a custody hearing? I referred each of them to Poindexter. I decided to go on line and see what was being said about the case. There were posts on message boards all over the place—Vick lied, Vick was guilty, he was in the business of breeding pit bulls. Some called on the NFL Commissioner Rodger Goodell to suspend Vick. One article said that it looked like the Feds were going to step in, which might be a very bad thing for Vick. The article suggested that this might be the only way to save the case, since it looked like Virginia was going let it pass.

On Tuesday, May 9, 2007, Brinkman called to say the Monday meeting with Poindexter had not happened. He hoped it would not matter and that an announcement would be forthcoming from the US Attorney's Office that they would be taking over the case.

The following day, I was in Hartford, Connecticut where I taught Animal Fighting Investigation for the NACA. The class was an enthusiastic group of about 40 ACOs, brimming with questions and eager to get out there and get the bad guys. At home the next evening, I finally had a chance to look through a bunch of files from Alison. These contained information about three individuals, Virginia O, Hardcore Benny Butts, and Michael Vick. I set to work trying to map out the connections. I knew Benny Butts, according to Brinkman and Dog Angel, had worked at 1915 Moonlight Road helping to train and condition the dogs. The man known as Virginia O set up the fights. We still had no idea who this man was.

To track fighting dogs and their owners, one can interpret the registrations and pedigrees, with the various designations of parenthood. These are cross referenced with the wins and championships noted in the underground magazines, as well as posts on internet message boards. It is both time consuming and challenging.

One of the online pedigrees Alison sent was for MV Kennels Maggie May. Maggie May's dam was listed as MV Kennels' Blaze. A notation on the pedigree said, "Absolute baddest bitch on the planet. She beat True Colors Champion Darkside in 14 minutes (doa). Her times, :15, :14. Three OTC :2, :8, :10. Also collecting Five Forfeits! Nothing lived long enough to scratch back!"

It was not hard to translate. According to the pedigree, Maggie May was a two time winner of official fights, having beaten two dogs in 15 minutes and 14 minutes respectively. In the 14 minute fight, she had killed her opponent, Darkside. Maggie May had also won three off the chain matches in 2, 8 and 10 minutes. An off the chain match is one for which there is no keep or training period. The dog goes straight from the chain to the fight.

One night after I had fallen into bed out of pure exhaustion, Mark Kumpf called. I never heard the phone. I listened to his brief message the following morning. "You owe me big time!" I wanted to call him that moment, but decided I probably should not wake him up at 5 a.m. his time! I contained myself until 9 a.m., and hurriedly dialed his number. Mark reminded me that he had testified as an expert witness in a case in Cumberland County, Virginia in 2004. The defendant, Dawn Allen, had been charged with felony dog fighting. Her boyfriend, Glenn Sweeting, a suspected drug dealer, was shot and killed by police during a drug sting operation. A short time later, authorities executed a search warrant at Dawn Allen's Mosby Road home where they found 26 pit bulls. One dog had no lips, and one had fresh wounds. They found a total of five dog carcasses buried in a shallow grave. Allen denied knowing how the dogs had died, suggesting that they may have been bitten by snakes. Allen pleaded guilty to a lesser charge of cruelty to animals and was sentenced to 12 months in jail with all but ten days suspended. Mark had been looking through his file copies of documents related to the case. One of the notations from Allen's paperwork contained something he felt might interest me. Mark said the fax would be waiting for me when I got to work. The rest would follow by snail mail.

I grabbed the fax as soon as I walked in the door, and called Brinkman. "You are going to love me. I am not positive, but I think I have Vick's telephone number. Mark sent it to me." Brinkman was speechless. When I read the notation, "Mike Georgia 1-678-[***-****]," Brinkman exclaimed, "That's an Atlanta area code!" He would be able to use the phone number to track Vick's travels and perhaps even telephone calls to other dog fighters. I told him there was also a note scrawled on a handwritten pedigree, "Michael Vick 7 months old no males."

Our elation lasted for only a brief moment. Brinkman told me that Poindexter had been to the Sheriff's office again demanding that Sheriff Brown fire him. Brinkman assured me he was all right for the time being. He was continuing to hope for some good news from the Feds. Later that day, I received an e-mail from Dog Angel. He reported that Vick was saying he was not worried about the local prosecutor; he expected all charges to be dropped. I deleted the message origin and sent a copy to Brinkman.

Dog Angel theorized that Vick could beat this case by having his cousin Boddie, Purnell Peace and Quanis Phillips agree to take the blame. They could agree to plead guilty to a lesser charge such as cruelty or failure to provide for animals. The men could claim Vick had no idea what was going on. They would pay a small fine, and the case would go away. Vick could make a few donations to animal welfare groups, and do some public service announcements like Rapper DMX had done several years ago. Vick could then go back to playing football and probably dog fighting, too.

Dog Angel learned that although the Vick crew discussed the plan, the sticking point was apparently money. According to Dog Angel, the going rate for someone to take a fall like this one would be anywhere from $50,000 to $100,000 for each year of imprisonment. If as expected there would not even be jail time, the cost could be considerably less. In any event, this amount should have been nothing to Vick. But, according to Dog Angel, he could not bring himself to do it. In-fighting erupted among the crew. Peace and Phillips still blamed Boddie for all of their troubles. He had been the one to bring the law to Moonlight Road. He should be the one to take the fall, they argued. But Vick did not want to pay anyone. For their part, Peace and Phillips began to resent being placed in the same category as Boddie. Their close association with Vick had convinced them that they were his equal partners. The mere suggestion that either of them should agree to do time for something they viewed as all Boddie's fault, was an insult. The heightened emotion in the camp may have prevented Vick from thinking clearly. In spite of the relatively small cost compared to his many millions, Vick did not take this opportunity to try to save himself. Dog Angel was delighted.

The next thing that occurred sent a chill down our collective spine. One of Dog Angel's contacts from the Midwest sent several e-mails to HSUS that contained informations about Vick's operation. These messages were shared with a short list of people. They were VAFTF President Richard Samuels, John Goodwin and Ann Cheynoweth of HSUS, Dog Angel, Gerald Poindexter, and me. A short time later, Dog Angel learned that Vick had told Peace and Phillips to find out the real name of that e-mail sender. *How did Vick know about these emails?* In addition to tipping our collective hand about how much we knew, the breach might have jeopardized the safety of the operative in the Midwest. Dog Angel was adamant that he knew the source of the leak, but he was never able to prove his suspicion. Our small group simply resolved to be more cautious in the future.

In late May Dog Angel reported that Vick may have engaged a man known as the Fixer to help him out of his problem. A shadowy underground figure, the one thing Dog Angel knew for certain was that the Fixer is an active dogman. One source said he has worked for the Gambino crime family; another that he is part of the Russian Mob. Some rumors suggested ties to Las Vegas organized crime. Dog Angel's attempts to track him led only to disposable cell phones that bounced off towers in Las Vegas, New York City, Atlanta and Norfolk. Dog Angel became obsessed with the Fixer. He insisted that he wanted to try to build a federal Racketeer Influenced and Corrupt Organization, or RICO, case against him. Dog Angel insisted the Fixer was part of an ongoing criminal conspiracy involving Vick. I struggled to keep him focused on our case. The Fixer, I argued, was secondary. It was the only disagreement that Dog Angel and I would have. Goodwin joked, "You have to keep Dog Angel focused. He can stray from the trail from time to time."

Poindexter continued to make statements to the media that puzzled us. He said he did not see where the evidence pointed to a dog fighting operation. Dog Angel told me that he heard Michael Vick was feeling pretty good and ready to celebrate the case being over. He was actually planning a press conference where he would announce he had been exonerated and would be happy to get back to football. He announced on ESPN that, "Everyone loves Michael Vick."

Brinkman called to say the meeting that had been cancelled on May 9 was re-scheduled. It would take place the following Monday morning at Poindexter's office, and he was counting on me to be there. The meeting was going to be tricky, Brinkman said. He did not trust Poindexter, and he planned to give him an overview only. He was still hoping that the Feds would take over. For me, events were about to happen that meant I would never attend that meeting.

CHAPTER 10 THE ROAD LESS TRAVELED

I never wanted to grow up to be an animal control officer or ACO. As the favorite villain of Walt Disney and other segments of the entertainment media, it was not something to which the average kid aspired. But I had always loved animals and people. I wanted to work at something that would allow me to serve both. At age 13, I began to volunteer at our local SPCA. It didn't bother me to scoop poop or do whatever was required. I loved helping the animals. That was the first time I learned that SPCAs did not find homes for all of the animals they received. There were simply too many. My family immediately became converts to spaying and neutering.

Later, I worked at a couple of pet stores. I found that I did not care for that as much because the animals were simply merchandise, or inventory. Anyone who had the money could purchase any animal they wished. A tiny yorkie puppy for a three year old child? Fine! A Saint Bernard puppy for an apartment dweller? No problem. The customer's last 2 dogs got off their chains and got hit by cars? Died from something, "Don't know what; we didn't take them to a vet." Here you go; sign here!

I tried dog grooming. I hated the days of shaving a dog only to discover an infestation of fleas, ticks or even maggots! But, I really enjoyed transforming shaggy mops into impeccably coiffed pets. After 7 years of this, I realized I needed to think about my future. The physical demands of grooming would be awfully difficult when I got to be 50!

One day, I saw a job posting for the City of Chesapeake. Animal Control Officer. I had absolutely no idea what the job required, but it had animal in the title. I decided to apply and was hired in 1978. I loved the job. We could really make a difference by protecting animals. I also soon found that my duties included having to euthanize animals. There never were as many people looking for their lost pets or wishing to adopt as there were animals coming in the door. Euthanasia never got any easier. I managed to cope by remembering that there were many worse things that could happen to them, and to cherish the happy endings that would never have happened without our efforts.

Four years later, in 1982, I became the director of an SPCA, a shelter that took in 12,000 animals a year. I worked there for 7 years, doing fund raising, budgeting, and public relations. Eventually, working for a 30 member board each with different priorities, and the constant euthanasia became too much. I had had enough. I decided to leave animal welfare. I was tired of breaking my heart over the things I saw every day. I put in my notice.

I have been an actor since I was about 14. Plays, industrials, a couple of small independent films, a little television, and commercials were some of my fare. It was never a lot—just enough to help pay veterinary bills. So, when I left the SPCA, I joined a children's theater troupe, sponsored by an arts program called Young Audiences of Virginia. It was fantastic. We toured the state doing workshops and performances for elementary and high school students. It was a wonderful year; fulfilling and rewarding. Some of these children had never seen a live performance of any kind until we arrived. After the show they would reach out tiny hands to touch us, not quite sure we were real. The response—the shining look in their eyes and the delight they showed to us were incredible. There was only one problem. It paid very little money. It was a painful decision, but I realized I had to find a real job again.

Next, I went to work for the American Red Cross in 1990 as the manager of the Patient Services office. Our office produced the written reports of the HIV tests that the laboratory performed every day, and sent them to the surrounding hospitals and clinics. Our other duty was to facilitate and schedule autologous blood donations. People scheduled for surgeries that might require blood transfusions could self donate as many as four units of their own blood. It was extremely rewarding to work with our patients and help them through this process. Sadly, the Red Cross decided to do away with our department, and we were all laid off. Henceforth, our patients would be sent to regular bloodmobiles. My staff and I felt that these people were patients, not donors. It saddened us that they would no longer get the special care we gave them.

I had never been out of a job before; had never collected unemployment. I was not prepared for the shame I felt. For a year I worked as a waitress and did odd jobs while I sent out resumes. Going on interview after interview only to be rejected was extremely depressing. It was also frustrating. I felt as though my management, fund raising, budgetary and personnel experience were all discounted because they had been performed in an animal care setting. I sensed the people interviewing me believed that all I had done at the SPCA was play with puppies.

One day I received a call from my old boss from Chesapeake. He had been Lieutenant Jeff Warren of the Chesapeake Police Department. He was now a major, and he was calling to tell me that there was an opening at Chesapeake Animal Control for the top position of Animal Control Coordinator. Did I have any interest in getting back into animal care and welfare? I was surprised to realize I did. I was excited to realize how much I missed it. I missed the animals and I missed being able to make a difference for them. Major Warren told me that if I were hired, I would be required to go through the full basic police academy. Gulp! I was 41 years old! Could I do it?

I applied and got the job. From my hire date in May 1994 until the academy started that September, my immediate supervisor, Sergeant Van Williams, would take me out to the side yard of the shelter each afternoon for a pep talk about what it was going to take to get through. I was concerned myself not just because of my age, but also because I was pretty "girly girl". I did not think of myself as tough or a fighter. However, I also knew I was stubborn and determined. I told the Sergeant he could be sure I was no quitter.

I made it through the four month long school. The academics were a breeze. The physical portion-the running, the pushups, the defensive tactics, firearms, officer survival, and the other skills were tough. In the beginning there were days I could not wait to get to my car so that I could cry in private all the way home. Amazingly, as time went on, I adapted and ended up enjoying one of the most memorable and rewarding periods of my life. I felt so much pride at the accomplishment of simply making it through. I made wonderful friends, and the bonds that our class forged are still strong today. I learned so much that I continue to use every single day. Shortly after graduation, our Chief of Police asked me if I wanted to transfer to the Police Department as a Police Officer. I did not hesitate to respond, "No, thank you, sir." I was happy in Animal Control.

In Chesapeake, our Animal Control also runs the shelter. Animal sheltering is emotionally brutal. We often refer to Monday as "dump the dog day". Sometimes the reasons that people surrender pets are heartbreaking. Other times they seem incredibly shallow. One of the most common reasons offered is moving. While plausible in some circumstances, most of us consider our pets our family, and would never move without them. Other reasons are also common. One woman turned in a six month old shepherd mix puppy because it jumped on her children and chewed things. The office assistant doing the paperwork, gently suggested dogs need training in order to have manners. She asked the woman if the dog had received any obedience training. The woman responded that she did not have time for that. The office assistant explained that we could not promise that we would be able to find a home for this dog. People do not usually come to the shelter looking for a huge six month old puppy, partially housebroken, with no manners and no training. The woman voiced not a single word of concern that this lovely dog might eventually be euthanized. She signed the papers, and then asked if she could look at puppies for adoption. The office assistant was so taken aback, she could not even reply for an instant. Pulling herself together, she replied that the woman was welcome to look. However, she would not be permitted to adopt another animal after relinquishing a young, perfectly healthy, friendly dog.

Another heart wrenching example of what shelter workers face each day was a woman who turned in her 13 year old Chihuahua because it was going blind. Although the office assistant explained that dogs are amazingly able to cope, the woman said it was too much trouble to keep this imperfect animal even though it had been a loyal companion for 13 years. Another person said she was turning in her Golden Retriever because she was simplifying her life. A man turned in his dog because it did not like the grandchildren. We met the grandchildren as they attempted to destroy our office. We agreed with the dog! Examples go on and on. Litters and litters of animals that should never have been born, because humans still fail to spay or neuter the adult animals.

People often respond with outrage when staff must tell them we might be unable to find homes for their animals, that they might be euthanized. Some call us murderers. In spite of this they still walk out our door leaving their animals behind.

Chesapeake Animal Control is an open admission shelter. We are not permitted to turn an animal away if the person presenting it is lawfully allowed to do so. Because we must always take animals in, we must do euthanasia. We handle about 4,500 animals a year. That is about 400 animals a month; an average of 13 animals each day. Because of the serious animal overpopulation problem, we must compete with other surrounding shelters, rescues and private individuals for the small number of available homes. Approximately 700 animals are adopted each year from our shelter. Another 800 or so lost animals are returned to their happy owners. But nearly 2,500 animals are euthanized each year, some for age, disease, injury, or temperament. Tragically too many are euthanized simply because they are extra and there is nowhere for them to go.

Euthanasia is a job that all our officers and shelter attendants rotate. At Chesapeake Animal Control we euthanize by injection of sodium pentobarbital. We also use tranquilizers to sedate any fractious, feral, or struggling animals. Every effort is made to make their passing peaceful, gentle and without fear. No one wants to do this job, but those who perform it have an odd sense of determination to ensure that if it must be done, it is done humanely. Virginia requires that anyone who performs euthanasia be trained and certified to do it competently and humanely. The certification is done by a veterinarian, and is filed with the State. Those who perform euthanasia must be re-certified every three years. Some of our Chesapeake officers have been with department for as long as 17 years, and still cry on euthanasia day. As an administrator, I do not routinely euthanize these days. This does not make it any easier when the time does occasionally come.

It is ironic that shelters and ACOs are routinely blamed for euthanasia as if they are the cause. The flood of animals that pours into shelters and pounds is not caused by the people who work there. While the general public deplores euthanasia, many of these same critics would never consider adoption from a shelter. They blame the messenger for euthanasia while continuing to purchase their pets from breeders, pet stores and puppy mills. The fact is the number of surplus dogs and cats is greater than the number of available homes. It is simple math. The number of animals coming in is greater than the number going out. No one hates euthanasia more than the people that actually carry it out, and many wonderful, caring people leave the animal welfare profession every day because of it. Low cost spay and neuter programs such as PeTA's SNIP program, our own Chesapeake Humane Society Care Clinic, and the many other community based initiatives are having an impact on the problem, but turning the tide takes time. Until Americans stop considering pets as fashion accessories, until pets are no longer considered disposable, until every pet owner makes a commitment to care for each pet for its lifetime, and until spaying and neutering is embraced by every American, euthanasia will continue.

There are organizations that call themselves "No Kill". In order to do this, many of these turn animals away that are old, sick, injured, or otherwise less than perfect.

Many people in animal control and the humane arena despise this term. They believe that No Kill is the cruelest hoax ever perpetrated on the American public. No Kill all too often means, "We refuse to euthanize, so we are going to shut our door and force the shelter down the street to take the animals we turn away. Then we are going to point the finger at that shelter for killing animals, while we use our No Kill status as a fund raising strategy."

No Kill can also mean manipulating numbers, designating certain difficult or less desirable animals unadoptable so that a shelter can advertise that they do not euthanize any adoptable animals. It can also mean warehousing animals, crowding them and keeping them in cages with little human contact for long periods. The more animals a shelter has, the less contact and attention humans can give them, and the more opportunity there is for disease. Some animals live like this for years.

A friend of mine in animal control confided to me that his shelter regularly received visits from representatives of a prominent SPCA. These people would select animals that they believed were adoptable and take them to their own shelter. This part was great, he said. It gave animals a second chance. However, if the animals failed to be adopted, someone from that SPCA would call my friend to come and pick them up again. That way, if the animals did have to be euthanized, the SPCA's hands were clean. They could continue their No Kill fundraising posture.

The thing that many of us in animal care and control dislike most about the myth of No Kill is that we fear it gives the public a false sense of security. It allows them to believe that animal overpopulation is a problem of the past, and there is really no urgency or need to spay and neuter dogs and cats. We worry every day where this misconception will lead us.

Still some of us stay. For better or worse, we make the decision not to give up. I made that decision when I returned to animal control. I continue to work with colleagues for change. This means education of the public, working to increase spay/neuter and adoptions from shelters, better laws for animals, and better conditions and compensation for ACOs.

And now, 12 years, 11 and one half months after first joining Animal Control, I was in the middle of the biggest case of my life.

CHAPTER 11 A MEDIA FEEDING FRENZY

After the April 27 search and discovery of the dog fighting operation on Vick's property, stories began to flood the media. It was the topic of news articles, editorials, commentaries, message boards, chat rooms and blogs. There was no escape. The frenzy had begun.

Vick was quick to deny any involvement and attempted to distance himself. "I'm never at the house. I left the house with my family members and my cousin. They just haven't been doing the right thing. It's unfortunate I have to take the heat. If I'm not there, I don't know what's going on. It's a call for me to really tighten down on who I'm trying to take care of. When it all boils down, people will try to take advantage of you and leave you out to dry. Lesson learned for me."

In an ESPN story, at least one of Vick's own teammates contradicted his denial, claiming that Michael Vick was not the only Atlanta Falcon involved in dog fighting; other players were connected to the sordid past time.

But, NFL Commissioner Roger Goodell was quoted as saying, "At this time based on what Michael has told me the league is standing by him."

On May 3, an editorial appeared on the front page of the sports section of our local paper, *The Virginian Pilot*. It included a scathing passage about Vick and his continued antics on and off the field that had now culminated in accusations of dog fighting. The writer seemed to join the ranks of those who were out of patience with Vick.

On May 9, Falcons new coach, Bobby Patrino spoke with reporters. "I need to believe in Michael. Since I've been here, a couple of situations have come up and we have talked about them. His track record with me is that he's told me the truth. I'm going to believe what Michael tells me. Michael is working very closely with his attorney to resolve the situation in Virginia. I've certainly spoken to Michael about it. We're hoping for a positive outcome."

Another Vick teammate was not as positive. Safety Lawyer Milloy stated cryptically,

"It's still up to the individual to make their choices. They reap the benefits when they make good choices. They suffer the consequences when they make bad choices. That's all I'm going to say about that."

By early May, I was so uneasy about the case, I was losing sleep. I kept going over and over the evidence, despising the lighted clock numbers that sneered at me from the top of my dresser. Brinkman and I were starting to agree this case had a one way ticket south. I agreed to an interview with *Sports Illustrated* writer George Dohrman.

I met George on May 10 at *Kelly's* in the Ghent section of Norfolk. *Kelly's* is a neighborhood watering hole that boasts the best made from scratch burgers in town. It was the kind of place where, like *Cheers*, everyone knows your name. Or at least your drink. Sue, one of my favorite waitresses greeted me with, "Is it a martini night? Vodka, very cold, very dry, shaken and shaken with 3 olives?"

"Yes, it is," I sighed.

George Dohrman is young, good looking, dark haired and passionate. I asked him what exactly he was writing about; what was the theme of his story? He told me that he had been home in San Francisco when his editor called him about doing a story on the emerging dog fighting case. As he listened to his boss, George said, he had one dog with its head in his lap, and a second dog using his foot as a pillow. George suggested that he might not be the most unbiased person to write this story. His editor replied, "George, who else at *Sports Illustrated* would be better than you? Nobody here at this magazine is going to condone dog fighting. We know you love dogs and know more about dog behavior than anyone here." Soon George was on a plane. Now we sat together and shared pictures of our dogs. George and I talked about the search at Moonlight Road and some of the evidence that the media had reported as having been recovered.

While George and I were talking, Brinkman called. He sounded desperate. He was under so much pressure, he said, with the daily threats to his job, and the case was not moving. There was still no word from the Feds. He planned to make another call to the US Attorney the following morning. George and I finished our meeting and went our separate ways.

SI.com posted a story on May 11, 2007. Falcons owner, Arthur Blank had met with Vick, he told reporters, and said he could not have been "more stern. I told him, 'You represent yourself as a person and you represent the NFL. It's not one single thing; it's a series of things." Blank was referring to a list of unsavory incidents. Vick had been accused of using the alias Ron Mexico when he sought treatment for himself after he had allegedly given herpes to a woman named Sonya Elliot. He had also been fined $20,000 for making an obscene gesture to fans. He had been stopped at the Miami airport with a water bottle, containing a secret compartment police said smelled of marijuana. Blank said he told Vick, "You're responsible for who you are with. You need to make some difficult choices and you need to make them now. I think you're at a critical point in your life."

On May 12, Vick told a group of reporters that he would not discuss the latest controversy in his life. "It's still under investigation, and once it is over, we will talk about it. I cannot talk about the situation. Don't plan on talking about me anymore unless it is about football."

That same day, WAVY TV 10 aired an interview with Poindexter. He laughed about the idea of dog fighting, and asked the reporter, "What dog fighting? What scarred dogs? Have you seen the dogs?"

The reporter replied, "Yes, we have seen the dogs." At that point, one of the scarred dogs appeared on the screen.

According a newspaper story, Vick's house was put on the market and sold for approximately one half of its assessed value. Appraised for over $700,000, it sold for about $350,000. Rumors flew about who might have purchased it. Many insisted that the buyer was Poindexter or a member of his family. One rumor surfaced that the buyer was in fact Poindexter's sister, but that she backed out of the sale due to the media spotlight. None of the rumors were ever be substantiated.

Patrick Terpstra from WVEC TV 13 went to Poindexter's office. Poindexter refused to go on camera, but did not notice that Patrick held an open microphone in his hand that captured a tirade by the infuriated attorney. Poindexter said he was not going to be pushed; he had been getting hate mail. Patrick asked why Poindexter had not had a meeting to look at the evidence, why had he not had a meeting with the investigators. Poindexter, Patrick said, did not respond.

I spoke to a reporter named Jason Cole from *Yahoo Sports*. This interview was to have far reaching consequences that I could never have imagined that day. When the article came out, Cole would misquote me and take statements out of context, such as saying that I had personally spoken with an informant who could place Vick at dog fights on the Moonlight Road property. But it was actually a statement that Cole quoted accurately that landed me in water that was at least simmering if not actually boiling. He had asked me what I thought of Poindexter's statement that he had not seen any evidence of dog fighting. I had replied, "Well, he was there on the property. He saw what we saw. It does make me wonder what in the world is going on in Surry County. It sure doesn't give me a warm and fuzzy feeling about the Surry Commonwealth Attorney."

Why did I say it? I have asked myself that question so many times. I knew better. In over 20 years, I had never before been so unguarded in speaking with the press. I had never discussed an ongoing investigation. Was it exasperation over the way the case was going? The specter of the Benny Butts case? I also asked myself if somehow this media attention had gone to my head in some way. Was I getting something out of the attention? I hoped not. This case was not about me; it was about a crime and the cruel exploitation of innocent animals. I know I made a conscious decision to do what I could to keep the media spotlight on this case. I was trying to walk a very fine line. Instead, I crossed it.

The day Cole's story came out, Poindexter called. He began by screaming at me that he thought we had had an understanding; that he thought we were on the same side. I snapped back, "So did I until I heard you don't think there is any evidence of dog fighting."

He denied saying that. I challenged him saying that when reporters had asked him about the scarred dogs, he had responded, "What scared dogs?" I had seen the stories. He asked me why I had been to the media, that I had tarnished his reputation. Me? I thought. What about his comments again and again that there was no evidence of dog fighting! I took a deep breath and replied that I had lost every bit of confidence in him. I felt he was going to do nothing. I wanted to make sure the light continued to shine on this case.

Although some stories asserted that he had been given all of the evidence, I knew that was not correct. He had seen the equipment, dogs and other items the day of the search, but he had not seen everything else that Brinkman had. According to Brinkman, he had not asked. I questioned him about this. He replied it was not his job to do so.

"Wait a minute. Wait a minute. You're the guy who has to go into court; you're the guy who has to go before the grand jury. You're the man. So, are you saying it is not your role, it is not your job to say, 'Hey guys show me what you got'?"

He replied that he had met with Brinkman already. He did not know that Brinkman had told me about that meeting. How ACO Smith had claimed he saw nothing wrong with the dogs at Moonlight Road, how Poindexter had discouraged the idea of a second search warrant suggesting he try to obtain consent, how later he had encouraged Sheriff Brown to fire Brinkman.

I chose my next words carefully. "You know, yes, I lost confidence in you, but if you tell me this case is going forward, and you are just proceeding cautiously, but you are proceeding then I am all for you. But, you say you need help, and I am told you have not contacted a single person who has offered it."

Poindexter did not respond. Instead he told me a meeting was planned for the coming Monday morning in his office. I was invited, he said. I did not tell him that I already knew about the meeting from Brinkman. I also did not tell him that Brinkman had his own doubts about Poindexter. I would watch Poindexter and listen carefully to what he said when we met. I still had no idea I would never attend that meeting.

On Wednesday, May 16 I got home from work to find five messages on my home phone answering service from reporters. *Associated Press, CNN, The Atlanta Journal Constitution*, and more. As I stood there marveling at how these people had tracked me down, the phone rang again. It was a radio station from Atlanta. I was on the air, the man said. He asked me some questions about dog fighting in general, and I described evidence that might be typical in these cases. The reporter said that I was being characterized in Atlanta as some sort of PeTA loving, animal rights fanatic. I laughed, and he asked if I would like to respond to that, tell him a bit about my background. I told him I had been in my present position since the mid 90's. I worked for a police department, and my job was to enforce the laws for the protection of the public, the protection of animals and the control of animals. I was also responsible for running a shelter to care for displaced animals. I did not think that would qualify me in any way, shape or form as an animal rights fanatic. That seemed to leave him with nowhere to go from there and he ended our interview.

Just as I began to dare to hope that our case might have a chance, a May 21, 2007 *Washington Times* news story quoted Poindexter saying, "The likelihood to me that Michael was there, with organized dog fighting and wagering and everything, I don't believe it."

That same day, Mary Kay Malloney of WAVY TV 10 did an interview with two Washington Redskins football players, Clinton Portis and Chris Samuels, who happened to be in town. Running back Portis seemed surprised that anyone would care if Vick were fighting dogs. "I don't know if he was fighting dogs or not, but it's his property, it's his dog. If that's what he wants to do, do it. I think people should mind their business."

Offensive Lineman Chris Samuels stated, "You can't accuse this man of something and go ahead and throw the book at him right now. He's got to be convicted first, and I don't think that's fair."

Portis went on to say, "You want to hunt down Mike Vick over fighting some dogs? I think people should mind their own business. I know a lot of back roads that have the dog fighting if you want to go see it. But they're not bothering those people because those people are not big names. I'm sure there's some police got some dogs that are fighting them, some judges got some dogs and everything else."

Samuels chimed in, "Politicians."

"Presidents," added Portis laughing.

Portis seemed genuinely surprised to hear dog fighting was a felony in Virginia. If Vick were charged and convicted, Portis said, "Then I think he got cheated...You're putting him behind bars for no reason—over a dog fight."

Later that day, Portis released a statement proclaiming, "In the recent interview I gave concerning dog fighting, I want to make it clear I do not take part in dog fighting or condone dog fighting in any manner."

Mark Kumpf called to tell me my name was surfacing on internet message boards. Among some of the comments were opinions that I was a bitch and I didn't know "nothing". I needed to go back to catching dogs. I needed to get back in the kitchen and cook something. I was a racist. I was some kind of PeTA clone and a humaniac, and I would soon be looking for a job. If they had really been fighting dogs, we would not have been able to handle the dogs because they would have torn us apart!

On May 25 Dog Angel reported that Vick was starting to worry. There was way too much attention. The media would not leave the case alone. An associate of Vick told Dog Angel that one of Vick's uncles was going to come forward to say, "It was all me." The public would have their villain, and Vick would walk away. His image might be slightly soiled, but he would be able to play. Dog Angel said I should watch for an announcement the following day from Gerald Poindexter. The man was about to do another about face.

On Saturday, May 26, just as Dog Angel predicted, *The Virginian Pilot* quoted Poindexter as saying that he was confident that dog fighting charges would be brought against someone. In the same article, the reporter noted his earlier comments. One day, it was yes, we have evidence; the next it was no we don't have evidence, and the day after that charges would be brought against someone!

The Vick camp had been scrambling for a favorable story to counteract the bad press. Dog Angel said they called in every favor they could to help spin the case their way. Their plan was to portray Vick as a kind hearted, but naïve young man who surrounded himself with less fortunate friends. Vick trusted these people, but they took advantage of his generous nature.

The front page of *The Virginian Pilot* carried a story that posed the question, "Is Michael Vick friendly to a fault?" The story suggested that his trust and loyalty to friends from his past may be his undoing. Vick was just a nice guy who may have been led astray by others. The paper went on to list some of the criminal charges that had been brought against some of his friends. James Johnson, a mentor from Vick's days at the Peninsula Boys and Girls Club was quoted as saying, "[Vick] saw how it felt to be without." That experience, he believed, explained why it was so difficult for him, when he had money, to say no to friends who did not. "Sometimes he's loyal to a fault. The guys that he chose as friends are guys he grew up with in the 'hood.'" Johnson also stated that he had heard Vick admit to having made bad decisions and needing to straighten up.

The Sunday, May 27 episode of the ESPN Program *Outside the Lines* featured a man who was described as a confidential police informant. His face hidden and his voice altered, the informant claimed that Michael Vick had been funding and gambling on dog fights since his college days at Virginia Tech. The informant claimed, "He's one of the ones they call the big boys because he bets a large dollar. As I'm talking about large money, $30, 40 thousand, even higher. He's one of the heavyweights.

"I've seen Vick. We beat him back in 2000, yes. That dog was Michael Vick's dog. Michael was not in the pit. Michael's thing is he came with all of the money. He was betting. He was betting with everybody. He was betting on his dog, $5,000 on his animal. Bets are coming from everywhere. They turned the dogs lose. They locked up. The fight went 40 something minutes. I won."

According to a federal agent, whose identity was also withheld, the informant was a reliable source who had supplied information in other dog fighting cases that had led to successful search warrants and convictions.

I was traveling again on Tuesday, May 29 when the *Sports Illustrated* article came out. I got a call asking if I had seen it yet. I had not, but I grabbed a copy at the airport. George Dohrman had titled it *The House on Moonlight Road*. The article was great, comprehensive and well written. It discussed the case brewing around Vick, the secret world of dog fighting, and the people involved. Included in this group were athletes such as former NFL Running Back LeShon Johnson of Krazyside Kennels who was convicted of dog fighting in 2005, and former NBA player Qyntel Woods who was accused of dog fighting in 2004. Woods pleaded guilty to first degree animal abuse. Former Dallas Cowboy Nate Newton was arrested at a dog fight in 1991. This was a case that Dog Angel worked on. He had spent several years investigating Nate Newton, who he said was known even among other dog fighters for his poor care of his dogs. Dog Angel was furious when the charges were later dropped.

George quoted an NFL running back, who asked not to be named. This individual stated that fighting dogs was a fun thing, a hobby, to some athletes. "People are crazy about pit bulls. Guys have these nice big fancy houses, and there is always a pit bull in the back. And everyone wants to have the biggest, baddest dog on the block." Also quoted was a former professional football player Tyrone Wheatley, who had praised the spirit of fighting dogs in a 2001 issue of Sports Illustrated. "Sometimes you just want to see how tough a dog you got."

The agent from Oklahoma said he was amazed at the cross section of people who attended dog fights—adults from all walks of life, little children, teenagers, and couples on dates. Comments from him and other experts on dog fighting investigations made it clear that dog fighting was not only a scourge, but that many professional athletes might be involved.

Though they were decidedly in the minority, Vick had his supporters. Linwood De-Brew, the executive director of the Moton Community House in Newport News told a *Daily Press* reporter, "I'm going to support him until he dies. I don't find as much fault in the situation as it has been made out to be. My research tells me that over four million dogs and cats are killed each year by PeTA and the Society for the Prevention and Cruelty to Animals." DeBrew went on to excuse dog fighting as a part of the local community, saying it had been going on ever since I was a young man, and I consider it a small thing, based on our culture. In Korea, they slaughter dogs like Smithfield slaughters hogs. And according to them, the best-tasting ones are beaten with baseball bats to tenderize the meat."

DeBrew's comments sparked outrage. Angry readers took him to task in posts on the newspaper web site, denying that dog fighting was any part of a culture, criticizing him for comparing humane euthanasia to the brutality of dog fighting, and proclaiming their overall disgust.

Vick's cousin, Davon Boddie, whose arrest had set off the explosive chain of events that continued to shock and divide the public since April, was interviewed by WAVY TV 10 on June 7. Though Boddie had lived at the house on Moonlight Road for several years, he denied any knowledge of the dogs. The reporter asked if he had not noticed that there were 66 dogs on the property. Who fed them and cared for them, the reporter inquired. What about the fighting paraphernalia? Boddie refused to answer any of those questions. He instead claimed that police were lying and had framed him the night they had found him with drugs. It was a conspiracy, he said, and now it was a conspiracy against Michael Vick. The reporter asked him if he was suggesting that police planted 66 dogs on the property. Boddie did not respond. Instead he replied that he wanted to go on record in the interview and state that he had not betrayed Michael Vick. Contrary to his intentions, everything Boddie said gave credibility to the entire case.

Butts' carpet mill found later at Moonlight Road

Butts' yellow treadmill found later at Moonlight Road

Butts' black treadmill found later at Moonlight Road

The Pit
Exercise Equipment
Medical and Drugs
The Hanging Tree
The Infirmary
Dog Kennels

Dog Kennels
The Hanging Tree
The Infirmary
Medical and Drugs
Exercise Equipment
The Pit

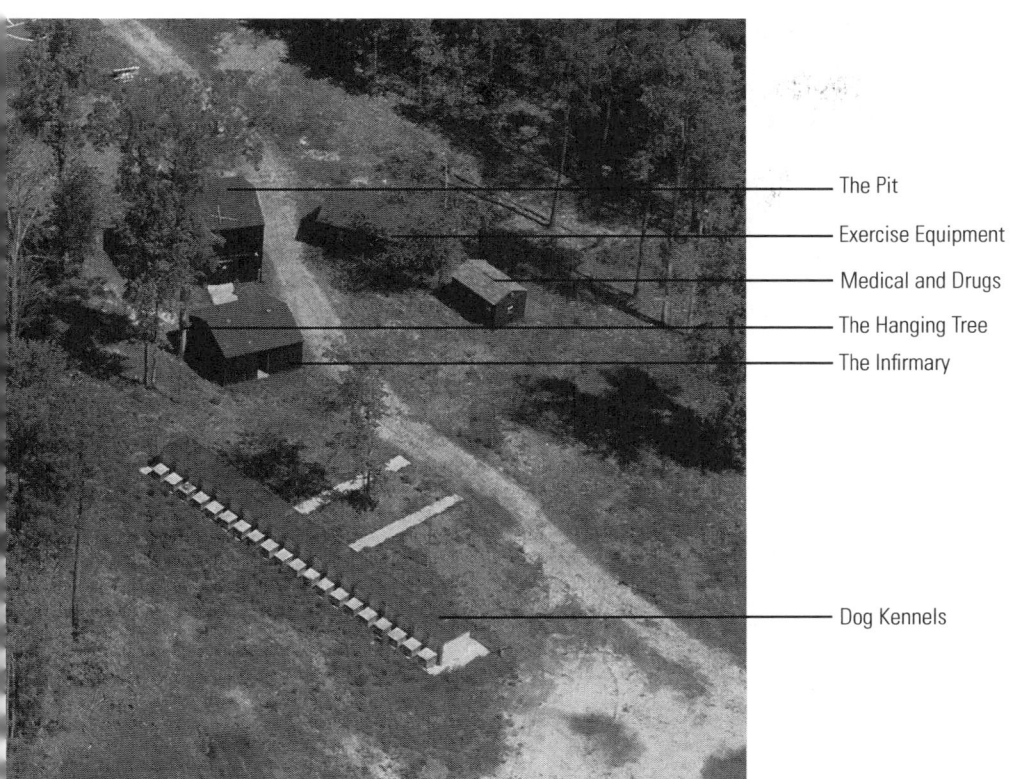

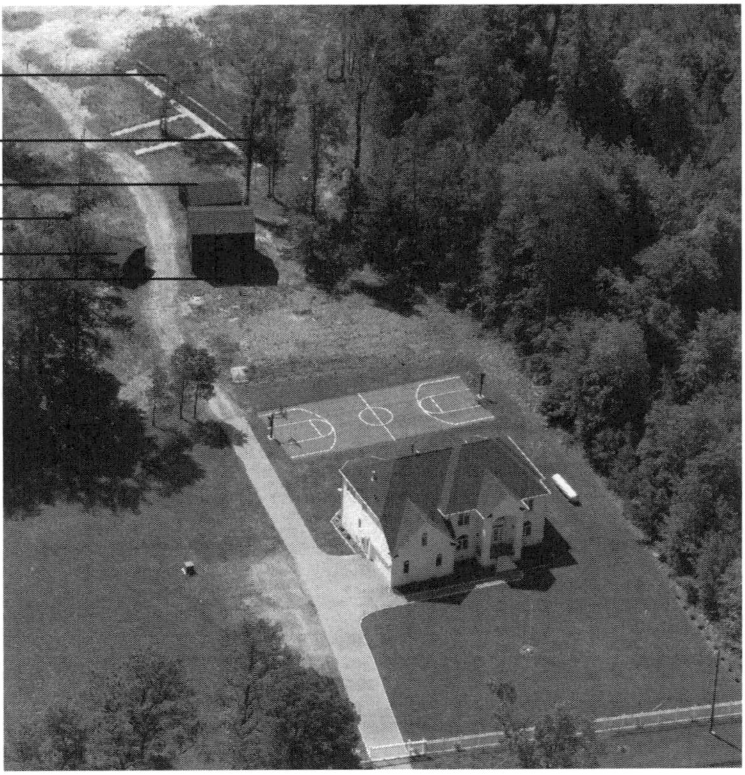

Surry, the puppy Agent Jim Knorr adopted from Deputy Bill Brinkman

Little Red

Bonita

Buster later named Johnny Justice

Big Fella

4 GENERATION PEDIGREE
VIRGINIA O'S PIPER

BREEDER: VIRGINIA O
OWNER: VIRGINIA O
SEX: FEMALE
COLOR: BLACK
ENTERED BY: ExtremeKnls
POSTED: 2005-12-05
LAST MODIFIED: 2005-12-05

2XW

Generations in Pedigree

First	Second	Third	Fourth
(Sire) CH HARDCORE'S BOZACK (POR)	GR CH TANT'S YELLOW (6XW) ROM	CH CHAVIS' YELLOW JOHN (4XW) ROM	CH BASS' TRAMP RED BOY (3XW) ROM
			MARLOWE'S RED FEATHER
		TANT'S MISS JOCKO (2XW) ROM	CH CHAVIS' JOCKO (4XW) POR
			CHAVIS' LADY ROSE (1XL)
	HARDCORE KENNEL'S BREAKER (ROM)	SHADY HILL KENNEL'S JEEP	CH CRENSHAW'S JEEP (4XW) ROM
			REECE'S LADY MORIAH
		SHADY HILL KENNEL'S WENONA	CH CRENSHAW'S RASCAL JR
			CRENSHAW'S KANSAS
(Dam) VIRGINIA O'S EBONY (2XW)	CH S.T.P.'S BLACK PAZMANIAN (4XW) ROM	CHEROKEE KENNELS' OILER JR. (2XW) ROM	GR CH MURPHY'S & HEIKKLIA'S OILER (5XW)
			BOYLES' BLACK GOLD POR
		MANN'S LADY BUG	CH BOYLES' BOLT ACTION (4XW-1XGL) ROM
			BURCH'S CINDY
	CH S.T.P.'S MISS RAGE	O.STEVEN'S OLD CHARLEY	CH O. STEVEN'S HOMER (4XW) ROM
			O.STEVEN'S GERALDINE ROM
		REID'S EASY (POR)	MALONEY'S MACHO
			ODK'S SUGAR BABE

Pedigree for Virginia O's Piper

4 GENERATION PEDIGREE
BADD NEWZ' JADA

BREEDER: BADD NEWZ & DYLAN
OWNER: BADD NEWZ
SEX: FEMALE
COLOR: BLACK
BIRTHDATE: 2006-01-19
ENTERED BY: rwkennels
POSTED: 2005-12-18
LAST MODIFIED: 2007-01-24
No OF VIEWS: 122 times
View Log

Generations in Pedigree

First	Second	Third	Fourth
(Sire) DYLAN'S CUJO	BAJAN BLACK ROCK	BAJAN RADAR O'QUINN 1xW ; 1xL (game)	GR CH SMITH & WILLIAMS' BADGER ROM
			Harold's ZUKI
		BAJAN NIGHTMARE	RAGING BULLS BLACK SABBATH
			ANDERSON'S OREO
	DYLAN'S ANGEL	BWK POINTY	CH HARDCORE'S BOZACK (POR)
			STONE CITY KNLS BABY
		BWK MAGGIE	CH HARDCORE KENNEL'S MYSTIC (POR)
			STONE CITY'S UGLY
(Dam) BADD NEWZ' NIGHTMARE	BAJAN BRIGAND	TOPLINE'S TROOPER	TOWNSENDS REVENGE
			BRITANNIAS LITTLE HOLLY
		BSKS ZETA	CHAMPION CARPE AND BAGGAR AND RICE'S ELMO
			CHAMPION RICKY B'S CULCHIE
	BAJAN BABY DOLL	BAJAN RADAR O'QUINN 1xW ; 1xL (game)	GR CH SMITH & WILLIAMS' BADGER ROM
			Harold's ZUKI
		BAJAN NIGHTMARE	RAGING BULLS BLACK SABBATH
			ANDERSON'S OREO

Pedigree for Badd Newz Jada

PICTURES

4 GENERATION PEDIGREE
CJ-SMOOTH'S JADA

BREEDER: CJ-SMOOTH.
OWNER: CJ-SMOOTH.
SEX: FEMALE
COLOR: BLACK & WHITE.
BIRTHDATE: 2006-01-19
POSTED: 2007-07-30
LAST MODIFIED: 2007-07-30
No OF VIEWS: 17 times

WAS BADD NEWZ PRIOR TO 7/30/07

Generations in Pedigree

First	Second	Third	Fourth
(Sire) DYLAN'S CUJO	BAJAN BLACK ROCK	BAJAN RADAR O'QUINN	GR CH SMITH & WILLIAMS' BADGER ROM
			HAROLD'S ZUKI
		BAJAN NIGHTMARE	RAGING BULLS BLACK SABBATH
			ANDERSON'S OREO
	DYLAN'S ANGEL	BWK POINTY	CH HARDCORE'S BOZACK (POR)
			STONE CITY KNLS BABY
		BWK MAGGIE	CH. HARDCORE KENNEL'S MYSTIC (POR)
			STONE CITY'S UGLY
(Dam) CJ-SMOOTH'S NIGHTMARE	BAJAN BRIGAND	TOPLINE'S TROOPER	TOWNSENDS REVENGE
			BRITANNIAS LITTLE HOLLY
		BSK'S (TOPLINE'S) ZETA	RICE & CARPETBAGGER'S CH.ELMO
			RICKY B'S CH.CULCHIE
	BAJAN BABY DOLL	BAJAN RADAR O'QUINN	GR CH SMITH & WILLIAMS' BADGER ROM
			HAROLD'S ZUKI
		BAJAN NIGHTMARE	RAGING BULLS BLACK SABBATH
			ANDERSON'S OREO

Jada's pedigree was altered July 30, 2007 to substitute the kennel name Badd Newz with that of CJ Smooth's

4 GENERATION PEDIGREE
VIRGINIA O'S STING

OWNER: VIRGINIA O
SEX: MALE
COLOR: RED BUCKSKIN
CHAIN WEIGHT: 55
ENTERED BY: jchood
POSTED: 2003-06-18
LAST MODIFIED: 2003-10-31

Generations in Pedigree

First	Second	Third	Fourth
(Sire) HOPE'S GABRIEL (2XW) ROM	CH CAROLINA KENNELS' TERMITE (4XW) ROM	CHAVIS' DANGEROUS DAN (2XW)	CH CHAVIS' JOCKO (4XW) POR
			CH CHAVIS' LADY SASSY MEAD (4XW)
		STEEN'S DELILAH	CHAVIS' BUCKY (2XW)
			CHAVIS' MARGARET (2XW)
	ROBINSONS PRETTY (1XW)	ROBINSON'S APACHE	GEORGE'S RED ACE (1XW)
			ROBINSON'S BED BUG
		ROBINSON'S MUGWIA	HALL'S TRAMP
			ROBINSON'S BED BUG
(Dam) VIRGINIA O'S EBONY 2XW	CH S. EP'S BLACK PAZMANIAN (4XW) ROM	CHEROKEE KENNELS' OILER JR. (2XW) ROM	GR CH MURPHY'S & HEIKKLIA'S OILER (5XW)
			BOYLES' BLACK GOLD POR
		MANN'S LADY BUG	CH BOYLES' BOLT ACTION (4XW-ENGL) ROM
			BURCH'S CINDY
	CH S. E.P.'S MISS RAGE	O.STEVEN'S OLD CHARLEY	CH O. STEVEN'S HOMER (4XW) ROM
			O.STEVEN'S GERALDINE ROM
		REID'S EASY (POR)	MALONEY'S MACHO
			ODK'S SUGAR BABE

Pedigree for Virginia O's Sting, son of Ebony, the only dog he brought to Virginia. Sting would sire Magic, another Badd Newz fighter

BADD NEWZ

4 GENERATION PEDIGREE
M.V.KNLS BLAZE

BREEDER: B.GOODSON
OWNER: M.V.KNLS
SEX: FEMALE
COLOR: RED
CHAIN WEIGHT: 47
CONDITIONED WEIGHT: 42
ENTERED BY: FOREFRONTKNL
POSTED: 2003-08-11
LAST MODIFIED: 2003-08-11

Very Good Brood Bitch !

Generations in Pedigree

First	Second	Third	Fourth
(Sire) GOODSON'S FRED	B&B'S MAURICE POR	TRENT & SEXTON'S JERRY	HOLT'S JEREMIAH (2XW)
			ART'S MISSY (2XW) ROM
		REUVER'S COLD COUNTRY DAYTONA (2XW)	CH LLOYD'S GATOR (RICK SORRELS)
			REUVER'S STRIPPER
	REUVER'S COLD COUNTRY DAYTONA (2XW)	CH LLOYD'S GATOR (RICK SORRELS)	GR CH DAVIS' BOOMERANG (ROM)
			J.CARVER'S MISS BOOMER
		REUVER'S STRIPPER	CH LLOYD'S GATOR (RICK SORRELS)
			DEVINE'S BRANDY
	GARNER'S BUSTER	GR CH GARNER'S SPIKE (5XW) ROM	WOOD'S SNOOTY (2XW)(2XL) ROM
			MIDDLETON'S BLACK BETTY (POR)
		CH EDWARD'S RED LADY (3XW)(1XL)	WOOD'S SNOOTY (2XW)(2XL) ROM
			GR CH BASS'(EDWARDS') MOLLY BEE (8XW)
		GR CH GARNER'S SPIKE (5XW)	WOOD'S SNOOTY (2XW)(2XL) ROM

Pedigree for the Infamous MV Kennels Blaze AKA Badd Newz Champion Jane

4 GENERATION PEDIGREE
CJ-SMOOTH'S NIGHTMARE

WAS BADD NEWZ BEFORE 7/30/07

BREEDER: BAJAN GAMEDOGS.
OWNER: CJ-SMOOTH.
SEX: FEMALE
COLOR: BLACK & WHITE.
BIRTHDATE: 2003-03-02
POSTED: 2007-07-30
LAST MODIFIED: 2007-07-30
No OF VIEWS: 18 times

Generations in Pedigree

First	Second	Third	Fourth
(Sire) BAJAN BRIGAND	TOPLINE'S TROOPER	TOWNSENDS REVENGE	GR CH CATES' NIGERINO (5XW)
			TOWNSEND'S PRINCESS
		BRITANNIAS LITTLE HOLLY	GR CH (CRENSHAW'S SLATER) BRABHAM & SINGLETONS' SNAKE
			CH SWETMANS HOLLY
	BSK'S (TOPLINE'S) ZETA	RICE & CARPETBAGGER'S CH.ELMO	RICE'S TONTO
			RICE'S MINNIE
		RICKY B'S CH.CULCHIE	ELWOOD'S BARNEY
			FARMERS' BOYS' FLOSSY
(Dam) BAJAN BABY DOLL	BAJAN RADAR O'QUINN	GR CH SMITH & WILLIAMS' BADGER ROM	SMITH & WILLIAM'S REUBEN (1XW-1XL) ROM
			T.L. WILLIAMS' MEJI POR
		HAROLD'S ZUKI	GR CH SMITH & WILLIAMS' BADGER ROM
			GRIFFIN & HAROLD'S CLEO
	BAJAN NIGHTMARE	RAGING BULLS BLACK SABBATH	HUNEYCUTT'S LUCIFER
			SOUTH RIVER'S MAMBA
		ANDERSON'S OREO	HUNEYCUTT'S LUCIFER
			ANDERSON'S LUCKY

Nightmare's pedigree was altered July 30, 2007 to substitute the kennel name Badd Newz with that of CJ Smooth's

PICTURES

4 GENERATION PEDIGREE
M.V.KNLS & FOREFRONTS 'MAGGIE MAY' 2xw

BREEDER: M.V.KNLS
OWNER: M.V.KNLS & FOREFRONT KNLS
SEX: FEMALE
COLOR: RED
CHAIN WEIGHT: 52
CONDITIONED WEIGHT: 45 / 46
ENTERED BY: FOREFRONTKNL
POSTED: 2003-08-11
LAST MODIFIED: 2003-08-11

Absolute Baddest Bitch on the Planet . She beat True Colors Ch 'Darkside' in 14 min (doa). Her times , :15 , :14 . Three O.T.C. :2,:8,:10 . Also collecting Five Forfeits ! Nothing Lived long enough to scratch back !

		Generations in Pedigree		
First	Second	Third		Fourth
	MILLBUSTER'S RUSS	CH CAROLINA KENNELS' TERMITE (4XW) ROM		CHAVIS' DANGEROUS DAN (2XW)
				STEEN'S DELILAH
		CAROLINA KENNELS' DALLAS		GEORGE'S RED ACE (1XW)
				ROBINSON'S BED BUG
	SPOOKIE	BOWMAN'S JR. 2XW ROM		CH ALEXANDER'S BATMAN (4XW2XLG)
				BOWMAN'S GERDY 2X
		JOHNSON'S CLASSY		BOWLING'S LONER (2XW)
				JOHNSON'S LIL ROM
(Dam) M.V.KNLS BLAZE				TRENT & SEXTON'S JERRY

Pedigree for MV Kennels' Maggie May, daughter of the infamous MV Kennels' Jane AKA Champion Badd Newz Jane, with notations referencing her kills

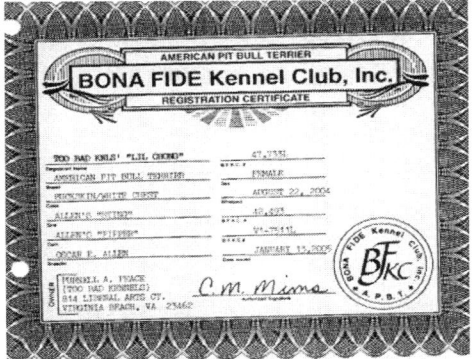

Registration for Lil Chong, the dog who jumped out of the pit at Moonlight Road and was subsequently killed by Peace who shot her in the head

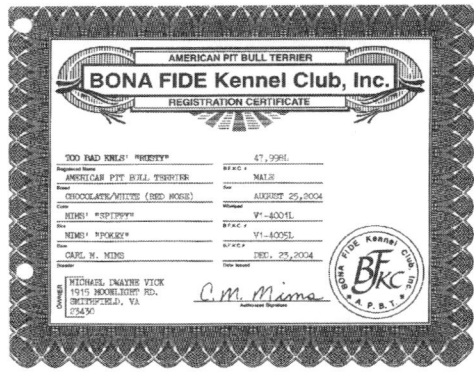

Registration for Rusty

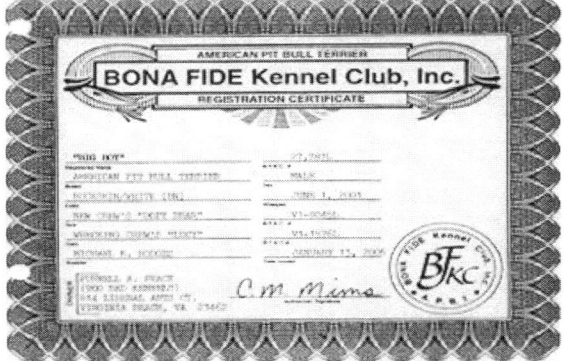

Registration for Big Boy who became a Champion

BADD NEWZ

CHAPTER 12 LIKE A BAD MOVIE

I felt feverish and miserable when I got to work on the morning of Thursday, May 17. I had an awful cold and longed to stay home, but had too much work to do. I had just turned on my computer when I got a call from Police Lieutenant Randy Farney telling me to report immediately to Internal Affairs (IA). I sat for a moment after I put the phone down. "Great," I thought. "This cannot be good."

When I arrived at Farney's office, Major Wright was already seated. I took the other chair, and Farney began to read some quotes from the *Yahoo Sports* Jason Cole story. Some were misquotes that had been attributed to me, and I told Farney as much. I admitted the statement about not feeling warm and fuzzy about the Surry County Attorney was not a misquote. I had said it, and I had no intention of lying, or trying to excuse it. I told Farney and Major Wright about the fears that the investigators themselves were having about what might happen to the case in Poindexter's hands. Beyond exchanging glances, neither Farney nor the Major made any comment. I told them I had tried to always identify myself as a member of the Animal Fighting Task Force, rather than an employee of Chesapeake when speaking to the press. After a brief pause, Farney said a full scale IA Investigation would be launched. The charges would be speaking to the press without authorization, speaking about an ongoing investigation, and making an unflattering comment about a government official. He ordered me not to speak with any member of the press, and to direct all media inquiries to him. I was no longer part of the Vick investigation, and I would not be attending the meeting in Surry the coming Monday to discuss the evidence in the case.

Farney ordered me to meet with Detective Mike Lawton, also of IA. I gave my statement to him, and when I finished Lawton ordered me to turn over my entire file on the Vick case, including e-mails. My voice was almost gone by the time the interview ended. Lawton suggested that I go home and go to bed. He said I could turn over the file when I returned to work.

It was almost surreal. IA detectives are portrayed as cold heartless villains on television and in movies. Maybe they really could be if one had done something horrible. I am certain there are police officers who might agree with the popular image. Yet, Farney, Lawton, and the Major all were the kindest, most cordial of gentlemen. They had been nothing less during the interviews. Lawton was even solicitous in suggesting that I should not be at work, but at home in bed. I decided to take his advice.

All the way home, I turned this latest development over and over in my mind. Two things struck me about our meeting. I was not told who the complainant was in this matter, and I was ordered not to tell anyone that the investigation existed.

Who had complained? Of course one name came to me immediately, but how was I to know? When I got home, I just wanted to turn off my brain. I crawled into bed with two dogs who were delighted to see me home so early. We were later joined by Oscar the wonder cat, and in spite of not being able to turn over or even shift position, I drifted off to sleep.

After a miserable weekend of nursing my cold, I was back at work on Monday, May 21. I stopped by the IA Office to turn in my notebook, and returned to my office. Brinkman called, and I had to tell him that I would not be at the meeting that morning. I told him I was out. He was shocked. He was counting on me. What did he know about dog fighting? Drugs were what he knew. I told him I was sorry, but could not say more.

That afternoon when I got home, I was stunned to be met at my door by Brinkman, State Police Officer Steve Tate, and Special Agent Jim Knorr of the USDA OIG. Did this mean the Feds were really coming in? I did not dare ask and they did not tell me. As we all sat around my dining room table they peppered me with questions. Most of these were about the materials I had already shared with Brinkman.

As we talked, both Brinkman and Knorr said they felt they knew exactly who had succeeded in removing me from the investigation. The meeting with Poindexter had not gone well, Brinkman said. Knorr had been there as well, and he signified his agreement by a nod. Knorr is in his mid 50's, medium height and slightly gray with a ruddy complexion. His demeanor is unflappable, and one gets the sense very little would ruffle that calm.

Brinkman said Poindexter seemed to act like a defense attorney rather than a prosecutor. He had even made a statement that he was better in that role. Brinkman gave Poindexter an overview of the case to date. It was vital, he told the prosecutor that he find and interview Tony Taylor, Virginia O, and an informant he had developed who had actually been present at the fights. Poindexter questioned the validity of the original search warrant and the fact that Brinkman had taken an ACO on a drug warrant. Brinkman said he responded by saying that he always took an ACO along if he knew he was going onto property where dogs were present. This was normal procedure, and this search was handled no differently. He said that he and the ACOs all saw items that they believed were related to dog fighting. They called for an expert to identify them. The expert identified them, and a search warrant for dog fighting was secured.

Poindexter stated that he was not willing to go forward unless investigators could put Vick at a fight on Moonlight Road. Brinkman replied the Virginia statute did not require that.

Under the Virginia statute, a person is guilty of a felony if he or she owns, possesses, trains, or intends to use dogs for fighting. However, Brinkman he said he was confident he could put Vick at a fight on the property if he could interview the people he had mentioned. Knorr told Poindexter that any necessary forensic examinations could be done by USDA laboratories. He also offered to assist Brinkman with the interviews. Brinkman reminded Poindexter that he needed to execute another search warrant on the Moonlight Road property.

I told Brinkman and Knorr I had given quite a bit of information to Poindexter, but did not know if he had followed up on any of it. Both Knorr and Brinkman exchanged glances oncemore without comment. Brinkman said he had more informants who could put Vick at fights on the property. He said that these were guys who were currently incarcerated. Several names came immediately to my mind. I realized that Brinkman had not shared all of these names with Poindexter. I looked at Knorr, but his expression was unreadable. Brinkman said he still believed that the only hope for the case was for the Feds to take it over. Knorr was noncommittal.

As the men were leaving, Brinkman told me he was determined to secure another search warrant in the coming days. He wanted to remove sections of the floor from the pit for examination. He also said that he had reason to believe that Virginia O's first name might be Oscar. He asked me to see if I could get any information on a dog fighter who might have that first name.

I was supposed to be out of it. And I tried, but as things would play out, not a day passed that someone did not call me with questions, offers of information, or requests for help. I was careful to do all my talking during my off hours.

On the way to work the next morning I got a call from John Goodwin. He told me he knew something had happened, but was not going to ask me about it. I thanked him and asked if he knew whether Dog Angel had made any progress on finding out Virginia O's real name. Goodwin said he had not.

Goodwin's next comment took me by surprise. Vick's crew suspected their inner circle had somehow been infiltrated. "Is Dog Angel in danger?" I asked.

"Of course," he replied as if that was the norm.

I remembered asking Dog Angel once how he felt about the danger, and his reply was surprisingly flip. "So what? Won't be the first time or last time, but I will tell you this about these guys. They're cowards, pitiful men; men that I have no respect for. Guys who think they're tough, but in reality they are nothing. Now the Soldiers of Silence or Hells Angels..."

"Okay," I said. "I get it." I guessed after almost 30 years his instincts must be pretty sound, but I was surprised at his casual dismissal of the risks.

I spent most of that day working on my letter to IA. Whenever an officer is under investigation, the officer is required to write a letter explaining his or her actions. I made no attempt to minimize or excuse anything I had done. I took full responsibility for my actions and expressed regret that anything I had done might reflect negatively on my department.

Mark Kumpf called me that evening. He knew I had not been at the meeting with Poindexter. He had worked for a police department himself, and guessed what must have happened.

There was no point in denying it. We knew each other too well for that. He said he wanted to pass on some messages from several local reporters who had called him to express their concern and well wishes. Apparently, they thought it was extremely odd that the person with the most local expertise on dog fighting had not been at the meeting with Poindexter and the rest of the team.

On Wednesday, May 23, 2007 I got a voice mail message from George Dohrman of Sports Illustrated saying that he understood I had been embargoed from the meeting in Poindexter's office. He had also heard that there might have been a USDA Agent in attendance at the meeting.

Where was all of this coming from? How did everyone know so much? The kind messages depressed me further.

Mark called again. A reporter had contacted him looking for a response to a statement that was expected to be released that evening. According to the reporter, Poindexter would be releasing a statement saying that there was no evidence of dog fighting on the Moonlight Road property; that every item authorities had removed had a legitimate use. This was bad enough, but worse was yet to come.

Brinkman called that evening as I drove home. I repeated what Mark had said. Brinkman thanked me for the heads up, and said he had bad news of his own. Exactly one half hour before he had planned to execute the new search warrant, Poindexter had ordered him not to go forward. He did not like the wording. Furthermore, the property may have been sold. Poindexter told him to wait and ask for the property owner's permission. I felt physically sick. "Well, that's it," I said. "It looks like we are dead in the water. It's over."

"No, it's not," Brinkman insisted stubbornly.

I wished I could believe him. Mark called a day or so later to tell me that the news media had gotten hold of a copy of the affidavit for the unexecuted search warrant. How had that happened? How had reporters known to go looking in the first place?

"What the hell is going on there?" Mark demanded. I was astounded. What a colossal blunder to allow the media to tip off the suspects in advance of a search. You might just as well announce, "This is what we will be looking for, in case you want to get rid of it!" Unless it had not been a blunder at all.

I had barely hung up when my phone rang again. It was Brinkman. His voice was heavy with exhaustion. The leak of the affidavit and the constant threats about his job were wearing him down. "You must be dodging land mines every moment of every day," I said.

"Yep, pretty much, pretty much." He still believed the Feds would take the case. I wished I shared his confidence, but I had heard this too many times by then. I thought Brinkman was clinging to an unrealistic hope.

Later that afternoon, I thought I had really entered the twilight zone. Dr. Melinda Merck, the forensic veterinarian called. She told me she just finished speaking with Poindexter, what a nice man he was, and what a good conversation they had. He asked her quite a few questions, and she was at pains to answer them in detail. She believed that he intended to go forward. Poindexter was telling the media one thing, Brinkman another, and her yet another. I thought she was getting a wonderful blizzard of a snow job and suggested she call Brinkman.

Brinkman called me a few days later. In another stunning flip flop, Poindexter and Brown were now pressuring him to go forward with the second search warrant. Oddly, Brinkman said that while Poindexter was now insisting on another search of the property, Poindexter was already picking his draft apart. I could not help thinking how convenient this was now that everyone not living under a rock knew what they would be looking for. Then I wondered what had happened to asking the property owner's permission!

Brinkman wanted to know if I could provide him with copies of search warrants that specifically sought carcasses. I referred him to Mark for advice. Mark said to request a search for dogs and any and all animals, living or deceased, wild or domestic. He said the affidavit should not mention breed, and should take into account the possibility that bait animals might be buried on the property. The affiant should articulate that in this officer's training, education and experience, persons engaged in illegal dog fighting activity often bury deceased animals on the property as part of their attempts to avoid detection.

Brinkman asked me to do a favor for him. He wanted me to call Dr. Merck. I was to tell her that she would be getting a call from him the next morning at Poindexter's behest. Brinkman would ask her if she was available to assist with the second search warrant. I was to instruct her to say, "No." Brinkman had decided to stall. He did not want to go forward with this warrant. So, it was vital that Dr. Merck say she would not be available for at least a couple of weeks. Brinkman explained he wanted to try to buy some time until the Feds could step in. At some point he would want very much for Dr. Merck to assist, but he wanted it to be the federal search. He pleaded with me not to ask him any questions, but to promise I would get the message to Dr. Merck. I said I would.

Brinkman and I hung up at last. I called Dr. Merck and relayed Brinkman's request. She was puzzled and annoyed that I could not answer her pressing questions. In the end, she reluctantly agreed to do as Brinkman asked.

Speculation continued on the sale of the house on Moonlight Road. Rumors were rife—Poindexter had bought it, a relative of Poindexter's had bought it. According to *The Virginian Pilot*, Vick co-owned the house with Charles Reamon, Jr., who was the nephew of Vick's high school football coach. Reamon had also been identified by the media as Vick's financial advisor. It was Reamon who had paid the fee for the 2006 kennel license purchased by Tony Taylor for the property on Moonlight Road. In 1997 Reamon had been fined for carrying a handgun in a vehicle. In 2002, he was caught up in a federal sting. He was one of 21 Norfolk International Airport employees charged with lying about their criminal records on security clearance applications. Reamon pleaded guilty and received a fine. In 2006, he received a six month suspended sentence for carrying a loaded .357 Glock in an airport.

On Thursday, May 24, I dissolved into tears for the first time. Mark had been right. *The Virginian Pilot* published a story attributing a statement to Surry County Commonwealth Attorney Gerald Poindexter that the investigators lacked solid evidence linking anyone to dog fighting. "I know everybody is saying, when are those fools in Surry County going to get up off their butts and do something? But what are we going to do?" There were no eyewitnesses, he said, who could state that dog fighting had occurred. Poindexter also said that although he had never met Michael Vick, he heard he was a nice guy. He claimed only one dog was scarred. The article quoted Mark Kumpf's rebuttal asserting that this case had more evidence than had been required to convict other people in Virginia; that the totality of the evidence spoke directly to dog fighting, and that it was not unusual to lack eyewitnesses.

If no one was to be charged with dog fighting, the dogs would have to be returned. Returned, I believed, to a life of brutality and cruelty. I felt myself to be at one of the lowest points of my career. I had given Poindexter names of potential witnesses—dog fighter Stacey Miller, Tony Taylor, Dawn Allen, Virginia O! If he wanted more evidence, why had he stopped the second search warrant, and how had it been leaked? I could not help remembering that I had never gotten a call from Poindexter inquiring why I had missed that all important meeting. I finished the final draft of my letter and delivered it to Internal Affairs.

On Friday, May 25, 2007 Brinkman called me. He too had seen the article in *The Virginian Pilot*, but he was too excited to care. He asked me to find out anything I could on Badd Newz Kennels. My mind jolted back to the day of the search warrant. I could see the beam in the shed that had housed the treadmills. I saw the writing. "TBK" for Too Bad Kennels and over it "BNK". The hair stood up on the back of my neck. Brinkman said he believed that Badd Newz Kennels was Michael Vick's kennel name.

CHAPTER 13 THE RISE OF BADD NEWZ KENNELS

It was only a few years before he earned the nickname, Virginia O, that the old school dog fighter retired from the New York Transit Authority, where he had been an engineer for many years. In the early days, he kept his pit bulls in an abandoned building. He tapped fire hydrants to give them water. The first time he entered a dog in a fight, he wagered $29. The fight took place in an old bank building somewhere in New Jersey. As time went on he learned how to condition his dogs and prepare them for the grueling battles they would face. The more he learned, the more he bet, eventually wagering as much as $1,200 a match.

In 1993, he moved to Virginia, bringing one dog with him. Her name was Ebony, and she was a two-time fight winner. During his previous travels to Virginia, he had met a dog fighter known as Hardcore Benny Butts. Butts agreed to allow him to keep Ebony at his Hardcore Kennels in rural Surry County.

Soon the older man became well known among dog fighters as Virginia O. He would breed Ebony to Butts' Champion Hardcore's Bozack, and keep a puppy out of that litter called Virginia O's Piper. Butts was deep into the fight game himself. He made treadmills for other dog fighters to use in training their fighting dogs. For his part, Virginia O worked to refine his own personal training program, or keep.

By 1994, Virginia O was regularly fighting dogs up and down the eastern United States. That year he conditioned and handled one of Butts' dogs in a fight, a son of Bozack named Big Red. In 1995, his own dog Virginia O's Miss Tee won a fight lasting 30 minutes. That same year Virginia O rode along with Butts one evening to meet "some Army guy" Butts said was looking to buy a dog. Butts introduced him to Tony Taylor telling him to call Taylor by his nickname, Chief. None of the men could foresee where that simple introduction would lead.

Virginia O decided to breed Ebony again, this time to another Butts dog, Champion Hardcore's Mystic. Virginia O co-owned a puppy from this breeding with another group of dog fighters who called themselves Gator Boys Kennel. The puppy's name was Gypsy. When the time was right, Virginia O entered her in a fight. Gypsy was declared the winner when the handler of her opponent picked his dog up conceding the fight after 53 minutes. Gypsy earned her second win in 1997 after a grueling battle that lasted an hour and 15 minutes.

Around this same time, a young athlete named Michael Vick also began to fight dogs. Former Virginia Tech students would one day tell an investigator that football was not the only sport that interested Vick. Known to his friends as Ookie, Vick and his cronies often traveled to rural Floyd County, Virginia on weekends when no football games were scheduled, to fight pit bulls. In 1998, a fight report appeared in *The Sporting Dog Journal* or *SDJ*. The entry reported a fight between two dogs called Mann's Deuce and Mitchell's Peanut. But, what had people talking was not the fight itself. It was the name of the referee, listed in the magazine simply as "Vick".

By 2000, Virginia O had gained enough respect in the fight game to be called upon as a referee. It was not uncommon to referee fights between dogs owned by people he knew very well. One such person was Fat Bill Reynolds of Dixie Line Kennels in Pittsylvania, Virginia.

Fat Bill was disdained by many dog fighters, but Butts apparently did not share these scruples. He and Fat Bill co-owned a dog named Mary Jane. In a fight refereed by Virginia O, the men were bitterly disappointed when Mary Jane quit after only 27 minutes.

From time to time, Virginia O and Butts would decide that a losing dog was not worth keeping. Virginia O had seen other dogmen electrocute dogs. He had also seen them drown dogs, but he felt this took too long. Hanging was also ineffective, he felt, because pit bulls have such strong, thick necks. He preferred to shoot the dogs in the back of the head with a .22 caliber pistol. He would kill several by this method.

By 2001, Allen was living in Williamsburg, and his three way partnership had come apart. Fat Bill Reynolds was on his way to federal prison. Butts, the other member of the partnership, was heavily using drugs. Virginia O did not like drugs, and he began to distance himself from the man. It was the drugs he thought that had made Butts careless. The authorities had raided his Surry County property in 2000, seizing marijuana plants along with 33 of Butts' dogs, mountains of training equipment, and paraphernalia for dog fighting.

Another event occurred in 2001. Virginia Tech quarterback Michael Vick was a first round draft pick for the Atlanta Falcons Football Team. It was the first time ever that an African-American quarterback had been a first pick. Virginia O knew the name, but paid little attention. He had a more pressing problem. He had to decide what to do with one of his dogs. A female red and white pit bull named Blaze had become too aggressive to keep on his property. In what he considered an intervention by providence, Tony Taylor, the army guy, called him. He wanted to buy a dog. Virginia O said he thought he had just what Taylor was looking for. When Taylor arrived at the house, he brought some other young men with him. One of them looked oddly familiar. The young man said nothing at all during the visit, but Virginia O was certain he recognized him from his pictures in the newspapers.

"You look like Michael Vick," he said.

"Yeah, man," responded Vick tersely.

After some discussion and haggling over price, Taylor paid $1,000 for Blaze. The young men loaded their new prize into their car and drove away. This dog would become MV Kennels Blaze, but the men would call her Jane. Jane would go on to become a champion.

That same year, the name Vick appeared again in *SDJ*. The magazine reported a fight between Vick Kennel's Mona and Elm Street Kennels Cindy. After 42 minutes, Mona's handler picked her up, conceding the match to Cindy.

Michael Vick decided that he wanted to reach out beyond the local area to buy some better dogs. It was around this time that he met a dog fighter who was also a Richmond, Virginia school teacher. One of the most influential and powerful dog fighters on the east coast, the teacher was well connected, and he introduced Vick to a certain Richmond barber shop owner. This barber shop was a favorite meeting place for local dog fighters to plan and discuss upcoming fights. Sometimes, the owner would hang up the CLOSED sign and pull the blinds so that he and the others could watch video tapes of dog fights. The barber shop owner had a champion dog called Secretariat that had beaten most of the local Richmond area fighters. The school teacher told Vick about dogs from famous kennels owned by the likes of Carl Mims of Bona Fide Kennel Club and David Tant, widely considered to be the number two dog fighter in the country at the time. The teacher boasted that he owned a dog that had beaten one of Tant's dogs. Vick was impressed. His fascination with these dogs was deep. He decided to take a trip to meet Carl Mims. He also paid a visit to David Tant.

Virginia O and Taylor continued to stay in touch. In 2001, Taylor told him that he and three other men had decided to form their own fighting kennel. The partnership included Taylor, AKA Chief or T, and his cousin, Purnell Peace, AKA P-Funk. Peace had several dogs under his own kennel name, Too Bad Kennels. The third member was Quanis Phillips, AKA Q. Michael Vick, AKA Ookie, was the final partner, and the front man. He would put up all of the money for improvement of the kennel property, the purchase of the dogs, and their care. He would also put up the stake money for the fights. The men had already begun buying dogs—four from North Carolina, one from New York, six dogs and six puppies from Richmond. They had begun to train them using live chickens and rabbits as bait.

Taylor had come up with the name for the new enterprise, Badd Newz Kennels. The kennel name, he said, was an inside joke. Michael Vick had grown up in Newport News, a city called, not so affectionately, Bad News. Taylor told Virginia O that he had had Badd Newz T-shirts and headbands made up for the men to wear at dog fights. Their headquarters would be a sizable property that Taylor had found in Surry County and that Michael Vick had purchased for approximately $34,000. The four men planned to breed, raise, train, fight, and sell pit bulls. Eventually, there would be a house constructed, where not only the dog caretakers, but visitors could stay, and there was plenty of land for dogs. Surry was a sleepy little county where the crew felt they could pursue their plans for a dog fighting empire away from prying eyes. The men had obtained a kennel license and even had a web site. The web site was called Vick's K-9 Kennels and offered pit bulls, beagles, Rottweiler's, and Presa Canarios for sale. Vick's K-9 Kennels would serve as a front for the illegal Badd Newz Kennels activity.

Virginia O listened to Taylor's raptures about the new venture. He had always preferred to operate quietly, making a conscious attempt to stay below law enforcement's radar. He usually kept only a few dogs at a time, but he believed in live and let live. These guys were young, energetic, and ambitious. Let them weave their plans. He was busy with his own.

Virginia O had a male dog named Sting. He was the son of Hell on Earth's Gabriel, who was allegedly owned by a man known as "White Mike" Stewart in Maryland. Sting's dam was Allen's own Ebony. Virginia O began to offer Sting at stud. For one breeding, he decided to take the pick of the litter instead of a stud fee. He chose the only female. The four remaining puppies were sold to the Badd Newz Kennels crew for $1000. One of these puppies was a male named Magic, who would grow up to become a Badd Newz fighter. Virginia O asked Taylor if he would keep his new female puppy for him out at the Moonlight Road kennel. Taylor was still a bit in awe of the older man, and was eager for a chance to ingratiate himself. He readily agreed to keep the puppy. Unfortunately, one of the Badd Newz dogs got loose and killed the puppy. Virginia O could only shake his head and wonder what was going on out there.

Taylor had been extremely nervous that the yard accident in which the puppy had been killed would sour his relationship with Virginia O. Testing the water, he made a number of calls asking for advice, relieved that the older man did not seem to bear a grudge. Finally, Taylor asked Virginia O to come out to the kennel and take a look around. Taylor would be interested to hear what he thought of the operation. By this time Taylor was working for Vick full time and living in the double wide trailer parked on the Surry county property. Vick had even provided him with a brand new Navigator to drive.

Taylor took Virginia O on a tour of the property. He could hardly believe his eyes. There were plastic cups nailed to trees for the dogs' food and water! What were these guys thinking? Of course, the dogs simply chewed them off. He gave Taylor some advice on immediate changes needed to provide for the dogs. He made suggestions on how a kennel should be set up. These young men were in a hurry to get their enterprise up and running. As far as Virginia O could see, money was flowing like water. Just not for the basic things a kennel needed like solid bowls for food and water, made out of something the dogs could not destroy, chain link kennels and decent shelters.

Hardcore Benny Butts found out about Virginia O's visits to Moonlight Road. He was dying to rub elbows with Vick and his entourage. Butts pleaded with Taylor and Virginia O to introduce him. The two finally agreed. Taylor suggested that Butts might build a jenny for Badd Newz Kennels. Butts eagerly accepted Taylor's suggestion, and promised to get to work.

Between 2001 and 2003 much changed on the Surry County property. Kennels were constructed—chain link with concrete floors. The Richmond school teacher worked with some of the contractors on setting these up. Several outbuildings were constructed. These included a training room with treadmills and carpet mills, an infirmary of sorts, and a building to store vitamins, supplements, first aid supplies, and a bank of stainless steel cages. The pit building was constructed. At first it was only one floor. Looking like a garage, it housed a treadmill, a set of pallets on which bags of dog food were stacked, and rolls of carpet. The carpet would be laid out for fights in order to provide traction for the dogs. A scale for weighing the dogs hung from the ceiling. The second floor would be built later and would become the infamous pit itself. Both interiors and exteriors of all the buildings were painted deepest black. The Badd Newz crew continued to buy and test dogs. Peace, Taylor, and Phillips killed those that did not perform. They shot most of them. Two were electrocuted; one by Peace and one by Taylor.

Virginia O began to visit Moonlight Road with increasing frequency. He was careful never to pop in, however. There always seemed to be a crowd of people just hanging around. He did not like it. He made sure that he always called first and that Taylor was there. He would see Vick from time to time and Quanis Phillips. Soon Vick began to greet Virginia O by name. In turn the older man came to know each of the crew by his nickname, Chief, Q, P-Funk, and Ookie. Occasionally, the Vick crew sported their specially made Badd Newz T-shirts and head bands.

The Badd Newz Kennels crew had begun hosting fights in 2002, but with the house completed they were ready to entertain bigger names in the dog fighting game. The men would meet opposing dog owners and crews at a neutral location. From there they led guests down the country roads to the Badd Newz Kennels property. Vick would usually stay out of sight until the fights actually started. Taylor, Peace and Phillips would charge spectators $20 a head to watch the fights. Occasionally Virginia O fought a dog here. One such fight was the result of a challenge from two men known as Little Mike and Bunka. Word was that the two wanted Virginia O bad. They hoped to make a reputation for themselves by defeating the great man. The fight was between two 51-pound male dogs. Virginia O's dog was Chaos. Little Mike had a dog out of Patrick breeding, a famous fighting line. Mahlon Pat Patrick and five associates would be arrested for dog fighting in 2008 in Arizona. Patrick and his girlfriend, Emily Dennis would be acquitted of all charges.

On the day of the fight it was snowing and so cold the dogs were shivering. The second floor of the pit building had not been finished, so everyone gathered on the ground floor. Little Mike was nervous and drinking heavily. His dog was overweight. According to the rules, Virginia O could have refused the fight because of this breach. Instead, he agreed to allow Little Mike to pay a forfeit of $1,200 and go forward. The bet was $3,500. The entire Badd Newz crew was present, including Vick. Bunka handled Little Mike's dog and Peace handled Chaos. In the beginning, the overweight dog seemed to have the advantage. Little Mike shouted out over the noise of the crowd, "I got you, Vick!" Vick scowled in disapproval. It was a breach of etiquette to acknowledge his presence. He sent one of his crew to take Little Mike aside and explain the facts of life to him. In the end, Little Mike's dog lost the fight to Chaos. The Vick crew cheered and hollered. They hoped the outcome of this fight was an omen for things to come. That same year their dog Chico beat a dog from Alabama for a bet of $1,000. It seemed like Badd Newz would be good news for the Moonlight Road crew.

Virginia O continued to pursue his independent ambitions in the pit game. In 2002, his dog Piper won another fight, a grueling match that lasted one hour and 46 minutes. Badd Newz hosted the fight in which Shorty lost to Floyd, but still managed to be named gamest dog in show. The award helped to take the sting out of losing close to $1,000. That same year, Phillips and Taylor traveled to North Carolina to match a dog named Seal against a dog named Maniac. The men lost $500 when Seal was defeated. Later that year, Badd Newz invited Maniac and his owner to Moonlight Road for a fight against another of their dogs, Zebro. This time the bet was $1,000 per side. Again Maniac beat the Badd Newz entry.

By 2002, the Badd Newz crew decided that Jane, the dog Virginia O had sold to Taylor, was ready for a real fight. By now Virginia O's role had become that of promoter. He was responsible for making the contacts, negotiating terms, and "hooking up" or arranging the fights. Peace, Taylor, Phillips, Vick and Virginia O traveled to Maryland for a match between Jane and a New York dog from Show Biz Kennels. Each side staked $1,000. Peace placed an additional side bet for $600. Jane won that fight. She won again in North Carolina against a dog from Lockjaw Kennels. This time both sides put up $1,500. Allen, Phillips, and Taylor traveled to New Jersey for Jane's third match against a dog from Size 'Em Up Kennels. This time the bet was $5,000 per side. But more was riding on this win than the purse itself. If Jane captured a third win, Badd Newz would have a real champion fighting dog. The men were ecstatic when Jane prevailed. An informant would later claim that Vick was present at this fight, as well as a famous rap music singer. Both men were confident that they were safe from detection because so many regular and narcotics officers from the local police department were also present.

Peace purchased a dog that he named Too Bad Kennel's Big Boy. Big Boy was the son of Wrecking Crew's Lucy. Wrecking Crew was the kennel of Darryl Sills, from Norfolk, Virginia. In 2001, Norfolk animal control and police officers had executed a search warrant for dog fighting at Sills' home. He was arrested and sent to federal prison for drugs and weapons. In 2003, in a fight hosted at Moonlight Road, Big Boy beat a dog from South Carolina for a stake of $1,000. Later that year, the crew took Big Boy to South Carolina where he won another fight for a bet of $3,600. Big Boy would win his championship in 2004 at a fight hosted by Badd Newz at Moonlight Road against a dog from New Jersey. The bet was $1,500.

The house began to go up. In 2003, a local television station covered the construction of the mansion being built by Michael Vick in Surry County. Ironically, the news footage showed kennels with pit bulls. Although ordinarily hidden from view by a tall wooden fence, the news helicopter clearly captured the fully operational jenny from the air, as well as a number of pit bulls bouncing and lunging on the ends of their heavy tow chains.

In March of 2003, Vick, Phillips, Peace, and Allen took two dogs to D. C. Kennels in Blackstone, Virginia for fights refereed by Virginia O. D. C. Kennels belonged to Derek Sadar Carter, a former Virginia Tech Hokies teammate of Michael Vick. Badd Newz Kennel's Bandit lost to Geehad Kennel's Red Rover. The fight lasted 32 minutes; the bet was $10,000. In the second fight, the Badd Newz crew pitted their recently purchased Black Chef's Pickle against Geehad Kennel's Mayla. This time the bet was $13,000. Pickle lost after one hour and 44 minutes. Her injuries were severe, so Peace, after consulting with Vick, hosed her down with water and matter of factly electrocuted her. In the meantime, Vick retrieved a bag from his car which contained $23,000 in cash and handed it over to the man from Geehad.

That same year, Peace and Taylor took Magic, the son of Virginia O's Sting, to North Carolina. Vick and Phillips came up from Atlanta to meet the others at the fight. The bet was $1,500. Magic won. Badd Newz dogs Tiny and Too Short were also winners.

The crew began to breed their dogs, hoping to produce their own brand of fighters. Champion Jane produced Maggie May who would grow up to be a fierce fighter, killing at least two of her opponents and described on her pedigree as the "baddest bitch on the planet".

As time went on, Taylor began to bring his children to the Moonlight Road property. They rode four wheelers and enjoyed a life that their father could not provide for them. But, trouble was brewing. Phillips and Peace did not like having the children around. There was always a parade of available girls who were anxious to get to know a rich professional athlete or even members of his staff. The parties were huge with plenty of sex and drugs for all. Having Taylor's kids around was a problem that continued to annoy Phillips, but he was afraid of Taylor, who was much bigger and stronger. He knew if he pushed the wrong buttons with Taylor, he would suffer, so Phillips devised a plan to turn Vick against the man.

Phillips began to poison Vick's mind against Taylor. According to one undercover operative, Phillips had known Vick since childhood and knew just the right approach. Vick was extremely touchy about money. Phillips and Taylor usually did most of the work caring for the dogs. Taylor also did odd handyman jobs around the property. Both men frequently stayed at the house. They used the money from the Badd Newz wins for living expenses. Phillips began to complain to Vick that Taylor was not pulling his weight with the care of the dogs, and was overcharging Vick for labor and materials for work around the house. He also accused Taylor of dragging out the jobs to bleed Vick for even more money. His words had their desired effect. Vick soon became distrustful of Taylor and suspicious of his every action.

Things came to a head in September 2004. Tony Taylor had a falling out with Vick and Phillips. Part of it was about the money. Taylor asked Vick for $14,000, as payment for power washing the house. Vick was annoyed. He believed Phillips' claim that Taylor had no real intention of doing the work. The final rift, according to one investigator, occurred when Phillips, Taylor, Peace and a couple of other friends went to a nightclub on Mercury Boulevard in Newport News called The Alley. Phillips was wearing a gold chain that a friend of Taylor's wanted to try on. At the end of the night, the young man refused to return the chain, and it was accidently broken. The crew became angry because Taylor refused to act as enforcer to make the young man return the jewelry, or to "beat the shit" out of him. The next morning when Taylor returned to Moonlight Road, all of his belongings and his little puppy were outside on the front steps. Still Taylor refused to leave. The men argued, and Vick stormed out of the house in a rage. According to an informant, once away from the house, Vick called on Derek DC Carter to throw Taylor off the property. DC was a monster of man and had a reputation as one capable of handling problems. He made quick work of Taylor. Tony Taylor was finished; he was out. Vick returned to the house only after it was all over.

The fall from grace for Taylor was enormous. He went from living in a mansion as Vick's right hand man, to once again having to make and scrape to survive. Little did Vick imagine that his treatment of Taylor would one day play a pivotal role in his own eventual downfall. It is not uncommon for professional athletes to have falling outs with their crew. The wise athlete, however, will avoid the kind of hard feelings that can lead to betrayal and future "tell all" books. The wise athlete keeps his friends close, but his enemies closer. He sets up the exiled crew member in a nice apartment, with a car, and walking around money for a year or so. Vick did none of this. In what would prove to be a pattern that surfaced time and again, Vick seemed unwilling to part with even the relatively small sum that might have purchased Taylor's silence.

Instead, Vick cut him off without a cent. Now, Taylor was a bitter man. His children no longer had a beautiful home, and he was known as an outcast.

Another example that seemed to illustrate Vick's reluctance to part with his money, said one informant, was the grudging care for his dogs. Always on the hunt for a bargain, Vick got a deal on some dog houses, so he bought in bulk. He had plans to one day move the entire dog fighting operation to another rural location. In the meantime he told Peace to let houses the dogs were using wear out first. Once the move was made they would set up the dogs with the new houses. So while Vick and his cronies luxuriated winter after winter in the warmth of the opulent mansion, the dogs shivered in dilapidated, leaky houses, the new ones stacked and empty against the pit building gathering dust, leaves and pine needles.

Despite problems with his associates and dogs, Michael Vick's professional star continued to rise. He signed a new 10-year $130 million contract with the Atlanta Falcons on Christmas Eve 2004.

Virginia O knew what had happened to Taylor. He began to visit the property less and less often. He was tired. He did not need to get involved in young men's disagreements. Besides all this, the fight game was changing. It used to be a man and his dogs. There were rules, and customs. It had always been said that a good dogman knew when to pick his dog up. If he decided that his dog was going to lose and wanted to save his dog to fight another day, no one would think less of him if he opted for a pick up. Not so anymore. The fight game was filled with young thugs, gang members, drugs, and weapons.

One day Virginia O would bemoan this sad state of affairs. "The Internet ruined the dog game. I don't even have a computer. I hear there's stuff on there all the time about me that isn't true."

These days, he would complain, you were afraid to end a fight by picking up your dog. "Nowadays if a man wants to pick up his dog, he doesn't know what these young fools might do. They bet big money on the side, and they don't wanna lose it. I don't like it." At the very least, he claimed, there was derision and argument. "Yo, man. You curring out before your dog does!"

He would also claim that the young men in the fight game did not care about their dogs like he and other old timers did. "They don't even pet their dogs." He would see no irony in the fact that he executed dogs that were not good fighters. Completely lost on him was that fact that every day of his life he had betrayed the loyalty, devotion, and affection that his dogs gave to him, up until the moment he put a bullet in their heads.

Despite Virginia O's misgivings about the younger generation of dog fighters, he continued to collaborate with the Badd Newz crew. When he bred Sting again to Piper, he sold a female puppy to Peace. The puppy would be called Too Bad Kennel's Lil Chong. This dog would fight at Moonlight Road against a dog named Trouble. Peace handled Lil Chong in the pit. The fight lasted over 2 hours. The Badd Newz crew was disgraced when Lil Chong tried to escape by jumping out of the pit. This disqualified her, but Vick insisted on her being placed back into the pit to be mauled by the opponent. Lil Chong was seriously injured and lost the fight, as well as the bet of $7,000. Vick paid the $7,000 and a side bet of $4,000 that Peace placed. Peace executed Lil Chong by shooting her in the head. Vick thought it had been a good fight. He was impressed with Trouble, and a few days later he offered to purchase her for $15,000. Her owner did not hesitate to refuse such a paltry offer.

Construction continued at Moonlight Road. The second floor of the pit building was finished. Access was gained by a ladder in the upper left-hand corner of the ground floor next to the pallets of dog food. Like the rest of the buildings, the walls and floor of the pit were painted black. The men installed a window unit air conditioner, so that spectators could keep cool in warm weather. Now Badd Newz had a working pit. Fighters traveled from New Jersey, North Carolina, South Carolina, Maryland, Alabama, Ohio and other states to fight their dogs here.

Although Vick came to believe his crew were experts at the inner workings of the dog game, in reality, they were amateurs. The crew had become a virtual laughing stock among serious dog fighters even before Taylor's ouster. Taylor had once tried to set up a match with a dogman out of the Washington DC area, known as Sly. During the negotiations, Sly proposed that they go for 10 dollars.

Taylor responded that they would rather go for more, but 250 was the tops.

Sly said that was out of his league, but he might be able to get his friends to cover some of the bet. Taylor and the rest of Vick crew secretly laughed that Sly apparently could not cover a $250 bet! A short time later, Sly called to say he had gotten some boys to cover the bet for $250,000! When Taylor realized that Sly had actually been talking about hundreds of thousands of dollars all along, he did his best not to appear surprised and began to back pedal as fast as he could. At this point it was Sly's turn to laugh, and the reputation of Vick and his crew as novices was sealed.

Despite plenty of urging by the crew, Virginia O kept most of his fight conditioning secrets to himself. He was reluctant to squander his hard-won knowledge on the Badd Newz crew. He was disgusted that Benny Butts, in his groveling attempts to curry favor, told the crew everything. Butts also made every effort to prolong his visits to Moonlight Road, trying to ingratiate himself and earn extra money. By 2004 he moved his treadmills and carpet mill along with a number of his own dogs to Moonlight Road.

What Butts did not know was that a Surry County Deputy Sheriff had his eye on him. Deputy Bill Brinkman remembered Butts all too well. The local prosecutor's handling of the 2000 Butts case was a sore spot for Brinkman that continued to fester over the years. Brinkman had reason to believe that Butts was running drugs, hiding marijuana and cocaine in bags of dog food that he transported across state lines. In October of 2006, Brinkman contacted USDA OIG Agent Jim Knorr. Together they began to work on building a federal drug case against Benny Butts. Brinkman knew that Butts had moved dogs and equipment to Michael Vick's property on Moonlight Road. Brinkman firmly believed that in addition drug dealing, Butts was still fighting dogs. He was convinced that Michael Vick was involved as well.

Oblivious to this potential storming brewing, Butts was doing his best to become indispensable to the Badd Newz crew, but Benny's drug problem was growing worse. He was not only dealing, he was also using heavily—marijuana, cocaine, heroin and prescription drugs such as valium, xanax, and oxycontin.

In the meantime, Virginia O was determined to chase his next win. He drove to Pennsylvania that year to enter Chaos in another fight. Vick, Phillips, and Derek DC Carter followed in a separate car. Allen didn't like their smoke and loud music and refused to ride with them. Allen lost $1,000 when Chaos failed to win. Later that year, DC was killed in a gun battle in Lawrenceville, Georgia, the result of a drug deal gone bad.

Butts' drug problem continued to escalate. Things came to a head at a dog fight in 2006, where he responded violently to Vick's order to hurry up while weighing a dog. Butts pulled his knife on Vick and threatened to burn down his house. It was an unforgivable act of disrespect, and the end of Butts' relationship with Vick. He was banned from the property. The following year in February 2007, Butts died of a drug overdose. Speculation soon surfaced about whether his death was an accident, suicide, or something else entirely. According to Brinkman, Butts had new drug charges pending in Maryland. He had gotten into trouble again with White Mike Stewart of Hell on Earth Kennels.

On February 17, 2007, an impressively ungrammatical post by "The Crew" appeared on the Online Pedigrees Message Board. It read, "Thanks guys for all your kind words, his family and I really appreciate it. Benny was the backbone of HARDCORE kennels, I get a lot of credit for BENNY's hard work and dedication...I couldn't have done it without him he taught me a lot about these dogs, he was way ahead of his time in conditioning and supplementation. He was by far one of the best conditioners in the game today. He was my friend, he was my partner, he personified the word HARDCORE in every aspect of his life. I love you and I will miss you BENNY BUTTS."

It was signed, BIG MIKE. Was it Michael Vick? Or could it have been White Mike?

Butts' death meant that Brinkman's potential case against him was over. He and Agent Knorr continued to talk regularly, but neither had really determined where to go from that point. They could not have imagined the turn of events that waited for them a short two months later.

Around the time of Butts' death, Vick had a conversation with Virginia O. Vick told the older man he was the only person who had sold him a good dog. Others merely tried to scam him, convincing him to pay big money for worthless dogs. He said Virginia O was welcome to leave any of his dogs at the kennel anytime he liked to have them cared for by Badd Newz.

One day the media would portray Michael Vick as the ultimate dog fighter, but in reality he was a minor league, even second string player. A man who was a major league dog fighter was Terry Kendrick of OG (Original Gangsta) Posse out of Ohio, and he attended some of the Vick fights. He confided in Dog Angel, unaware that he was talking to the man who was building a case against him. Kendrick would be arrested in 2007 and later convicted of marijuana trafficking and dog fighting. Kendrick told Dog Angel that Vick was "rank and wet". "Rank", in gang slang, meant Vick was no good at all as a dog fighter. "Wet" meant wet behind the ears, an old term used to describe someone who knows nothing. Kendrick's opinion was that Vick knew nothing about the dogs, and the ones he had were no good. He bought poor quality fighting dogs, and he bet chump change. Considering that he had almost unlimited money to use in indulging his pastime and a full time crew to condition and handle the dogs, Kendrick found this shocking. According to Kendrick, "Vick had a crew around him that were stupid, man. They ripped him at every point, skimmed large, and then tried to show they were cool on the business front of the game. If that Nigger had a better crew he would be James [King]."

Dog Angel agreed with Kendrick. At one time, he said, Vick had the opportunity to purchase the famous Barracuda, who later sold for $80,000, along with some of his promising offspring. Other dogmen might sell their cars, fail to pay their mortgage, or even trade their girl friends for a quality pit bull, but Vick could not bring himself to pay the price for a top quality dog. Nonetheless, he still expected true gameness from his dogs, and if they failed, the penalty was death.

Another thing separated Vick from real professional dog fighters. The informant C claimed Vick had a penchant for throwing pet dogs into the pit with his pit bulls. Other breeds of dogs usually fight to defend territory, food, possessions, or to establish dominance. These fights are usually of very short duration and end as soon as one dog signals submission. On the other hand, game bred pit bulls will fight for hours demonstrating a tenacity and ferocity that is prized by dogmen. But, real dogmen make a sharp distinction between pit bulls and all other breeds. It would be beneath them to pit one of their game dogs against any other breed or pet. A professional dogman believes such a practice would cause his fighting dogs to develop bad habits. An analogy would be a professional boxer sparring with an average Joe. The boxer could easily destroy this opponent, but that would not prepare him to meet another professional fighter. This is not to suggest that dogmen will not use other small animals like rabbits, chickens and cats, to bait their pit bulls during training. That is often done, but in the ring, pit bulls fight pit bulls.

For Michael Vick and his crew to put a house pet into the pit with a game bred pit bull to be mauled as it screamed in pain and terror was behavior that made professional dogmen regard Vick with loathing. The irony that an often troubled quarterback, who some said was not living up to his own potential as an athlete, would mete out such vicious deaths to less than perfect canine athletes, was apparently lost on him.

Despite Vick's expressed confidence in him, Virginia O was increasingly uneasy. There were too many things he watched the Badd Newz crew do that he did not like. Phillips had taken a much bigger role in leadership of Vick's operation since the departure of Taylor. Virginia O did not trust the man and likened his intelligence to that of a table top. By 2007, Virginia O began to limit his visits to Moonlight Road, coming by only about once a month. He stayed in touch with Peace, who had now become Vick's yard man. Peace would occasionally ask him to care for the dogs, while he and the rest of the crew traveled to Atlanta to watch Vick play football.

One warm evening in April of 2007, Peace called to ask Virginia O to stop by. He said Vick would be there and that they would be testing some dogs that night.

CHAPTER 14 MICHAEL DWAYNE VICK

Michael Vick was born in Newport News, Virginia on June 26, 1980. His parents were young unmarried teenagers, Brenda Vick and Michael Boddie. Brenda was only 16 when she became pregnant with her famous son, but she was already the mother of a young daughter, Christina. Two more children would follow, Marcus and Courtney. The elder Michael served in the army and later worked in the shipyards and as a carpenter. Brenda worked also and received public assistance. Although his parents would marry when Michael was still a young child, he and his siblings chose to keep their mother's surname. Vick was called Ookie by his family, a name that would later be identified as his dog fighting alias.

    Michael Vick grew up in Ridley Circle Homes, a public housing project in the east end of the city nicknamed Bad News. Nowadays, it is accessible via Terminal Avenue off of I-664 just past the Monitor Merrimac Memorial Bridge Tunnel. The multi-family units are clustered behind the Waterfront Lumber Company not far from the marine terminals. The buildings are meanly constructed, the faux stucco finish a bluish gray. Roof shingles ripple and curl. Vehicles with flat tires and sheets of plastic stretched over missing windows are common sights. The landscape is strewn with trash and dotted with dark brown open dumpsters, out of which more trash overflows and spills. Every now and then there are glimpses of forlorn attempts to make the homes more attractive and homey. A few flowerbeds and occasional lawn ornaments can be seen. The shriveled and stunted stalks of a potted flower lie limply over the sides of a basket hanging from a clothes line. Nearby, clean laundry hung out to dry in the sunshine flutters in the breeze.

    Behind a six foot spiked metal fence at the Family Center, children play under the watchful eyes of several young women. Other children play in the scrabble and packed earth yards nearby. A young man pushes a toddler in a stroller. Here and there, other men, young and old, stand talking in groups or sit in old kitchen chairs staring as the world passes. The relatively new Achievable Dreams Tennis Center provides education to at risk kids inviting hopes and dreams of escape to a better future. Churches are plentiful, The Solid Rock Church, The Gospel Spreading Church of God, the Zion Baptist Church, and the imposing United House of Prayer for All People. This building boasts ornate filigree cornices over the first floor windows and beautiful inlaid mosaic stonework. Flanking both sides of the front entrance are two impressive white stone lions.

Several blocks away, across from the Head Start Center on Hampton Avenue, is the Boys and Girls Club where Michael Vick spent much of his free time as a boy, and where he first played football. It is a neat and well kept building, painted gray and blue with a cheerful brick red stripe painted all around.

Around the corner on Jefferson Avenue boarded up businesses, thrift stores, and tiny confectionaries featuring hand painted signs and bars on the windows are scattered here and there. A pall of depression seems to hang in the air. It is an area well known for drugs and crime. Michael Vick sought to escape these surroundings. In later years he would talk about going off by himself to fish, and about discovering the nurturing support of the Boys and Girls Club.

As early as seven years old, Michael Vick began to demonstrate amazing ability playing football here. Adults at the club took notice. Vick would later say, "Sports kept me off the streets…It kept me from getting into what was going on, the bad stuff. Lots of guys I knew have had bad problems."

In the 6th grade, Vick met a young boy he would come to call his best friend. Quanis Phillips, or Q, also loved basketball and football. The boys would play together starting in middle school and on into high school. When Vick was 11, he met 18 year old Tony Taylor, a known dog fighter in the neighborhood. Occasionally, Vick and Phillips would watch dog fights held in nearby streets or open lots. Both Vick and Phillips were fascinated by Taylor and by the lure of this blood sport. Fate had intervened, and the three would become irrevocably linked until their downfall years later.

By the time Vick was a freshman at Homer L. Ferguson High School in Newport News, he was proving himself to be an astonishing athlete. He threw for over 400 yards in a single game. He attended Warwick High school his junior year after Ferguson High was closed. Here he played as a Raider under Coach Tommy Reamon. During his high school career, Vick passed for 4,846 yards with 43 touchdowns. In one single game, he ran for six touchdowns and threw for three more.

Coach Reamon knew he had something extraordinary in the young Vick. He believed his protégé could go all the way to become a professional football player. He helped the boy with his SAT tests. He urged him to choose Virginia Polytechnic University over Syracuse University, where he thought Virginia Tech Coach, Frank Beamer, would be better able to guide and develop the young football player.

Vick followed his mentor's advice. He left home in 1998 to accept a full scholarship as a Virginia Tech Hokie. His best friend, Phillips, accompanied him, and lived with him for several months before returning home to Newport News. Coach Beamer had promised to "redshirt" Vick the first year, in order to allow him time to develop. Vick would later tell a *Sports Illustrated* reporter that as hard as it had been, he learned important lessons being forced to sit out that first season. "Before I took my first snap, I wanted to be in control of the offense, know where the players were, how to read defenses. These are all things I learned when I sat out."

Completely unknown to the world at large, 1998 was also the first year that *SDJ* featured the name Vick. A fight report included this name as the referee for a particular match. It was during this period that Vick, according to former Virginia Tech students, began to travel to rural Floyd County for dog fights. In those days, no one really noticed him. He had not yet achieved the fame he would one day enjoy.

By spring of his freshman year, Vick's amazing speed and athletic ability led him to tapped for quarterback. In 1999, in his very first game, Vick scored three touchdowns against James Madison University. On the third touchdown, Vick executed a crowd pleasing flip, but he injured his ankle forcing him to miss the rest of that game and the next. Vick went on to lead the Hokies in an 11-0 season, and from there to the Bowl Championship Series national title game in the 2000 Nokia Sugar Bowl against Florida State. The Hokies lost this game 46-29, but Vick was responsible for a brief recovery bringing his team up from a 21 point lag to a brief lead.

In spite of this loss, Vick set an NCAA freshman record that year of 180.4 yards for passing efficiency. It was also the third highest all time record for college football. He received an ESPY Award as the nation's top college player, and the first-ever Archie Griffin Award for college football's most valuable player. He received the third highest number of votes for the 1999 Heisman Trophy. This was the highest finish ever achieved by a freshman. It would not be until 2004 that Adrian Petersen would break Vick's record for votes, finishing second that year.

The following season Vick achieved his career rushing high of 210 yards against the Boston College Eagles. In the Black Diamond Trophy game against West Virginia, Vick was responsible for 288 total offensive yards and two touchdowns for a 48-20 win.

He led the Hokies to a win against Syracuse at the Carrier Dome, where they had not won a game since 1986, bringing his team back from a 14-0 lead by the opposing team. With only a little more than a minute left in the game, Vick scored the winning touchdown in a 55-yard run.

It seemed that Vick was invincible, but in the following game against Pittsburgh, Vick was injured again. He missed the rest of that game, the game against Central Florida, and did not start against the Miami Hurricanes, where he saw the Hokies' only loss of the season. Vick's last game as a Hokie wended in a 41-20 win against the Clemson Tigers in the 2001 Toyota Gator Bowl.

Vick decided to leave Virginia Tech. He was determined to become a professional football player. His family was still living in public housing in Ridley Circle Homes in Bad News. Michael Vick said he wanted to buy his mother a home and a car. In the 2001 NFL draft, Vick was the first overall pick. He signed a six year contract worth up to $62 million and became an Atlanta Falcon.

Vick continued to stay in touch with Tony Taylor from the old neighborhood. They often discussed their mutual passion for dog fighting. Taylor told Vick he had the real dogs, and that he kept them at his grandparent's home in Smithfield, Virginia. Taylor introduced Vick to his cousin, Purnell Peace. That year Vick accompanied Taylor to the home of Virginia O, where Taylor purchased the female pit bull Virginia O called Blaze.

The name Vick would continue to find mention in SDJ. T.B.K. or Too Bad Kennels, the kennel name of future co-defendant Purnell Peace would also appear. The men decided that together they could establish a dog fighting empire. In 2001, at the urging of Tony Taylor, Vick purchased the property in Surry County, Virginia that would be the future home of Badd Newz Kennels for $34,000.

Vick met the Richmond school teacher from whom he hoped to learn more about the fight game. He was determined to be a big player in the game of professional dog fighting, as well as the NFL. Just as he was being molded as an NFL quarterback, he also sought mentors to teach him the ins and outs of the dog world.

Back in Atlanta, Coach Dan Reeves hoped to gradually introduce young Vick to professional football. On September 9, 2001, Michael Vick made his NFL debut in San Francisco. He completed his first NFL pass and scored his first touchdown on September 23 against the Carolina Panthers. The pass was only 18 yards and the touchdown the result of a two yard rush, but they helped the Falcons win 24-16.

Reeves was forced to change his plans when starting quarterback Chris Chandler was injured. Suddenly Vick was pushed into the starting lineup. He started against the Dallas Cowboys on November 11 and threw the first touchdown pass of his career, a mere nine yard toss, but the Falcons won 20–13. He also started against the St. Louis Rams and played in five other games that year. He completed 50 of 113 passes for 785 yards with two touchdowns and 3 interceptions that year. But Vick had problems. He turned the ball over too often. The young man also reportedly had problems memorizing Reeves' plays. Vick would tell a *Sports Illustrated* reporter, "There was so much verbiage, and instead of studying routes or coverages, I came to practice just worried about getting the names of the plays out. As the backup (to Chandler) I'd get eight reps, and I'd hold up practice because I screwed up six of them."

The Sporting News reported that Falcons management had other worries about their young star. Apparently, concerns had already surfaced about Vick's immaturity and some of his associates. Vick dismissed his well wishers saying, "I think things out. I do my research. I don't have a lot of friends. I don't trust everyone. I know I have to be careful about who I am and the company I keep, and I will be. I have a responsibility to a lot of people, and I won't let them down. And if I see that some of my friends change, I can change too. In a hurry." Tucked away in *The Sporting News* story was a small notation about one of Vick's favorite off the field hobbies, breeding pit bulls.

"There's more to me than people think."

His words were eerily true, but it would be another six years before the sordid story of Badd Newz Kennels would come to light. In the meantime, when Vick would attend fights, he took care to dress and look like any other dog fighter in attendance. With the baggy pants, gold necklaces and his crew around him, he managed to blend in completely. But, after *The Sporting News* article came out, Vick was suddenly recognized by many of the dog fighters who had seen him at these shows. Quickly, any number of people began offering to sell him dogs. In dog fighting, it is all about the bloodlines. Desirable dogs are those that come from proven fighting stock. But just as some of his NFL teammates claimed he had difficulty memorizing plays, Vick had trouble remembering the various kennels, bloodlines and pedigrees. According to Dog Angel, Vick's teammates talked about his habit of wearing the different plays on a "cheat sheet" taped to his arm. Dog Angel asked another NFL quarterback he knew about this practice. The man responded that it was fine if a man followed those plays. Vick, he said, could not keep the plays straight even though they were taped to his sleeve. Instead of throwing the ball to a receiver, he said Vick would forget the play, forget where to throw the ball, and take off running down field. Vick's similar struggles in the game dog world meant he was unable to make sound choices when purchasing dogs. Like his unplanned runs down the field, Vick would just take off and buy dogs based on bargain basement price and a nod from one of his buddies.

In 2002, the Falcons released Quarterback Chris Chandler, and at only 22, Vick became a full time starter for his team. "I always knew I had the physical ability to perform, but my confidence wasn't where it needed to be. I knew that I had to work the entire off-season to prepare. I studied my playbook every day, even if it meant locking myself in my bedroom when Mom came to visit. I watched all my plays from last year. It's what I had to do." The pressure was on, and Vick applied himself. By the next season Vick would not need the nod from his wide receiver to help him. In the dog game, however, he continued to rely on nods from his home town crew.

His hard work on and off the football field paid off. Vick led his team to the playoffs his very first season as a starting quarterback. He completed career highs of 231 out of 421 passes for 2,936 yards, and 16 touchdowns. His record that year also included 113 carries for 777 yards and eight rushing touchdowns. He had a number of single-game career-highs, including 24 passes completed out of 46 pass attempts at Pittsburgh on November 10. He passed for 337 yards against Detroit, and completed a personal career record pass for 74 yards for a touchdown against New Orleans on November 17. Vick scored an NFL record of 173 rushing yards by a quarterback against Minnesota on December 1. In January 2003, Vick led his team to an upset 27-7 victory over the Green Bay Packers in the NFC playoffs, a game that ended the Packers' undefeated playoff record at Lambeau Field. The Falcons would later exit the playoffs in a 20-6 loss to the Philadelphia Eagles.

Michael Vick quickly became the adopted favorite son of both the NFL and the city of Atlanta. He was not only a major football star he was a poster child for young African American males. Michael Vick had escaped the projects to become a celebrated and feted young millionaire. Thousands of young men watched their idol and aspired to achieve his success.

But, despite his fame and predictions for a bright future, there were clouds on the horizon. In early 2004, two men driving a Ford F-150 truck were arrested in Virginia. Harry Leon Snead, Jr., the driver, was carrying $1,420 in cash. The other occupant, Jerry Lee Garner, 23, had just over an ounce of marijuana. Both men were charged with possession with intent to distribute drugs. The truck the men were driving was registered to Michael Vick and Charles W. Reamon, Jr., the nephew of Tommy Reamon, Vick's former high school coach.

On October 10 of 2004, an Atlanta airport security worker named Alvin Spencer placed his Rolex watch on the X-Ray scanning belt. At about the same time Michael Vick, Quanis Phillips, another man identified as Todd Harris, and a young child were going through security prior to boarding an Air Tran flight to Newport News. When Spencer went to retrieve his watch, it was gone. Spencer later told police he watched the video tape and saw Vick's companions Phillips and Harris take his watch and give it to Michael Vick. He reported the incident to his supervisors and then to Atlanta Police, although no police report was filed. Instead, the investigating officer was believed to have contacted the Falcons Director of Player Programs, Billy Johnson. Spencer would claim that Johnson assured him the incident was a mistake, and that if he kept the story away from the press, the watch would be returned. Spencer also claimed that Johnson repeatedly offered him a cash settlement, but that he insisted on the return of his watch. Spencer added that he spoke with Vick by telephone at the Atlanta Police station. "I asked him did he have any intentions to bring me my watch and do you understand the watch is stolen? I couldn't get through to him that I wanted the watch back."

The watch was finally returned to Alvin Spencer by Billy Johnson six days after the incident. No charges were filed against Vick or his companions. A news report prompted an Internal Affairs investigation regarding the handling of the entire incident by the investigating officer. Vick was able to make this entire little problem go away.

Football was the ticket that allowed Vick and his friends to indulge their other pastimes. One of Vick's crew told Dog Angel that the NFL stood for National Fun League. It allowed the crew to travel, party, meet women, and of course, fight dogs. The dog game had become an obsession for Vick. He made travel plans and arranged his schedule so he could see his dogs fight. He took late night calls before important football games, to find out how a dog did in a roll or fight. His fans had no idea about his obsession, one that would lead him to build a home for the sole purpose of fighting and breeding dogs. The choice of location, the design of the pit building, the painting buildings black in the belief that this would keep any air surveillance from detecting his elaborate set up-everything was focused toward this one passion.

On Christmas Eve 2004, Vick signed a new 10-year contract with the Atlanta Falcons worth $130 million in salary and bonuses, making him one of the highest paid football players in history. His star was at its pinnacle. Vick seemed to be untouchable, but there was trouble brewing.

In April 2005, a 26 year old health care worker named Sonya Elliot filed a lawsuit against Vick claiming that he had knowingly infected her with herpes in 2003. According to her claim, the young woman met Vick at a Virginia Beach nightclub in 2001 and become involved with him. It became widely circulated that Vick, while withholding information from his victim, had sought treatment for himself under the false name of Ron Mexico. Soon fan orders for Vick's famous number 7 jersey began to include special requests for personalization featuring the name Mexico. The NFL was not amused and soon put a stop to the craze. The Elliot lawsuit was settled the following year for an undisclosed payment to the woman. Again, Vick was able to make an unpleasant incident go away.

In November of 2006, the Falcons suffered a humiliating 31-13 loss against the New

Orleans Saints. It was the fourth straight loss for the Falcons. Although Vick rushed for 166 yards, he was only able to complete nine out of 24 pass attempts. He got sacked three times, and the opposing offense hit him 12 times behind the line of scrimmage. As the Falcons left the field, the remaining Georgia Dome fans loudly booed their home team. Vick responded by showing his tormenters the middle finger of both his extended hands.

Later Vick would apologize saying, "First and foremost, I would like to apologize for my inappropriate actions with fans today. I was frustrated and upset at how the game was going for my team, and that frustration came out the wrong way. That's not what I'm about. That's not what the Atlanta Falcons are about. I simply lost my cool in the heat of the moment. I apologize and look forward to putting this incident behind me."

The NFL was apparently not impressed with his display of contrition and imposed a $10,000 fine. Vick also agreed to donate an additional $10,000 to charity. Vick responded by quipping, "I can't really say whether it's fair or not, but the league makes the rules and I broke the rules. It is what it is—20 Gs. I shouldn't have done what I did. I broke a rule, and now I'm paying the price. The good thing is I get to donate a portion of it to charity."

In January 2007, security personnel seized a 20 ounce Aquafina water bottle that contained a secret compartment from Vick at a Miami airport checkpoint. According to the officers, the compartment contained a dark residue and a strong odor of marijuana. Vick was allowed to board the Air Tran flight. Vick would claim that the compartment was for the purpose of carrying jewelry. The water bottle was seized by Miami Dade Police, and a report was filed. A laboratory analysis would find no evidence of drugs, and no charges were filed.

In spite of these problems on and off the field, Vick's star continued to rise. He achieved his dream of moving his mother out of the projects, when he bought her a home of her own. In addition to his Surry County Virginia property, he purchased a palatial home in an exclusive gated community in Duluth, Georgia. His number 7 jersey was one of the most popular NFL items offered for sale through Reebok. His endorsement deals at one time or another included such companies as Air Tran, Nike, Coca Cola, EA Sports, Hasbro, Kraft Foods and Rawlings (sporting goods). Don Russ and Upperdeck marketed his football trading card. He became a young entrepreneur investing in real estate and companies such as Atlantic Wine and Package, Divine Seven, a rental car company, and a restaurant called The Tasting Room.

In early 2007, Michael Vick was looking forward to training camp and the fall football season when his world came crashing down with the raid on his Moonlight Drive home in Surry County, Virginia on April 25.

CHAPTER 15 THE CASE COMES TOGETHER

Thursday, June 7 at 1:30 p.m., I was at my desk wrestling with end of the year bills when ACO Melanie Tobin burst into my office. "The Feds are at Vick's house!" she shouted. Since the night she had been part of the Chesapeake team for the original search, Tobin had been anxiously following the case. I immediately brought up the live video feed from the WAVY TV 10 Chopper on my computer. The Feds were executing a search warrant at Moonlight Drive. The warrant had been issued by the U. S. Magistrate's Office in Richmond, Virginia earlier that morning.

Multiple agents could be seen cautiously digging carefully defined areas in the shade provided by plastic tarps. They were sifting dirt, bagging unknown items and carrying those bags somewhere. I called Brinkman. "Where are you?" I demanded. "Are you there?"

"You bet I am!" he answered. He told me they were looking for dog carcasses he believed to be buried on the property. Shades of the ill fated County search warrant! They also intended to remove a section of floor from the pit to test for blood.

Brinkman said he had barely been able to stand the suspense while waiting for the Feds to act. The informant C had told him that approximately two months ago, a number of dogs had been ruthlessly killed for being poor fighters and subsequently buried on the property. Brinkman said the more he had been forced to wait, the greater his fear that someone might move the bodies. So, he had made it his practice to drive by the house on Moonlight Road at least once each day. One day, he said, he saw two men standing in the yard. One appeared to be very agitated, pacing back and forth as he talked on a cell phone. Brinkman immediately called Assistant US Attorney Mike Gill. "You know, we got movement out here. They're in the back where all the evidence was and everything." Brinkman said he had made absolutely certain that the two men saw him. Brinkman pleaded with Gill on the phone; it was now or never.

What he did not know at the time was that the decision had already been made. Once Poindexter refused to let the second search go forward and the information contained in the affidavit had been leaked to the media, the Feds decided to step in. Brinkman's call simply cinched the matter of when they would move.

"Well, are you finding anything?" I asked excitedly. "From the Chopper 10 live feed, it looks like you are."

"Oh, yeah," he replied. The relief in his voice was clear. He said he could not talk more, but would call me later.

WAVY TV 10 reported that federal authorities removed bags of evidence. Poindexter said he was, "Absolutely floored. What is foreign to me is the federal government getting into a dog fighting case. I know it's been done, but what's driving this? Is it this boy's celebrity? Would they have done this if it wasn't Michael Vick? There's a larger thing here, and it has nothing to do with any breach of protocol. There's something awful going on here. I don't know if it's racial. I don't know what it is."

Poindexter seemed to suggest every possible reason for the Feds' involvement except the obvious one. There was overwhelming evidence that multi state felony activity had been routinely originating from property in his jurisdiction.

Dog Angel was incredulous. "Have you ever seen or heard of a case where the prosecutor is making statements defending the main suspect?" he asked. I had to admit, I had not.

ACO Tobin and I were ecstatic. After two months of false starts, contradictions, speculation, and denials, it had happened at last. The Feds had entered the ring! The vise grip on my chest finally released. I did not speak to Brinkman again until the day after the Feds' search, Friday, June 8. He told me the Feds had completely taken over the investigation. Poindexter, he said, was enraged. Brinkman said he and the Feds had found exactly what C described. Three dogs were in one grave together. More dogs were in other graves. They found a board nailed to a tree from which, C said, dogs had been killed by hanging. They had gone to their deaths because they had not been ferocious enough fighters. They had not been game. Brinkman said they had removed an approximately four by six foot section of the pit floor. They had also taken a section of the wall.

One thing troubled me about the search. Dr. Merck had not been there. "Look," I said to Brinkman, "are you playing me? Why was I on the phone to Dr. Merck pitching this elaborate plan to her, asking her to be unavailable for the local warrant, but to be ready for the Feds two weeks down the road? Then ya'll go yesterday? I look like an idiot, at the very least. You put me in the middle and I feel like I lied to her."

"Wait a minute," he said. "I swear, even I didn't know it was going down yesterday. They kept it totally quiet."

Dog Angel later explained why not even Brinkman had not been alerted in advance of the search. The Feds, he said, had been worried about previous leaks in the case. They knew about the delays at the Sheriff's office the night of the first search, and they were well aware of the leak of the e-mail to the Vick crew. The Feds had taken no chances.

Brinkman then laughed and said he had to tell me one thing. He had read the federal warrant, and remarked to one of the agents, "Well this looks familiar," meaning the language. The agent smiled and said, "Well, it ought to. I got it off of yours." So, the very language that

Poindexter had rejected when he refused to let Brinkman's earlier warrant go forward, posed no problems for the federal magistrate.

I received a call from Dr. Merck. As expected, she was shocked that after clearing her schedule at Brinkman's request, the Feds had gone forward without her. In spite of the fact that I had nothing to do with leaving her out, I felt guilty. I told her I was so sorry, that neither Brinkman nor I had known until it happened.

The federal search was all over the news. When the news hit, Dog Angel was sitting with two of Purnell Peace's closest friends. The Vick camp, they said, was very depressed. Peace had just called them to describe in a profanity filled rant how bad this was for all of them. Next, Dog Angel placed a call to one of Vick's old teammates from Virginia Tech. He asked him how Vick was reacting to the news. The man said Vick was shocked that this had been allowed to happen. To Dog Angel this meant that someone was supposed to have been able to stop any further warrants.

One person came immediately to mind, the underground figure known only as the Fixer. Dog Angel detested him. He was determined to discover the identity of the Fixer, expose him and bring him to justice. Within hours, Dog Angel reported he had confirmed Vick's arrangement with the Fixer. Vick believed there was a leak in his own camp, and had engaged the Fixer to track it down. I often laugh at how relentless Dog Angel can become when on the hunt. Goodwin describes him as a tracking dog who barks and howls as he gets closer and closer to his quarry. When Dog Angel has no trail, he is quiet and I do not hear from him. When he is on the trail, he can single handedly run down the battery of my cell phone!

Goodwin called to pass on a message from Dog Angel. "The Vick camp really, really hates you," he told me.

"Be careful," John warned. I assured him that I would. Later that day, I finally spoke with Dog Angel again. He had been trying to find out exactly what Vick and his crew might be planning for me. He confirmed that the Vick crew believed I was responsible for all of their problems. I did not need any further convincing, but Mark Kumpf also called me. One of his sources confirmed Dog Angel's report that the Vick camp blamed me for the investigation.

"Are you being careful?" he asked. "Do you take a different route to work, and are you varying your hours? What about when you are home?"

Heck, I didn't even lock my doors half of the time when I was home. I had always felt safe. My service weapon was close by, and I had two little yappy dogs. They did not have to be big or ferocious. They just had to announce, and they did—anyone who walked by, any squirrel on the deck, any leaf that blew. No one would be able to sneak up on me. And, no, I was not varying my routine. Perhaps I should start, I thought. Then I thought, what if someone harmed my dogs or tried to steal them?

The next morning was Monday morning June 11. I decided to talk to Lynn Roberson, the first line supervisor at Animal Control about whether I should really be concerned. Lynn's response was to suggest that I call Major Wright immediately. The Major was out of the office, but I spoke to Lt. Farney. I told him I felt a little foolish, but Lynn had urged me to call. To my surprise, Farney seemed to take the matter in a serious light. He had a lot of questions. No, I had not received any calls, letters or any other kind of direct threats. I had only been warned by third parties. In answer to his question, I responded that we had an alarm system and panic buttons at the shelter. In addition, people had to be buzzed in the front door. Farney said he could not believe how huge this case was getting. He would let the Major know I had called.

I found Lynn on the phone to Police Supply. She was explaining that I needed body armor or a vest. Within an hour one of my officers picked up a vest. It had just been delivered when I got a call from Police Officer Lenny Stolecki. Lenny had been assigned to the police academy when I went through in 1994. He is a big guy with lots of muscles, a broad New York accent and the heart of a big teddy bear. I remembered him during the first few days of the academy when he tried to be so mean, maintaining a permanent deliberate furrow right between his eyebrows. Those first few days, we spent a lot of time in the parking lot doing pushups. In the academy, you did pushups anytime anyone in the class did something wrong. We did hundreds. That first week I could not lift a tea cup to my lips or take a shirt off over my head—my arms and chest muscles hurt so much. Stolecki knew I did a little acting on the side so he would stand over me yelling, "Are you acting like you're doin' a push up Strouse?" He tried so hard to be mean. One day we were coming back from some kind of field trip on the Big Blue Bus that the academy used. We got to the academy parking lot, and Stolecki ordered everyone off. "Strouse, you stay!" My stomach began doing flip flops, as my mind scrambled for what I might have done wrong. "Damn!" I thought. I hoped I was not about to be the cause of more pushups for my teammates. When everyone had gone, Stolecki barked, "Get up here." I stood before him at attention in the aisle of the bus. Still seated in the driver's seat, he continued to stare straight ahead. "You got heart Strouse. Now get the hell outta here."

Over the years, Stolecki and I remained in touch because he was in charge of vehicles for the Police Department, which included Animal Control trucks. Now he was calling to check on me because he heard I had been threatened. I explained that I was just taking precautions, and that there were no direct threats. I asked him to please not tell anyone else. "Well I was just checking on ya'. You know I keep track of all my kids, and you're still one of my kids. So I had to check." I laughed. I was several years older than Stolecki, but I was one of his kids!

On Friday, June 15, I received a call from USDA OIG Special Agent Jim Knorr. It was the first time we had spoken since our first meeting at my house. I could expect an order in the very near future, he said, authorizing the seizure of the pit bulls by the federal government. A federal guardian for the dogs would eventually be appointed, but in the meantime I should work with Special Agent Beth Dinkins. He expected to move the dogs that were still in the custody of Surry County in the very near future. Could I help, perhaps, by sending the word out to VACA asking if any of our members might be willing to provide housing for them? I did so immediately. Next, Brinkman called to say that he expected Vick to be indicted in August on charges stemming from the dog fighting. The Feds were moving quickly.

Several days later, I tried to call Brinkman back, but his phone went straight to voice mail. That was odd. I had never known him to keep his phone off. I realized that it had been almost a week since I had been able to reach him. He had always called me back promptly. I was worried.

By June 22, there was still no word from Brinkman. Goodwin called me. I told him I was concerned about Brinkman. Goodwin had not spoken to him either. I called Mark, but got the same response. Finally, I placed a call to Agent Jim Knorr. Murphy's Law meant I did not reach him either. I left a message.

On Saturday, June 23, the phone rang. It was Knorr. He laughingly told me everything was fine. Brinkman was on a much deserved vacation. He said he understood my concern perfectly. There had been several times when he had difficulty contacting Brinkman. "Don't do that," he had warned when he finally spoke with him. "You make me nervous when you don't call me back."

Knorr had a lot to tell me. They had an informant, he said, who they were putting up in a hotel in another state. Knorr had designated him a federal informant as soon as Poindexter had called off Brinkman's second search. I said nothing to let on that I had already knew about C. Knorr said that C had stated Vick, Purnell Peace, and Quanis Phillips had killed the a number of dogs because they had been disappointing fighters. Vick had personally participated. C also stated that on at least two occasions, Vick had taken pet dogs and thrown them into the ring with Badd Newz pit bulls. He and his crew thought it was funny to watch the pit bulls maul and kill helpless pets.

Knorr had been trying to keep C under wraps since May. He had asked his boss, Special Agent in Charge (SAC) Brian Haaser for some money to cover the hotel bill where C was hidden, pay for meals and provide some cash for the valuable information C was providing. Haaser had replied, "I'm not the Marshall's Service, and I'm not going to spend my money on a two bit dog fighting case." Knorr was incredulous at Haaser's refusal to help. In spite of this, he knew he had to keep C hidden. He had already infuriated Poindexter by refusing his request to interview C. "He's my witness," Poindexter had argued.

"No, he is a federal informant. My informant, and you will not get to talk to him," Knorr replied. Once Poindexter had refused to let the second search warrant go forward, and the information from the affidavit had been leaked to the media, there was no way Knorr was letting the man near his informant. Finally, Knorr told me, SAC Haaser found out that he and Brinkman had been speaking with Assistant US Attorney Mike Gill. In addition this case was generating intense media scrutiny. Haaser finally relented agreeing to provide some money to take care of C.

When Brinkman returned from vacation, the first thing he did was track down Tony Taylor. Using information from the Virginia Employment Commission, he located an address for him in Emporia, Virginia. Taylor showed no surprised at the sight of his visitor, nor did he have any illusions about the reason for this call. He had been following the stories in the press. Brinkman explained the facts of life to Taylor and told him he would be back in touch in a few days.

Vick's treatment of Taylor would now come back to haunt the beleaguered athlete. Taylor had lost virtually everything-the mansion, the high end SUV with a TV in the dash, the women and the rolls of cash in his pocket at all times. He had been humiliated by the bum's rush he had received from DC Carter, and he had been branded a thief. Since then Taylor had been struggling. Jobs for ex-crew members of famous athletes are hard to find.

Dog Angel described the difference between Taylor's treatment and that of an ex-crew member of another athlete. Dog Angel had once trailed a famous NFL linebacker who he believed was connected to dog fighting in the Lakeland, Florida area. In time, Dog Angel worked his way into the linebacker's crew, or so he thought. He had been certain, he told me, that he could get a certain ex-crew member to share the details of the linebacker's involvement in dog fighting. It seemed the ex-crew member had been thrown out of the inner circle for stealing. But in stark contrast to Vick's treatment of Taylor, Dog Angel said, the linebacker continued to take care of this man. In turn, the man refused to say a word against his benefactor. Failing to take care of Taylor was Vick's critical mistake. He forgot, that an ex-crew member still knew all of the dirty secrets, the women, the drugs, the guns and, in Vick's case, the dogs.

A few days later, Taylor's attorney contacted Brinkman to set up an interview. When they all finally sat down at the US Attorney's office in Newport News, Taylor's attorney said simply, "My client's going to tell you everything you want to know."

Taylor's formal interview took place on June 28, 2007. He admitted his role in the Badd Newz Kennels organization, and implicated his partners Quanis Phillips, Purnell Peace, and Michael Vick. Finally, Brinkman learned the identity of Virginia O, the man who set up and refereed fights for Badd Newz Kennels. C had been right. His first name was Oscar. Taylor told Brinkman his last name was Allen. Oscar Allen was a 67 year old African American who loved near Williamsburg, Virginia. Taylor gave Brinkman the address.

Brinkman would soon serve Oscar Allen with a subpoena to appear before a federal grand jury. The Feds were just about ready to present their case. There was no doubt in Brinkman's mind that he needed Oscar Allen AKA Virginia O. Taylor had been out of the gang since 2004. A good defense attorney might paint Taylor as a thief and a leech, who was merely lying to seek vengeance over being ousted and disgraced by Michael Vick. He needed more recent information, and he hoped that Oscar Allen could be convinced to provide it.

Knorr drove to Surry to serve the order for the federal seizure of the dogs to Surry County Administrator Tyrone Franklin. Franklin was angry about the seizure, Knorr said. He wanted me to know that Franklin blamed me for the Feds involvement. "What? How?" I asked. Franklin, he said, knew that I had sent out the message to the VACA e-mail list seeking housing for the dogs that remained in Surry. Knorr said Franklin believed I had written negative things about Surry County in my request for housing. I had done nothing of the kind. Knorr went on to say he was absolutely convinced that he knew the origin of the campaign of negativity against me. He did not need to say more.

Tuesday evening, July 3, Knorr called me again. This time he sounded exhausted and disheartened. He was not sleeping, he said. This case was making him stressed and crazy. He spoke about the turf war between federal agencies. The FBI had different priorities than USDA. They were interested in gambling, drugs and money laundering, not dog fighting. Knorr felt that if the USDA could convict Michael Vick and his co-horts, they could send a powerful message that might begin to put an end to dog fighting in this country. That was important to him. I was touched and surprised to find someone outside of animal welfare who cared so much about this issue.

Knorr said he was worried about the media attention surrounding the federal search warrant. He was afraid it might inspire Poindexter to indict Vick on state charges before he could go before a federal grand jury. "I'm not sure I understand," I said. Knorr replied he thought Poindexter would make a deal with Vick's attorneys to plead any felony dog fighting charges down to the most minor of misdemeanors. This would effectively make the case go away, while allowing Poindexter to claim he had done his job with due diligence.

"We would be finished," he said. I was still lost. If the Feds could prove Vick and the others transported dogs across state lines, could they not still go forward?

"Probably not," Knorr said.

Knorr asked me if I knew someone named Mark from Montgomery County, Ohio. He had information that this person had a video tape of Vick at a dog fight. "Do you mean Mark Kumpf?" I asked. "That's the only Mark I know, and there's no way he would not have told me if he had a tape." I gave him Mark's number anyway. Then Knorr dropped a bombshell. He told me that he planned to execute yet another search warrant at the Moonlight Road property. Dr. Merck would accompany them. This time they would be removing the bodies of the dogs. Previously, they had only taken samples. Just before we hung up, Knorr said he wanted to assure me that Assistant US Attorney Mike Gill was a dog lover himself, and his heart was also very much in this case. He apologized for bending my ear, and said we would talk soon.

I called Mark immediately after hanging up with Knorr. As I expected, he did not have a video tape. In fact, no video tape ever surfaced, though rumors of its existence persisted throughout the case.

Brinkman called on Thursday, July 5. He still sounded exhausted. He was trying to keep a low profile, he said. Poindexter definitely planned to go before the grand jury on July 24 in an attempt to secure an indictment on state charges against Vick and his friends. Brinkman said he was just holding his breath hoping the Feds would indict first. Despondently, Brinkman said that Poindexter would be coming up for re-election soon. Brinkman felt he would be unchallenged, even in light of recent events.

Brinkman asked if I was back to officially working on the case. "No," I responded, "But, I think I get calls from different people every single day." Brinkman said he would be in touch soon. He did not mention the upcoming search warrant Knorr had spoken about, so I kept my peace.

Friday, July 6, the Feds returned to Moonlight Road. USDA Agents Kristin Hamman and Jim Knorr were there along with Dr. Merck. Knorr had deliberately kept Brinkman away in order to shield him from the ongoing wrath of Poindexter. The WAVY TV 10 video showed people digging and sifting through dirt from carefully sectioned off areas. More people were carrying away boxes and bags. I spoke with Knorr later. He said he had been very pleased with the way the search turned out, and he was glad to have had Dr. Merck. I told him about a news report I heard that day. A reporter asked an unnamed federal agent what they had found on the property. The agent responded, "What we were looking for." Knorr laughed and said that pretty much covered it. They exhumed at least eight dogs.

In the next instant he asked if, when I had been there, I had seen a board nailed to one of the trees. Yes, I had, I said. There was another board, Knorr said, nailed to a tree in the woods where the 30 pit bulls had been chained. Knorr said disgustedly that he believed dogs had been hanged to death from these boards. Dr. Merck would perform necropsies on the dogs that they exhumed to try to determine the causes of death. Some of the bodies still had flesh and fur on them, meaning there was a good chance she would be able to do so.

Knorr said Brinkman called him after they left the scene. Brinkman told him Poindexter was furious that the Feds had executed yet another warrant. Brinkman was worried, Knorr said. Time was running out. The Feds needed to move fast and indict before Poindexter. As a stalling tactic, Brinkman told Knorr, he had suggested to Poindexter that there was no point in going to the grand jury until the laboratory reports on some of the items of evidence came back. Knorr said he hoped to serve Surry with a federal subpoena within the next few days allowing him to take custody of all of the evidence in the case. He would be in touch, he said.

When we hung up, I sat with the phone in my hand. I could not get the thought of those poor dead dogs out of my mind. To be so brutally killed for the sin of not being vicious enough. The hangings must have been carried out in full view of other dogs-chained to buried car axles or confined in kennels. They had no escape. I could only imagine the terror those highly intelligent animals would have felt as they watched the other dogs go to their deaths. There was absolutely no way they would not have understood what was happening.

On Monday, July 9, Alison Gianotto e-mailed me. She was worried because several news outlets were reporting that sources close to the case were saying Vick was unlikely to be indicted on any charges related to dog fighting. I begged her not to worry, but could not say more. When Knorr called later, I asked him what was going on; meaning the stories claiming Vick would not be indicted. "Don't worry about the stories. You and I know better," he said, laughing.

"Is there some sort of campaign of deliberate misinformation?" I asked jokingly. Knorr just chuckled.

On Tuesday evening, July 10, I talked to Knorr again. He was very tired. He had been driving all day. He had brought C to Norfolk where the Feds had put him up in a hotel closer to the investigation. I said I had been going through some more pedigrees from Alison, as well as the ones she had sent before. I had already sent most of these to Brinkman, but I asked Knorr if he had seen them yet. He had not, so I promised I would send them to him the following day. Then we could talk about what they meant, what dogs and what people were connected. We hung up promising to speak the next day.

I sent Knorr pedigrees for several MV Kennel's (Michael Vick) dogs. These were for Jane/Blaze daughter Maggie May, Bitch, and Nala. Nala, according to a notation on her pedigree, was a winner of three off the chain matches. There were also pedigrees Alison found for Badd Newz Kennels dogs. Badd Newz Jada was a granddaughter of Benny Butts' Hardcore Kennels' Champion Mystic. Badd Newz Rahim was a two time winner, according to his pedigree. Alison also sent me a list of other Badd Newz dogs, including Badd Newz Nightmare, Rahim, Sly, Scare Dem, Shorty, and Cleo. My mind flew back to the day of the search and the notation on the wall of the building that had housed the treadmills. "Cleo 1:10".

It turned out to be a good thing Alison captured the pedigree files. On July 30, 2007, the web site hosting the pedigrees was updated. The kennel name for Jada, Nightmare and Rahim was changed from Badd Newz to C. J. Smooth's. I sent both versions of each document to Knorr, and we had a good laugh.

Wednesday, July 11 was the day the cavalry finally rode into town. Brinkman and Knorr drove to Surry County and served the federal order for the seizure all of the evidence recovered from the dog fighting search. When Brinkman called me early that evening, he said Poindexter was beside himself. "This is making us look like we're incompetent," Poindexter lamented. Brinkman retorted, "I'm not incompetent. I'm the one working this case. Ya'll are the ones trying to bury it."

Brinkman had more news. He had just gotten a huge break in the case. He was on his way, he said, to pick up a photograph showing Michael Vick, Purnell Peace, Quanis Phillips, and Tony Taylor posing in their Badd Newz Kennels T-shirts and head bands.

Knorr called that evening, too. He was hot, sweaty and very tired. But, is spite of the comedy of errors that had been his day, he was elated and excited. He and Brinkman drove a truck with a U-Haul trailer to Surry, he said. They picked up all of the evidence from the original search. Unfortunately, the vehicle hauling the trailer broke down. A fireman friend of Brinkman came to their rescue and gave them a tow. In the midst of all this, Knorr received a call on his cell phone from Poindexter, screaming and cursing. Later when Knorr checked his voice mail at work, Poindexter had left a similar screaming, cursing message. Knorr assured me that I was going to be very happy at the way this case was going to turn out. He ended the conversation by saying that he had seen a litter of puppies at Brinkman's house. Brinkman, he guessed, had not heard about spaying and neutering one's pets. Knorr was quite taken with one of the puppies and was seriously considering taking her home with him when she was old enough. He would later adopt her and name her Surry, joking that she was the only dog that ever had reason to be grateful to Michael Vick.

On Sunday, July 15, I spoke with a confidential informant of my own. He told me he had a conversation with a man claiming to be Michael Vick's cousin. The man said Vick was not worried so much about the dog fighting, but he was afraid the authorities were looking at other things such as tax evasion and gambling. I contacted Knorr and passed on the information. He asked if I thought the cousin would cooperate. I really did not know, I said. He seemed more concerned about protecting Vick.

On Monday, Knorr called me. He was sitting, he said, with Brinkman and Officer Steve Tate from the State Police. His next words were the ones I had been waiting to hear for almost three months. The federal indictments were finished and would be released later in the week. Assistant U.S. Attorney Mike Gill would prosecute the case. Michael Vick, Purnell Peace, Quanis Phillips, and Tony Taylor would all be indicted under 18 U.S.C. §371 on one charge of conspiracty to travel in interstate commerce in aid of unlawful activities and to sponsor a dog in an animal fighting venture. Other charges might follow later. Knorr said he had the photograph of the Badd Newz crew that Brinkman had told me about, but they were keeping this very quiet.

"Be ready for Wednesday," he said. I hung up thinking about Mike Gill. The notoriety surrounding this case meant that the eyes of the entire country would be on the young prosecutor. The pressure would be intense, and his every move subject to scrutiny and dissection. A case like this one could make or break a career. I admired Gill's courage and determination.

I was at the office of HSUS in Gaithersburg, Maryland on Tuesday morning, July 17 for a meeting. It was a madhouse. The indictments had been filed that morning, a day earlier than Knorr predicted. The media was already going crazy. Televisions were tuned to the news reports, and people were rushing in all directions responding to calls, and requests for interviews. Rank and file members of HSUS were calling the office asking what they could do. They had called companies such as Kraft and Nike that used Vick as a spokesperson, as well as the NFL, they said. People were appalled at the details of the indictment.

All over the radio, the sport shows, the news shows, commentators expressed how sickened they were by the brutal killings of the dogs as described in the federal indictments—dogs drowned, electrocuted, hanged, shot and bludgeoned to death.

Dog Angel called. Vick was in a panic he said. The moment had finally come. Vick's close knit group of family and friends believed the case now exceeded the ability of his longtime Virginia attorney, Lawrence Woodward. The Feds were in, and the home team needed a heavyweight, someone who had gone up against the Feds before and might be able to put some fear of losing into them. Vick and his circle desperately clung to the hope for exoneration that would allow him to report to camp and get on with football. Other NFL players began to call Vick urging him to retain the services of attorney Billy Martin.

Martin spent 15 years as an Assistant US Attorney. He was a Special Attorney for the Organized Crime Strike Force in San Francisco, before moving to Washington, D.C., where he eventually joined the firm of the Atlanta based Sutherland, Asbil and Brennan. Martin has represented a number of high profile defendants. He defended Atlanta Mayor Billy Campbell against RICO, tax evasion and wire fraud charges. The case ended in convictions for only three counts of tax fraud. Other clients included basketball player Allen Iverson, Monica Lewinsky's mother, Marcia Lewis, and the parents of murder victim Chandra Levy. He would go on to represent Senator Larry Craig in his unsuccessful attempt to have his disorderly conduct conviction, stemming from an incident in an airport bathroom, overturned.

The fact that Martin himself had been a federal prosecutor might make the stakes even higher for the government. Added to all of this was the realization that every animal welfare group in the country would be watching this case. It was going to be the Super Bowl of dog fighting cases.

In the meantime, speculation was rife about what would happen next. Would Vick play? Would he be suspended? What would Arthur Blank do? Goodell? Some commentators referred to the April meeting between Vick and Goodell, when Goodell asked Vick about his dog fighting involvement so that the league might prepare for the eventual fallout. It was now clear that Vick had blatantly lied.

CHAPTER 16 CRASH

The NFL released a statement saying, "We are disappointed that Michael Vick has put himself in a position where a federal grand jury has returned an indictment against him. We will continue to closely monitor developments in this case, and to cooperate with law enforcement authorities. The activities alleged are cruel, degrading and illegal. Michael Vick's guilt has not yet been proven, and we believe that all concerned should allow the legal process to determine the facts. This matter will be reviewed under the League's Personal Conduct Policy."

The Falcons issued a statement of their own. "Obviously we are disturbed by today's news from Virginia. However, we are prepared to deal with it, and we will do the right thing for our club as the legal process plays out. We have a season to prepare for and training camp opens next week. Our plan is to do everything we can to support our players and coaches."

In a storm that seemed to gather momentum with each new revelation, people all over began to clamor for companies such as Nike and Rawlings to cancel endorsement deals with Vick. AirTran, Coca Cola's PowerAde, and Boys and Girls Clubs of America had already severed ties with Vick. Nike released a statement that they planned to go forward with the release of the Air Zoom Vick V shoe. But, on Wednesday, July 18, 2007 Kraft and Coca Cola released statements making it clear that their relationships with Vick ended in 2005.

Cries and demands for the NFL to suspend Vick became a thunderous roar. Sports figures had run afoul of the law in the past. Drugs, assaults, DUIs,--Pacman Jones involved in a nightclub shooting that left a security guard paralyzed, Ray Carruth convicted of conspiracy in the murder of his pregnant girlfriend—but nothing had ever captured the public in the way that this case had. Sports commentators wondered over the airwaves how these men could have done what they were accused of doing to helpless animals. It was the number one story in the country.

Many people were remembering Falcons owner, Arthur Blank's support and faith in

Vick, how he mentored the young man and defended him. The 2003 photograph of Blank wheeling an injured Vick around the sidelines of the Texas stadium resurfaced. Many felt Blank had been especially betrayed.

Even members of Congress weighed in. West Virginia Senator Robert Byrd did not mince any words when he released the statement, "I am confident that the hottest places in hell are reserved for the souls of sick and brutal people who hold God's creatures in such cruel and brutal contempt."

Senator John Kerry wrote a letter to the NFL urging the league to suspend Vick immediately.

"Dog fighting is one of society's most barbaric and inhumane activities...This illegal and despicable activity has no place in civilized society...As the most popular team sport in America, professional football has a responsibility to showcase the highest levels of behavior and sportsmanship...On behalf of millions of sports fans and dog lovers, I urge you to treat Mr. Vick's dog fighting indictment with the very serious attention it deserves and suspend him from the League until the resolution of legal proceedings."

Apparently the indictments were causing other dog fighters to worry. ESPN reporter Kelli Nagi reported that even before the indictments had been released, one source told her, "Everybody in the dog world is worried about Michael Vick talking. Michael Vick is making large money; he's making millions, OK? And if he has to tell on some people [to avoid prison time], I think he would tell. I don't put nothing past him."

On July 20, Nike suspended the planned release of the Air Zoom Vick V shoe, but the company did not sever ties with the embattled quarterback. "Nike is concerned by the serious and highly disturbing allegations made against Michael Vick, and we consider any cruelty to animals inhumane and abhorrent. We do believe that Michael Vick should be afforded the same due process as any citizen; therefore we have not terminated our relationship."

On Monday, July 23, protesters began to picket Atlanta Falcons headquarters, calling for Vick's suspension and carrying signs that bore phrases such as, "Kick Vick", "Tackle Cruelty", and "Sack Vick". Not much was heard from other professional athletes. Perhaps they had been told to keep mum after Clinton Portis' and Chris Samuels' disastrous comments to the press. Former Green Bay Packers Safety LeRoy Butler evidently felt he could risk a comment. Speaking about the reaction of his seven year old daughter to the events surrounding the case, he said, "Now, I had to explain it as a parent. I said that sometimes people do stuff that is so terrible that you've got to offset that guy by doing something good. She just kept wiping tears. She was really bothered by it. It's a stupid thing to do, obviously. But these guys get so arrogant, they don't think about it. You got $30 million, $40 million in the bank, they're on top of the world, no remorse, and no one can stop them."

Many in Atlanta were heartbroken. Michael Vick was the very symbol of Black Atlanta. He had been a hero and a role model for so many of its citizens. One supporter said, "You would think that Michael Vick is the largest criminal this country has ever encountered, by the media play. The way they have portrayed this, you would think he's guilty until proven innocent because now it's his goal and his responsibility to convince America that he's innocent." Another asserted that the media coverage surrounding Michael Vick amounted to an electronic lynching.

What would happen? Vick had signed a 10 year $130 million contract in 2004. At the time of the indictment, he had already been paid close to $44 million including bonuses and was expected to continue to earn nearly $6 million a season.

The press announced that Vick's lead attorney would be Billy Martin.

Knorr called, and somehow we got to talking about WAVY TV 10 Mary Kay Malloney's story of the first search of Moonlight Road. I reminded him that in that report she had included some footage from her own 2003 story of the construction of the house. Clearly visible in the 2003 clip were the dogs, the black outbuildings, the jenny and the fencing with the "beware of dogs" signs. I had sent the video file of the story to Brinkman, I said. Knorr asked if I thought Mary Kay would mind if he contacted her. I said I was sure she would not, and gave him her number. I also promised to send him the file of the story.

One sports commentator remarked that even if he were allowed to play, Vick might have difficulty focusing. Then too there was the issue of security. Might there be a risk to players or fans if he played? Could some nut case out there decide that two wrongs made a right? Would fans have to pass through metal detectors, or even be searched? So many people had taken such firm stands on the whole issue. The only one who had yet to stand up, issue any statement, or put the good of the team and the fans ahead of his own self interest was Michael Vick.

Brinkman returned from a trip to Richmond where he had gone to transfer the bones from the first search to Jim Knorr so they could be sent for analysis. When Brinkman arrived back at his office, Sheriff Brown asked, "Where you been?"

Brinkman answered, "I've been up in Richmond."

"Poindexter said you were. What were you doing up there?"

"I was transferring bones. I was giving them evidence to get it sent off."

"Oh, okay." Brown paused for a moment. "Poindexter wants me to fire you."

"I already know that," Brinkman snapped. "You do what you gotta fucking do. I mean, I don't give a shit. If he runs your department, do it."

On Monday, July 23, Arthur Goodell wrote Vick a letter ordering him to stay away from the Falcons training camp which opened on Thursday. "While it is for the criminal justice system to determine your guilt or innocence, it is my responsibility as commissioner of the National Football League to determine whether your conduct, even if not criminal, nonetheless violated league policies, including the Personal Conduct Policy." Goodell also stated that he would hire an independent investigator to explore the allegations in the federal indictment.

Of course Vick would not have been available for opening day in any event. His arraignment was set for Thursday, July 26, 2007. I stayed away. Jim Knorr and Assistant US Attorney Mike Gill, said, as a potential witness, I was not to be there. When Vick appeared that day, over 500 people lined up outside for a chance at a seat inside the courtroom. Areas of the street had been blocked off. Demonstrators both in support of and against Vick began assembling early in the morning. Knorr sat in the courtroom directly behind Vick's mother. Mike

Gill rose from his seat to make a statement that another indictment would be forthcoming in August. It appeared highly unlikely that the case would go to trial on the November 26 date set by Judge Henry Hudson. Vick, Taylor, Peace and Phillips all entered pleas of not guilty. Each was required to surrender his passport.

Quanis Phillips and Purnell Peace were ordered by the court to wear ankle bracelets. Phillips had prior convictions for possession with intent to distribute marijuana. Peace's record also included a drug conviction. After the brief hearing, Defense Attorney Billy Martin made a statement to the media on Vick's behalf. As he began reading, he made it clear that he would be taking no questions. In the written statement, Vick apologized to his mother for the stress the case had caused her. He said he looked forward to clearing his good name. He apologized to his teammates and said he would rather be with them at training camp playing football. He urged his fans to wait for all of the facts to come out before judging him. Billy Martin said his client was innocent, and this would be a hard fought trial. As he spoke, Martin was flanked by Davon Boddie, Vick's mother Brenda, and Vick's other attorneys, Tom Shuttleworth and Larry Woodward.

In a shocking upset for the Vick camp, it was announced a few days later that one of Vick's co-defendants, Tony Taylor, would change his plea to guilty. He would be back in court the following Monday for a plea agreement hearing. Commentators agreed that this was bad news for Vick. That same day, Nike and Reebok suspended their sales of Vick jerseys and shoes. Nike went so far as to suspend Vick's contract without pay, but left the door open in the event he was exonerated. Donruss Trading Card Company announced that it was pulling Vick's card from their 2007 releases. A representative of the company commented that she regularly took her five dogs with her to work with her.

There was more fallout. A Long Beach minor league baseball team held a Michael Vick Animal Awareness Day. Anyone presenting a Michael Vick jersey received free admission to the game on Sunday, July 29. The jerseys were used as pooper scoopers for attending dogs. The team also pledged to make donations to promote responsible dog ownership. The team's president and general manager, Steven Bash, said his players wanted to bring awareness to the intolerable injustices associated with dog fighting. Fans also brought toys, treats and cleaning supplies for abused and abandoned dogs.

As anticipated, Tony Taylor pleaded guilty to the charges in the indictment on Monday, July 30, 2007. As part of his plea agreement, he pledged to cooperate with federal authorities, and swore that the charges outlined in the indictment were all true.

Taylor's plea meant the collapse of the entire Badd Newz house of cards. Vick was stunned. He had truly expected all of his co-defendants, his cousin, everyone to take the heat and fall on their swords for him. Even Tony Taylor whom he had exiled in 2004. After all, he was Michael Vick. He had no idea who might be the next defector. Vick gave a radio interview that day. He acknowledged that he had put Arthur Blank through a difficult experience, but hoped he would be able to play again. "I know I... I put the city through a lot, the owner Arthur Blank, who I love sincerely; I put him through a lot." He thanked the people who continued to support him, and added, "It's a crisis situation for me, but I'm gonna get through it."

I wondered which of the remaining two Vick co-defendants would be the next roll. Surely it would dawn on them that they stood in a very precarious position. Here was Vick with his dream team of lawyers. They, on the other hand, were alone. The NAACP turned out to demonstrate on Vick's behalf. A southern church organization also came out to support him. No one was coming out to support Purnell Peace or Quanis Phillips. When would it occur to them that they were about to take the fall for Michael Vick? Perhaps it was time to cut a deal.

Oscar Allen was scheduled for an interview. Knorr said the man was prepared to cooperate. I sent him everything I had on Allen-his Virginia O dogs, breedings, fights he had entered or refereed, and any connection to the case. It would be good for the agents to have information with which to confront him, if he should prove less that cooperative.

I sat back and breathed a sigh of relief. We were on the home stretch. The score was two down and three to go.

CHAPTER 17 VICK TAKES A PLEA

When Quanis Phillips and Purnell Peace had arrived at the United States Courthouse in Richmond on July 26, 2007 they were shocked to see the crowds of demonstrators. Phillips looked at the throngs of people and exclaimed, "God, I can't believe they hate us this much!"

When Tony Taylor entered a formal plea of guilty to one count of conspiracy to transport dogs across state lines for the purpose of engaging in illegal dog fighting, Phillips and Peace knew that the ground was being cut away beneath their feet. The world was closing in around them.

Dog Angel was doing his part to undermine Peace's and Phillips' faith in Vick by working through their friends and families. He expected both men to turn to them rather than Vick or his attorneys for advice. Dog Angel used a technique he called his mental poison pills. He avoided any direct attempts to flip Peace or Phillips as these would be bound to backfire. Vick might even find out and for once use the power of his great wealth to keep them in line. Dog Angel was cautious never to directly suggest of any course of action. His targets must think any ideas they might have were their own. This took time. Dog Angel casually mentioned how Vick had thrown Taylor out and then had cut his own cousin, Devon Boddie, loose. "But, he won't do that to these guys," he assured the families, deliberately planting the opposite seed of doubt. Later when he asked the family members what Peace and Phillips were saying, they responded in disgust. "Nothing; they just sit there with their mouths open." Dog Angel suggested to the families that Peace and Phillips needed to find out what Oscar Allen was saying.

Peace and Phillips became increasingly worried over July and early August. Thanks to Dog Angel, their families and close friends were warning them that Vick would hang them out to dry. Then Dog Angel added more poison. He asked one of Peace's closest friends, "What if Vick makes a deal first? Makes a deal with PeTA and HSUS to donate big money to them, and then says Peace and Phillips were the master minds of the entire operation?" It was a complete fabrication, but it worked.

He continued to add more poison feigning anger at anyone who might dare to question Vick's loyalty to his crew. Friends of Peace and Phillips snarled in response, "Fuck that shit. You are talking about my home boys, my guys who have covered for that cheap ass mother fucker for years; my blood that takes care of all his shit. Fuck that."

Families and friends of Peace and Phillips began to call Dog Angel more frequently. When they asked how much an attorney might cost for both of the men, he replied innocently, "Why should it matter? Vick is paying for it, right?"

"That cheap ass mother fucker ain't paying for shit." Dog Angel had counted on this, and he was not disappointed. He had Peace and Phillips exactly where he wanted them. Only now did he suggest what he would do if he were in their shoes, hinting at what might be going through Vick's mind in terms of strategy.

True to form, Vick did exactly as Dog Angel predicted. He cut Peace and Phillips loose. The two scrambled to find their own attorneys. Dog Angel pointed out that they had only one ray of hope—cooperation with the Feds. Massaging their gangster pride, he assured them they were not rats, they were just smart.

Peace and Phillips knew the authorities had talked to Oscar Allen on August 7, and that he had said plenty. Of course he did receive some encouragement. Allen was already 67 years old, and took care of his elderly mother, a victim of that cruelest of diseases, Alzheimer's. When first interviewed, Allen was inclined to simply deny everything. Investigators lost no time in laying their cards on the table. They had him. If he refused to cooperate, he would go to prison. His mother, they told him, would die in a nursing home, and he would never see her again. Faced with that reality check, Allen gave up and admitted his involvement. He confessed to what investigators already knew and that he had been present the night the dogs named in the indictment had been killed. He admitted watching the tests and seeing the dead bodies being driven to the site of their graves. He described the roles of Peace and Phillips in the dog fighting operation, and confirmed that Vick was the leader. He knew about the falling out between Taylor and Vick. He also told authorities that he had just talked with Purnell Peace. Peace was worried, he said. He was a single father with a young daughter. He did not want to go to jail. Allen related how he had told Peace that he needed to step up and do the right thing; plead guilty and make a deal. He needed to do this for his daughter.

Realizing that they really had no way out, Peace and Phillips agreed to try to make a deal. Had Vick been generous, both Peace and Phillips claimed they would have remained loyal. If the three, Vick, Peace and Phillips, had stuck together, they might have been able to successfully discredit Taylor as a disgruntled ex-employee. That left Oscar Allen, an admitted lifetime dog fighter; hardly a sympathetic witness.

On August 14, 2007, Jim Knorr interviewed Peace and Phillips. A condition of any plea agreement would be that both agree to cooperate with the government. Peace was first. Instead of showing any remorse or empathy for the dogs that had been killed, Peace was cold and sullen. Knorr began by asking questions for which he already knew the answers. As he expected, Peace lied. He minimized his actions, denied killing the dogs, lied about the number of dog fights involved, and denied that Vick had any part in the activities.

When Knorr confronted him and told him he knew Peace was lying, Peace sprang up from his chair and with his contorted face inches from Knorr yelled that he was not lying, almost daring Knorr to repeat his words.

Knorr stayed perfectly still and returned Peace's stare. "This agreement is for you to tell the truth and cooperate. This meeting is going to be over." Peace's attorney, Claire Cardwell, took him out into the hallway for a heart to heart. When both returned to the interview room, Knorr began again. This time Peace admitted that he had been fighting dogs since 1990. He met Michael Vick in 2000, and Vick introduced Peace to Phillips. Known by his nickname, P-Funk, Peace was a partner in Badd Newz Kennels. The partnership included Vick, Phillips, and Peace's cousin, Tony Taylor. After Taylor's ousting from the group in 2004, Peace took over the day to day care of the dogs. For this, Vick paid him $3,000 a month. Throughout the time that Badd Newz Kennels was in operation, he and the other partners traveled to North and South Carolina, Georgia, Alabama, New Jersey and other states to fight dogs. Peace attempted to portray himself as better than his co-conspirators. He claimed that he tried to convince the crew to allow him to find homes for the dogs that would not fight. It was Vick, he insisted, who refused to allow this saying merely, "They got to go."

Knorr did not buy it. He questioned Peace about the purpose of the board that was nailed to the tree near the dog kennels. At first Peace claimed he and the others had weighed the dogs here. Knorr called him on this lie; he told Peace he knew the scale had been hanging from the first floor ceiling of the pit building. Peace finally admitted that the board had been used to tie the ropes from which the dogs wetre hanged to death. Over the years, Peace said, he had killed dogs by shooting, drowning and electrocution. On the April night in question, Peace said that Vick participated in the killings, but would not say what his actions had been. Though he conceded that one of the dogs would not die, he refused to admit that Vick or anyone else slammed it into the ground, despite the fact that Knorr had Dr. Melinda Merck's medical report documenting the skull, neck and rib fractures sustained by the dog.

Knorr's interview with Quanis Phillips went a little better. Phillips said he and Vick were childhood friends. Phillips was Q and Vick was Ookie. The two had been introduced to dog fighting by Tony Taylor. He readily admitted that the all of the men had drowned and shot dogs. Vick, he said, had even purchased five stun guns for use on the dogs. Phillips said that the men killed the dogs because there was no purpose keeping the ones that were poor fighters. On the April night in 2007 when the men tested and killed the eight dogs, all three-Vick, Peace and Phillips-participated. He and Peace drowned some of them. He and Peace, along with Mr. Vick, as he called his childhood friend, killed some by using a nylon cord to hang them from the board nailed to the tree in near the kennels. Then Phillips made the most shocking statement of all. He said that Mr. Vick took the nylon cord off of the hanging dog that would not die. Together he and Vick lifted it into the air and slammed it into the ground, killing it.

After the interviews with Peace and Phillips, Vick's attorneys were given the "bad newz". They were advised that Michael Vick had until Friday, August 17 to make a decision on whether or not to enter a plea of guilty. If he failed to do so, Assistant US Attorney Mike Gill would go forward with a superseding indictment. Vick's attorneys knew they could expect charges stemming from suspected tax evasion, structuring a criminal enterprise, or money laundering. Still Vick was stubbornly reluctant, dragging his feet. Particular sticking points were the gambling and the killing of the dogs. A gambling charge would carry with it a lifetime ban from the NFL. The killing of the dogs would create a public relations nightmare that Vick might find impossible to overcome. Vick apparently still believed he could beat this. His attorneys did their best to convince their client otherwise. He should not go to trial, and this case should definitely not go before a jury. They focused their own efforts on trying to negotiate for no jail time, but on this point Assistant US Attorney Mike Gill adamantly refused to budge.

Refusing to let up, Dog Angel continued to apply pressure to Vick's family. "This case just keeps getting worse and worse," he told them. If only Vick had faced things early on. He could have paid off Peace and Phillips. He could have spun the press with a penitent announcement, "Some bad things took place at my home, something I did not approve of, or know about. These two life time friends today plead guilty and admit that I had no involvement in this." The Feds would never have come in. Poindexter would have taken a deal, and the case would have been over, he theorized. Vick might have been slightly tarnished, but he would be playing football. Dog Angel warned that the government could still make this a RICO case. Badd Newz had been an ongoing criminal enterprise. The winnings had never been reported as income and no taxes had been paid on any of it. Vick could be looking at up to 20 years. A gambling charge could mean a lifetime ban from the NFL. The thought that he might never play again began to take shape in Vick's mind as a real possibility.

On Friday, August 17, Purnell Peace and Quanis Phillips entered guilty pleas to the single charge named in the indictment. They each agreed to testify against the ring leader of the operation, Michael Vick. After Judge Henry Hudson accepted the pleas, he ordered that Quanis Phillips be taken into custody for failing a drug test, which was a violation of the terms for his release pending trial. Peace was allowed to remain free pending sentencing.

Jim Knorr steadfastly insisted that Oscar Allen should be charged in spite of his cooperation with the government. Allen was a much bigger player than Vick or any of the other three. He had been fighting dogs up and down eastern United States for many years. He set up the fights, and even refereed. Mike Gill agreed. He prepared the indictment.

The media continued to speculate on what Michael Vick would do now that all three of his codefendants had turned against him. I knew that Vick was balking at admitting to the gambling and the killing of the dogs. I also knew that Mike Gill had vowed he would accept nothing less. "Oh, Lord," I thought, "this thing is going to trial."

Dog Angel was the only member of our team who continued to insist that Vick would plead guilty. His poison pills would work. Vick would save his brother and seize his only chance to ever play football again.

Dog Angel was right. The news broke on Monday, August 20. Vick admitted to crossing state lines to participate in dog fighting. He admitted financing the bets on the dog fights, but denied profiting from any wins. The reality of his losses actually helped him here. The irony was that Vick was such a bad dog fighter. Vick admitted that he participated in the executions of the eight dogs but did not elaborate on what exact role he played. Reporters and commentators from across the country could talk of nothing else. Reactions ranged from shock, to sorrow over the waste of a young and talented life, to relief for those who had worked so hard on the case.

Lead defense attorney, Billy Martin released a statement. "Mr. Vick has agreed to enter a plea of guilty to these [federal] charges and to accept full responsibility for those actions and for the mistakes he has made. Michael wishes to apologize to everyone who has been hurt by this matter." We could only wonder at his feelings having to make this announcement in stark contrast to his earlier one that Michael Vick was looking forward to proving his innocence.

Vick's mother, Brenda Vick Boddie wept as she told reporters, "I gotta be strong for him. It is tough on everybody. They are trying to put my baby in jail, and for what? Everybody makes mistakes. Everybody deserves a second chance. He has given his life over to God. He is not a criminal ... He's a good person. He has a big heart, and it just hurts." Dog Angel felt sorry for her, but I could not share his sentiment. How could she not have known what her son was doing, I wondered. Had she ever tried to stop him?

The Atlanta Journal-Constitution interviewed Vick's estranged father, Michael Boddie. He claimed Vick had fought dogs in the back yard of the family home. Boddie said he nursed some of those dogs back to health. "I wish people would stop sugarcoating it. This is Mike's thing. And he knows it ... likes it, and he has the capital to have a setup like that."

Boddie claimed that he had asked Vick a number of times to give up dog fighting. The story mentioned that despite the strained relationship between the two, Vick continued to pay for his father's apartment. Boddie's own credibility was called into question by the story's mention that he had asked Vick for $1million over a twelve year period; a request that Vick refused.

The NFL released a statement that read, "We totally condemn the conduct outlined in the charges, which is inconsistent with what Michael Vick previously told both our office and the Falcons. We will conclude our own review under the league's personal conduct policy as soon as possible. In the meantime, we have asked the Falcons to continue to refrain from taking action pending a decision by the commissioner."

The Falcons released their own statement. "We are certainly troubled with the news today concerning Michael Vick's guilty plea to federal charges. [NFL] Commissioner [Roger] Goodell has asked us not to take any action until he has completed his own review of Michael's situation. Accordingly, we will have no further comment until that time."

By Friday, August 24, the NFL made their decision. Michael Vick was suspended indefinitely and without pay. Commissioner Roger Goodell wrote in a letter to Vick, "Your admitted conduct was not only illegal, but also cruel and reprehensible. Your team, the NFL, and NFL fans have all been hurt by your actions." Goodell said that he would review the status of the suspension after the legal proceedings had concluded. Goodell said that the Falcons might try to recover as much as $22 million of Vick's signing bonus.

Falcons owner Arthur Blank said Vick's actions as they were outlined in the proposed plea agreement were incomprehensible and unacceptable. He went on to say that the suspension made a strong statement that conduct which tarnishes the good reputation of the NFL will not be tolerated.

Nike announced that they would sever all ties with Vick.

I called Jim Knorr. "Jim," I said, "I want to be there when he pleads. I have worked very hard on this and I want to be there."

My own phone began to ring incessantly. Friends and colleagues from all over the country were calling to say, "Congratulations! You stood up for the dogs and for professional ACOs all over the country." Some credited me with keeping the case alive. The truth was many, many people had sweated blood over this case. Still, the calls made me feel good. It was a vindication after four months of doubt. It was a very good thing I was scrubbing the bathroom and vacuuming up bird seed while these calls were coming in. It is the little things that keep you humble!

On Monday, August 27, Vick was to appear in federal court to enter his plea of guilty. I drove to Richmond and met Knorr at the US Attorney's office on Main Street. He introduced me to Assistant US Attorney Mike Gill. I was surprised at how young he looked. Mike Gill is tall and slender with a runner's build. He is dark haired, fresh faced with a charming smile, and looks barely old enough to have even graduated college. Although he does not physically resemble him in the least, he has a Jimmy Stewart earnestness. He said he was pleased to meet me and grateful for all of my help along the way. Agent Beth Dinkins was there from USDA, and Dr. Melinda Merck. Deputy Bill Brinkman was there and Agent Ryan Messer from the FBI.

All of us had arrived early, so we passed the time sitting around the conference table reminiscing about the journey that had brought us here. Strangers stuck their heads in the door to congratulate us. Finally it was time to go. We walked the four blocks to the court house. The streets nearby had been completely closed off to traffic. We headed for the rear private entrance in the back of the courthouse, the door of which faces the hill where the General Assembly sits. Here we confronted a sea of trucks and tents where the media was camped. All around us reporters were doing stand ups in anticipation of the commencement of the day's events. We picked our way carefully through a tangle of cables and electrical cords, keeping our heads down and avoiding eye contact. A US Marshall opened the door for us and led us up the old narrow marble stairway. From there we proceeded left then right and around through a labyrinth of offices until we finally reached the richly wood paneled court room. It was already crowded. Knorr directed Dr. Merck and me to seats on the front row of the prosecution side. Reporters were seated behind us, so Dr. Merck and I conversed in careful whispers. In front of us, to the right of the bench, was a section of seats that was nearly full. No cameras were allowed, so a host of artists sat here ready to sketch the action. It was fascinating to watch them, painstakingly drawing the background of the court room. Later they would add the players in the drama we were about to watch to their portraits. I wondered if any of them knew that their drawings might include the face of Dog Angel, who quietly slipped into the room.

The US Marshals scurried about, counting empty seats and directing the lucky ones to this spot or that. A group of people filed in and took their places in the first and second rows on the defense side. Brenda Boddie was there, a couple of young men, and several young women, one of whom was very pregnant. Someone whispered that she was Vick's girlfriend,

Kijafa Frink. At 10:25 a.m. Michael Vick entered the courtroom with his attorneys, Billy Martin, Larry Woodard, and Tom Shuttleworth. Dressed in a blue suit with a blue shirt and striped blue tie, Vick crossed to his mother and hugged her. The young man behind her raised his fist, calling out, "Be strong, Mike!" Vick clasped the fist in his own hands before turning to take a seat beside his attorneys.

A young clerk called the court to order and instructed us to, "All Rise!" Judge Henry Hudson entered and took his seat on the bench above us. He is a small man with white hair, and a benevolent, grandfatherly demeanor. His voice is gentle and almost caressing, and he smiles soothingly as he speaks.

Michael Vick and Billy Martin walked to the podium. For the next 17 minutes Judge Hudson asked Vick a litany of questions.

"Have you read the indictment? Do you understand what you are charged with? Have you read the statement of facts? Is the statement true? Is this your signature on the statement of facts? Are you satisfied with your attorneys? Have you conferred with them and had an opportunity to ask them questions? Have your attorneys answered your questions?"

To each question, Vick whispered quietly, "Yes sir."

The judge continued. "In the last 12 months have you been treated for drug or alcohol abuse? Have you been treated for any psychological problem or mental disorder in the last 12 months? Are you under the influence of any substance today?"

"No sir."

And finally, "Are you pleading guilty because you are in fact guilty of this charge?"

After a pause and a glance to his attorney, the response, "Yes sir."

"Do you have any questions of me at this time?" Hudson asked. Again Vick glanced at Billy Martin before responding, "No sir."

Judge Hudson reminded Vick that the plea agreement included his promise to cooperate with the government in this case. He reminded him of things he would be giving up by pleading guilty, such as the right to vote.

Finally Judge Hudson spoke about the fact that by pleading guilty, Vick would no longer have any right to appeal. He emphasized that there were sentencing guidelines in place for this type of offense, but that they were just that, guidelines. Hudson could go higher, or he could go lower. Did Vick understand that?

The plea agreement contained a recommendation, but the judge was not bound by that. It was his decision and his alone. Did Vick understand? Did Vick understand that whatever Judge Hudson decided, he had no right to appeal?

"Your attorneys can object to what I decide, but if I don't like their objection, I don't have to listen to it. It's up to me. I decide."

In the end, Judge Hudson accepted the plea agreement and set a sentencing date of December 10.

It was over. I do not know what I expected to feel. I certainly did not feel any elation or happiness. It was just sad, and such a waste of talent and life. And he had done it to himself. He was so young, and he could have been a beacon for others, a true role model for children. He could have had a great life, a career, opportunities, and the ease that wealth would have brought him and his family. It was all gone. He had thrown it away to torture dogs. How had he become this person? The waves of pain and sadness that emanated from him were palpable. But, an irritating little voice nagged in my head. Was he sorry for what he had done, or was he just sorry he got caught?

From the court room, Vick and his supporters moved to the Omni Hotel, where before a forest of microphones and reporters, Vick spoke to the assembled audience.

"For most of my life, I've been a football player, not a public speaker, so, you know, I really
don't know, you know, how to say what I really want to say.

"You know, I understand it's-it's important or not important, you know, as far as what you say but how you say things. So, you know, I take this opportunity just to speak from the heart. First, I want to apologize, you know, for all the things that-that I've done and that I have allowed to happen. I want to personally apologize to Commissioner Goodell, Arthur Blank, coach Bobby Petrino, my Atlanta Falcons teammates, you know, for our-for our previous discussions that we had. And I was not honest and forthright in our discussions, and, you know, I was ashamed and totally disappointed in myself to say the least.

"I want to apologize to all the young kids out there for my immature acts and, you know, what I did was, what I did was very immature so that means I need to grow up. I totally ask for forgiveness and understanding as I move forward to bettering Michael Vick, the person, not the football player.

I take full responsibility for my actions. For one second will I sit right here-not for one second will I sit right here and point the finger and try to blame anybody else for my actions or what I've done. I'm totally responsible, and those things just didn't have to happen. I feel like we all make mistakes. It's just I made a mistake in using bad judgment and making bad decisions. And you know, those things you know, just can't happen.

"Dog fighting is a terrible thing, and I did reject it. I'm upset with myself, and, you know, through this situation I found Jesus and asked him for forgiveness and turned my life over to God. And I think that's the right thing to do as of right now."

"Like I said, for this-for this entire situation I never pointed the finger at anybody else, I accepted responsibility for my actions of what I did and now I have to pay the consequences for it. But in a sense, I think it will help, you know, me as a person. I got a lot to think about in the next year or so."

"I offer my deepest apologies to everybody out in there in the world who was affected by this whole situation. And if I'm more disappointed with myself than anything it's because of all the young people, young kids that I've let down, who look at Michael Vick as a role model. And to have to go through this and put myself in this situation, you know, I hope that every young kid out there in the world watching this interview right now who's been following the case will use me as an example to using better judgment and making better decisions."

"Once again, I offer my deepest apologies to everyone. And I will redeem myself. I have to. So I got a lot of down time, a lot of time to think about my actions and what I've done and how to make Michael Vick a better person. Thank you."

Never was a statement by a non politician so scrutinized and dissected. Some took a completely skeptical and cynical view of his apparent contrition. He could have apologized months ago. He could have honored and respected the faith that Arthur Blank and Roger Goodell placed in him. He could have told the truth when they asked him directly about the dog fighting accusations. Instead he abused both men by callously lying to them. Contrary to his assertion that he had taken full responsibility for his actions and had never pointed the finger at anyone else, the truth was he had tried to do just that. Up to the very end, he denied being at the Moonlight Road house and blamed any wrongdoing on friends and family members who he claimed deceived him and took advantage of him.

It did not escape some listeners that Vick had said not one word of apology for the cruelty, pain, and suffering he had inflicted on helpless animals. To those listeners, his statement was simply too little too late. Only when he had been completely cornered with no other way out; when it was clear that the other defendants, his cousin, and the informants were not going to fall on their swords for him, had he finally come clean and admitted some of his actions.

Dog Angel said that the attorneys had done their best to help Vick craft his statement, warning him what points to avoid. Vick left his notes at the podium that day, which were later auctioned off on EBay. The proceeds were reportedly donated to HSUS to help combat dog fighting. The words may not have been his own, or sincere, but the paper on which they were written would be used for the victims he failed to mention.

Everywhere people wondered, could Michael Vick redeem himself and play football again? He certainly still had well wishers and supporters who hoped for that. He had the next three and one half months to prove the sincerity of his words. He could stand up and cooperate with the government, as he promised. If he had truly found Jesus as he claimed, he would no longer lie and deny, but would take responsibility and be truthful. Suggestions for his atonement abounded. Perhaps he would contribute to animal care and rescue groups. He might sell the Surry County property and donate the proceeds for the care of abused and displaced animals. He might do public service announcement about the evils of dog fighting and cruelty to animals. The truth was that nearly two years later he had yet to do one of these things.

CHAPTER 18 VICK FUMBLES

In spite of promises to cooperate, Jim Knorr really got very little from Peace, Phillips, Allen or Vick. Knorr was disgusted with Vick. In his interview with the man, Knorr said he had done nothing but deny and lie. Authorities got no information on other dog fighters, especially other NFL players. The FBI had hoped that the men would have some information on two murders-one from North Carolina and one from Baltimore, Maryland. But if the Badd Newz crew did have any knowledge, they kept it to themselves.

Things were not going well for Michael Vick. In early September, he failed a drug screen. The arbitration ruling cleared the way for the Falcons to recover nearly $20 million of Vick's signing bonus, and two banks were suing him for default on loans. Because Vick's plea agreement included his pledge to cooperate with the investigators and he had failed to do so, Knorr arranged for a polygraph examination, which was also provided for under the agreement.

Vick abysmally failed his polygraph examination on October 12. Vick had arrived that day, confident that he could beat the machine. Robert Hillard, the examiner, pretended to befriend Vick. He complained about having to do the examination over a bunch of stupid dogs, but told Vick he had a job to do whether he liked it or not. During the examination, Vick denied that he had taken any part in actually killing the dogs. He also denied that he knew of any other NFL players involved in dog fighting. Both responses registered deception.

When the test was over, Knorr, Vick and the others were standing in the hallway. Confronted with the results of his test, and Knorr's intention to include them in his report, Vick became enraged. "Yeah, fine. I killed the dogs. I hung them. I slammed them. I killed all of them. I lost fucking millions, all over some fucking dogs." His attorney, Billy Martin hustled him out of the building.

On Wednesday, October 24, 2007 traffic was miserable. I was on my way to Richmond for Oscar Allen's arraignment and plea. I would be allowed to interview him immediately following his court appearance. Traffic crawled. I was frantic. I was supposed to meet Knorr at the US Attorney's Office on Main at 9:30. Of all days! I finally made it to the parking lot at Franklin and 5th. I called Knorr to say I would meet him at the US courthouse. I scrambled out of my car, only to be dismayed that there was no parking attendant. One of those annoying slotted metal boxes had been installed instead. I did not have exact change, and there was no time to get any. I swore as I stuffed my one and only $20 bill into the slot for space number 37, and set off to the courthouse, a four block walk in high heels.

Cameramen and reporters holding microphones stood outside, calling out to every African American male who passed. "Virginia O! Are your Virginia O? Oscar Allen?" I hurried inside, and gave up my cell phone as hostage to make it through security.

I took my seat in the tiny wood paneled courtroom. Assistant US Attorney Mike Gill entered followed closely by Knorr. They waved to me and took their seats at the prosecutor's table. The defendant and his attorney took their places.

Oscar Allen was dressed in a black suit jacket over a limp white shirt, and gray pants. He clutched a baseball cap in front of him that he twisted and folded throughout the brief proceedings. He was very light skinned, bald with a short gray beard and mustache. He looked quite small as he stood beside his attorney, Jerry Zerkin.

This was the arraignment and bond hearing. Magistrate Judge Hanna Louch released Allen on a personal recognizance, or PR bond, and adjourned the court. The entire group of us trooped through the maze that is the US courthouse to Judge Henry Hudson's courtroom for his plea. The questions began.

"Did you associate with others with the intent to sponsor dog fighting?" asked the judge.

"Yes," replied Allen, twisting his hat.

"Did you travel in interstate commerce for the purpose of participating in dog fighting?"

"Yes."

And so on, through the questions by which Judge Hudson assured himself that Allen was not mentally ill, was not under the influence, and was pleading guilty because he was in fact guilty. By 10:50 a.m., Allen had pleaded guilty, and his bond was continued until sentencing in January.

We all met back at the US Attorney's Office. There was an agent from the FBI, Knorr, and two other USDA agents from other offices. The USDA agents had questions about the murder of a dog fighter who had been killed execution style at his North Carolina home before the first search of Vick's property. The FBI agent had questions about gang member dog fighters in Maryland. I had my own questions about other dog fighters.

None of us came away with much. Oscar Allen, AKA Virginia O described the Striper dog fight that had taken place off route 258 in North Carolina. He recognized one gang member, who was deceased. He admitted to having met a dog fighter we had convicted in Chesapeake. They met at a pig pickin', he said, at Benny Butts' place. He told us he had heard that Surry Commonwealth Attorney Gerald Poindexter had bought Vick's house in a many layered transaction. Mostly, Allen simply denied. He lied about the number of fights he entered, the times he refereed, and the other dog fighters and kennels he knew.

Dog Angel was furious. Allen could have given up some big players--Bring Da' Pain Kennels and Grand Champion Firecracker, Jamaican Joe and Grand Champion TK, Terry, OG Possee Kendrick, and even the Fixer. All got a pass from Allen.

On Monday, November 17, Vick surrendered to U.S. Marshals in Richmond. From there he was transported to Northern Neck Regional Jail, a state facility about an hour northeast of Richmond, to begin serving his anticipated sentence. This facility has a contract with the U.S. Bureau of Prisons to hold federal inmates awaiting sentencing. Maybe it was a desperate attempt on Vick's part to show Judge Hudson that he was contrite. Maybe he hoped to avoid a possible lengthy or even maximum sentence. Or maybe it was simply a move to get some time under his belt, because he still hoped to return to football for the 2008 season.

Eleven days later, Purnell Peace and Quanis Phillips were sentenced. The charge to which both pleaded guilty carried a maximum sentence of five years. Sentencing guidelines called for a period of incarceration of 12-18 months. Judge Hudson said that due to the nature of the crime both had committed, he believed sentences on the higher end of the range were appropriate. Peace was sentenced to 18 months in federal prison for his role in Badd Newz Kennels. Hudson told him that he was concerned that the pre-sentencing report stated Peace told investigators he saw nothing wrong with dog fighting. Quanis Phillips received a sentence of 21 months, due in part to his extensive criminal record. "You may have thought this was sporting, but it was very callous and cruel," Judge Hudson told him.

What sentence would Judge Hudson hand down for the ringleader of Badd Newz, Michael Vick?

CHAPTER 19 THE SENTENCE

On Monday, December 10, 2007, Michael Vick returned to court to be sentenced for his part in the Badd Newz Kennels enterprise. At 600 Main Street a disparate cast of characters assembled in the US Attorney's Office early that morning. Some had been here the day of Vick's guilty plea. All of them had worked on this landmark case and each one wanted to be present for its resolution. Mike Gill; Jim Knorr and Beth Dinkins from USDA; Deputy Bill Brinkman from Surry County and the State Drug Task Force; State Police Officer Steve Tate; Robert Hillard, the polygraph examiner; two agents from the FBI; John Goodwin of HSUS; Dr. Merck and Dr. Randall Lockwood from the ASPCA. Mark Kumpf flew into Norfolk from Ohio. He and I drove to Richmond together. At 9:30 a.m. we took the now familiar walk to the courthouse, threading our way through the same jungle of television trucks and cables. We were admitted via the back door and wound our way to the packed court room. Once again the artists were assembled already busily sketching. I did not know that Dog Angel was also in the building, disguised as a food vendor.

Instead of arriving in a shiny black SUV, this time Michael Vick was escorted by US Marshals. Instead of the expensive blue suit he had sported previously, he was dressed in horizontally striped black and white shirt and pants. The shirt was worn over a white long sleeved T shirt. On his feet he wore pristinely sparkling unlaced white tennis shoes. They made me think of the unlaunched Nike Michael Vick shoe. The court room had been buzzing with chatter, but when he appeared a hush fell as he took his seat at the table with his attorneys, Billy Martin, Lawrence Woodward and Tom Shuttleworth. Perhaps it was simply shock at seeing him in prison garb, or perhaps his appearance at last made his stunning fall from grace a reality.

Judge Hudson entered the room and the court was called to order. The judge spoke of the report from the US probation officer that included information about Vick's failed drug test. It also cited Vick's failure to abide by the terms of the plea agreement that required him to be truthful and to cooperate with investigators. Hudson reminded those assembled that the sentencing guidelines called for a term of 18-24 months. Billy Martin approached the podium. He objected to the report and said that from the very beginning, Vick had accepted responsibility for his role in the dog fighting conspiracy. Martin admitted that Vick knew that the dogs would be killed that fateful night, but that he had merely been present only handing the dogs off to Quanis Phillips. Hudson did not agree. He said Vick had not cooperated with investigators as he had promised and had given inconsistent statements about his level of involvement.

Judge Hudson continued by saying that Vick repeatedly denied his level of responsibility, lied about his drug use on two occasions, and denied his involvement in the killing of the dogs. Only much later had Vick finally admitted hanging one dog and drowning a second. He also admitted his drug use. Afterwards he again denied the drowning. His statements continued to be inconsistent with those of his co-defendants.

Those of us in the court room were suddenly stunned to hear Martin take issue with the fact that Vick alone of the defendants had been polygraphed. Those who were familiar with the terms of the plea agreement remembered that they allowed the government to order a polygraph if they believed that Vick was lying or was failing to cooperate. Vick had been ordered to submit to a polygraph, and he had failed.

The other defense attorneys looked shocked. Mike Gill was stunned. He would never have been allowed to discuss the results of that polygraph, which were inadmissible in court, but now the defense had done it for him. Martin argued that Vick was a young man who was clinically depressed over all that had happened to him. He had used drugs merely as an attempt to self medicate. "What we have is a young man who tries to please everyone." What he really needed, Martin argued was continued counseling and therapy to help him deal with issues that ultimately were the result of his dysfunctional family.

Mike Gill spoke next. He stated that his office stood behind the request for an upward departure from the sentencing guidelines based upon the findings outlined in the probation report. Part of a good faith plea agreement, he said, was that the defendant must not lie and must accept responsibility. Vick had done neither. When presented with evidence that refuted his lies, he continued to maintain those lies. His conduct led to the polygraph examination and its finding of deception. Vick finally admitted only that he had personally dropped one dog, after Phillips put the rope on it, causing it to hang until its death. Vick's false statements about his drug use and level of involvement in the dog fighting, as well as the killing of the dogs, represented not the promised cooperation with the government, but a calculated ongoing effort to hide the truth. Michael Vick had given the government no choice.

Martin responded that by meeting with law enforcement, Vick had been trying to cooperate and atone. He denied that Vick had made conflicting statements and argued for a downward departure from the sentencing guidelines.

Everyone now waited for Judge Hudson to make his decision. He paused for a moment staring down at the paperwork before him. When he spoke, he began by reiterating that Vick had not been forthcoming as he had promised, but on the contrary had been deceptive and inconsistent. Therefore, Hudson said, he had decided to uphold the findings of the probation report. Vick had denied many aspects of his own active participation in Badd Newz Kennels. Yet his admitted role had been just as serious. He had funded the operation. The judge reasoned that when those prone to criminal conduct were given inexhaustible funds, these dangerous individuals became even more dangerous. That is what Vick had done. He had denied much and made a conscious choice not to be forthcoming, but he was in it up to his neck. The sentencing range was appropriate.

Defense attorney Larry Woodward approached the podium next. He asked the judge to remember that he was sentencing a person, not just an offense. "Michael Vick grew up on some of the roughest streets in the Commonwealth [Virginia]", he said. He had only two things going for him—the pure unmitigated blessing that was his mother and his own talent. That talent was a blessing and a curse. Here was a young man who had never been in the criminal justice system. He had protected his little brother. There was no shame or disgrace, Woodward said, in asking for mercy. There was also none in giving mercy. Just this past Saturday Vick had said to him, "I don't want anybody to pity me." Woodward asked Judge Hudson to consider the low end of the sentencing guidelines.

Finally Vick spoke. He apologized to the court, his family and his children for what he had done. He stated that he would deal with the consequences of his actions, but asked the judge to consider the good he could do outside of prison. He suggested that he could serve as an advocate against dog fighting and animal cruelty. He vowed to make better choices in the future.

Judge Hudson was unmoved. He wryly suggested that Vick should "apologize to the millions of young people who look up to you." He told the assembled spectators that this was a tragic case, and one that was truly unique in United States Federal Court history. He had received thousands of letters about this case. The vast majority of those wrote to condemn Michael Vick and his actions. A few, however, wrote to support the young man and the good works he had done. These writers included such people as Hank Aaron, George Foreman and the mayor of Atlanta. They asked for mercy. However, Hudson said, he believed that the sentencing guidelines were right on target.

"You were instrumental in promoting, funding and facilitating this cruel and inhumane sporting activity, and I am convinced it was not a momentary lapse in judgment. You are at least equally culpable." Hudson said that Vick denied his involvement in the killing of the dogs even after the government stressed to him the importance of abiding by his plea agreement. He recognized the monumental consequences that Vick had faced and would continue to face because of this case.

Judge Hudson sentenced Michael Vick to 23 months in federal prison, one month short of the 24 month maximum set forth in the sentencing guidelines. He fined him $5,000 with a special added assessment of $100. Upon his release, Vick would be on supervised probation for three years. The government's motion to place $928,000 in an escrow account to cover the costs of caring for and re-homing the dogs was uncontested. With good behavior it was possible that Vick would be released from prison in the summer of 2009. Vick's mother wept as the sentence was announced, while his brother Marcus tried to comfort her. As the spectators left the court room, other family members began to cry. Vick looked towards his family and supporters and tapped his fist lightly to his chest two times before he was lead away.

As news of the sentence spread to the spectators lining the street outside, some were elated. Many of them held up signs that depicted injured pit bulls and demanded justice for these animals. Others wept or chanted, "We love Mike!"

Larry Woodward told the assembled reporters, "Mike is taking his medicine like a man." He said that Vick did not want people to feel sorry for him, but asked that he be given a chance once he finished his sentence.

I drove home from Richmond that day feeling so many things, relief, sadness, joy, exhaustion.

One week later on December 14, 2007, Tony Taylor was sentenced to two months in prison for his role in the Badd Newz Kennels enterprise. Mike Gill argued for probation, because Taylor had cooperated with authorities from the very beginning. Judge Hudson disagreed, saying, "You were as much an abuser of animals as any other defendant in this case." While he agreed with Gill that Taylor deserved a break for his cooperation, probation would have represented a gross disparity in sentencing for one who had helped to develop the operation and had admittedly killed dogs by both drowning and electrocution. Hudson also imposed a special assessment of $100 and ordered Taylor to be under three years of supervised probation after his release.

On January 25, 2008, in consideration of his elderly mother and his plea agreement, Oscar Allen was sentenced to three years of supervised probation, and ordered to pay a fine of $500. He was also assessed a special fee of $100.

If I expected Dog Angel to be satisfied with the outcome, I was disappointed. Something was wrong, he insisted. We had missed something. Dog Angel said he did not believe that dog fighter Benny Butts committed suicide, or died of an accidental overdose. He believed something much more sinister was involved, and he swore that he would get to the bottom of it. He fumed that in the end, Peace, Phillips and Vick did little more than try to fit their stories to what Allen had already said. And Allen lied repeatedly during his interviews, claiming not to know this or that dog fighter, even when there was clear evidence that he had fought against them. The Vick crew was connected to drug dealers such as Terry OG Posse Kendrick and the men of Bring Da' Pain Kennels. They had told none of this.

Dog Angel was angry that despite all of this, the government kept their side of the plea agreement bargain. He swore he would get some of the guys the Vick crew protected, and he did. Kendrick was later was sentenced to 13 ½ years for marijuana trafficking and dog fighting. Investigators revealed that Kendrick had refereed dog fights up and down the east coast, including ones at the home of Michael Vick. Earl Simmons, AKA Rapper DMX, pleaded guilty in December of 2008 to felony theft, possession of marijuana and narcotics, and one misdemeanor count of animal cruelty. He was sentenced to a mere 90 days.

CHAPTER 20 THE DOGS GO TO NEW HOMES

The seizure order to place the dogs in federal custody had been issued on June 20, 2007. Fifty three pit bulls had been seized from Badd Newz Kennels. Judge Henry Hudson appointed a guardian for all of the dogs. Animal-law expert Rebecca J. Huss of the Valparaiso University School of Law was tapped for this assignment. Early in the case, one dog escaped from its kennel in Surry County and fought with a second pit bull killing it. The attacking dog was euthanized due to its injuries. The remaining dogs were later removed from the custody of Surry County. Two other dogs also died after they were seized. Champion Jane was euthanized because of her extreme aggression, and another was euthanized when it was discovered to have a large tumor. It would be Professor Huss' job to evaluate and recommend the disposition of the remaining 47 pit bulls.

Approximately two months after the dogs were first seized from Moonlight Road, Anne Cheynoweth of HSUS called me. She said a man named Reamon had come forward claiming ownership of the nine beagles being housed at Virginia Beach Animal Control. I suggested that anyone making such a claim be required to prove ownership via pictures, rabies certificates, licenses, or other documentation. That person would be responsible for the boarding bill for these nine dogs that had been in the care of Animal Control since April. Anyone who had not been living under a rock since April would know that the dogs had been taken into custody. If the owner had visited the house even once to check on his dogs, he would have known they were gone. In addition, the owner might be facing charges for inadequate shelter and water.

      I discussed the beagles with Jim Knorr. I asked Knorr if he knew that Reamon was the name of the man listed as the co-owner of the house on Moonlight Road. This man, Charles Reamon, Jr., claimed to be a financial advisor for Vick. His uncle had been Vick's high school football coach. Then I told him that according to ACO Melanie Tobin, the beagles had been wearing collars with name plates when they were removed from Moonlight Road. The name on their collars was not Reamon. We did not hear from Reamon again.

Professor Huss traveled to Virginia to evaluate each of the dogs. The ASPCA put together a team that included ASPCA Animal Behaviorist Stephen Zawistowsk, three other behaviorists and three members of a pit bull rescue group to perform the assessments on each dog. Professor Huss would use her own evaluations, and those performed by the ASPCA team to make recommendations on the placement or ultimate disposition of the dogs.

The Feds severed ties with HSUS. HSUS had posted a picture on their website of a staff member clearly wearing a HSUS T-shirt holding one of the dogs in his arms. The web site asked for donations to help care for the Vick dogs and to support other efforts to combat animal fighting. HSUS was soon roundly taken to task, accused of misleading the public into thinking that the dogs were in their custody. In fact, HSUS gave $20,000 to Surry County to help care for the dogs, but the damage was done. Forgotten was the intelligence HSUS had provided early in the case that had helped investigators.

On Saturday, November 2, 2007, four of the ten Vick dogs from our shelter in Chesapeake left to go to Bad Rap, a pit bull rescue group. These were 86, Buster, Miss Petey and Tessa.

Miss Petey and 86 went to one foster home. Miss Petey was eager to please, easily learning "sit" and "stay", but 86 pretended to ignore her new guardian when she tried to work with him. He preferred racing around the yard in lightening like circles. Both dogs were even doing well with their housebreaking, which surprised all of us, because they had lived outside on a chain. Buster was in San Francisco where a young teacher and her friend had fallen in love with him. Tessa was with yet another family and also doing well.

Back at our shelter, an amazing transformation was taking place with Sneaky Eyes. The shy little tuxedo style pit bull seemed to blossom. Every single day he made progress. He learned to love his walks. He no longer crouched and crept but strolled with complete confidence through the shelter. He tore around the fenced yard, chasing and tossing his toys. He developed an interest in people around him and became eager to be petted and nuzzled. The tail that used to live tucked so tightly that it touched his belly was carried higher and higher everyday.

In all, Bad Rap was approved by guardian Dr. Rebecca Huss to take a total of 13 of the Vick dogs from shelters in Virginia. Ten of them stayed with Bad Rap, and three more went to the SPCA of Monterey County in California.

The next two dogs to leave our shelter were Socks and Big Fella. Socks went to our local Animal Rescue of Tidewater (ART), and Big Fella went to the Georgia SPCA. Representatives from both groups picked up the dogs just a few days before Christmas.

Dr. Huss approved the release of dogs to several other groups. Richmond Animal League in Virginia took four; Recycled Love in Baltimore, Maryland three; Our Pack, Inc. one; and Best Friends Animal Sanctuary in Utah 22 dogs, including the remaining four from our shelter.

Shadow, Bonita, Little Red and Sneaky Eyes were scheduled to leave on January 2 for Best Friends Animal Sanctuary in Utah. It was expected that they would all be going into sanctuary. This meant that they would not be considered for foster homes or adoption in the near future. This was a disappointment. We had hoped that Sneaky Eyes could eventually be adopted. We had been so impressed with his progress, and hoped that Best Friends would recognize Sneaky Eyes' potential. He had done so well with our shelter cat, Angus, and with the small poodle that belonged to Deb in our office.

Best Friends would change Sneaky Eyes' name to Curly. From time to time, Deb in our office would receive updates on his progress. Sneaky Eyes was making progress in both obedience and agility. He caught on quickly, and seemed to love being put through his paces.

HSUS worked with Virginia Beach to facilitate the adoption of the beagles, Rottweilers, and Presa Canarios in their custody. The dogs were transferred from Animal Control to Virginia Beach SPCA. Worried that potential interest in the dogs might be due solely to them being Michael Vick dogs, Director Sharon Adams effectively camouflaged them by putting signs on every cage and runway in her shelter, including those for cats, rabbits, gerbils and more. "Am I a Vick dog? Maybe I'm a Vick dog."

Other groups could not resist the temptation to capitalize on the fact that they had one or more of the Vick dogs. Bad Rap would soon announce how many they had taken, and invite donations for their care. Best Friends soon featured a number of the "Vicktory" dogs on their web site, also inviting donations for their sponsorship. Back in Virginia, we wondered why sponsorship was necessary when $928,000 had been set aside for the care of the dogs. Divided by 47 dogs, that worked out to about $19,700 a dog. It begged the question, had the attraction of these dogs been the incredible fund raising opportunities that having one or more Vick dog guaranteed?

Another point that rankled was the suggestion by some groups that the dogs had never received anything but the poorest of care until their arrival at these rescues. This was particularly difficult for my shelter attendants, for ACO Stevens and for Deb in our office. Each of them had worked so hard to earn the dogs' trust, to provide toys and enrichment, and to give the affection and attention they deserved.

Some groups claimed to have rescued the dogs. Completely forgotten were the ACOs and the shelters. The ACOs were the ones who rescued the dogs when they cut the chains and removed them from Moonlight Road.

CHAPTER 21 THE AFTERMATH

On August 7, 2007 the Commonwealth of Virginia decided to nolle prosequi (not prosecute) two charges against Davon Boddie for possession of marijuana. On October 3, 2007, Boddie pleaded guilty to one count of possession of marijuana with intent to distribute. Hampton Circuit Court Judge William Andrews handed down a five year suspended sentence. Despite his now infamous interview with WAVY TV 10 news, in which he claimed he had not betrayed Michael Vick, Boddie was almost unilaterally considered to be a snitch whose suspended sentence was payment for his cooperation with the Feds. Cutting him loose was just another tactical error on Vick's part.

In September of 2007, Surry County Commonwealth Attorney Gerald Poindexter indicted Vick and his crew on state dog fighting and cruelty charges. Vick's lawyers announced they would seek a jury trial. Two months later in November, Poindexter and Sheriff Harold Brown were both re-elected to their respective offices.

That November, NFL Arbitration ruled that the Atlanta Falcons could go forward with action to seek repayment of $19.97 million that the team had paid to Vick in bonuses since 2004.

Shortly before Vick was sentenced in federal court, he put his exclusive $3.8 million home in the gated Sugar Loaf Country Club community in Duluth, Georgia up for sale. The asking price was $4.5 million.

The house on Moonlight Road was sold to Todd Builders and was unsuccessfully offered for auction on December 15, 2007.

For some of us, life returned to normal with Michael Vick's transfer to Leavenworth Federal Prison in Kansas, that is if life at Animal Control can ever be described as normal.

Less than a week after Vick was sentenced, on December 15, 2007, Surry County Deputy Bill Brinkman was fired by Sheriff Brown. Brinkman joked to me that it was some Christmas present. He told me the Sheriff simply said his services were no longer needed and the Sheriff's Office was going in a different direction. Brinkman retorted, "Oh, that must mean you're going to let ALL of the criminals go!"

When I tried to tell Brinkman how sorry I was he said it did not matter anymore. He reminded me that Poindexter had clamored for his ouster since the beginning of the case. "Every time I met with [Poindexter], it was all about race, the investigation was racially motivated. It made me uncomfortable. It wasn't race; it was crime—criminal activity. But, he kept demanding Brown fire me. That's why I went to the Feds." Brinkman would later accept a job in Iraq training that country's police officers. I worried every day and tried to send good thoughts for his safety.

Brown denied that Poindexter urged Brinkman's firing. Poindexter denied urging Brown's action, or that he had ever made any statement that the case was motivated by racial bias.

Several banks brought suit against Michael Vick for allegedly defaulting on loans. Wachovia Bank claimed Vick and his partners in Atlanta Wine and Spirits failed to make payments on their loan for a $940,000. The Royal Bank of Canada claimed Vick had defaulted on a $2.3 million loan for real estate investments, and 1st Source Bank of Indiana sued for repayment of $2 million that was to have funded the start up of a rental car business.

In July 2008, Michael Vick filed for bankruptcy Under Title 11 naming as some of his creditors the Atlanta Falcons, Royal Bank of Canada, Wachovia Bank, 1st Source Bank, Divine Seven LLC, American Express, AT&T, Atlanta Wine and Package LLC, IRS, his attorney Lawrence Woodward, Isle of Wight County in Virginia, the Office of the US Attorney, and Radtke Sports.

With Vick suspended and imprisoned, the Atlanta Falcons tapped Joey Harrington for quarterback. Byron Leftwich also filled in. Matt Schaub had already been traded to the Houston Texans. Coach Bobby Patrino resigned one day after Vick was sentenced in federal court. His final game with the Falcons ended in a 41-14 loss against the New Orleans Saints. The Falcons ended the 2007 season with a painful 4-12 record.

I received a new title and a raise. I was now superintendent of Animal Control. The City also re-classified the position of ACO at a higher salary grade. I was delighted by this recognition of the valuable service performed by the 11 Chesapeake officers.

Major Kelvin Wright became Chief of Police in April of 2008.

The outcome of the Internal Affairs investigation against me ended with counseling and a letter in my personnel file. I received the Chief's award of excellence for my work on the Vick case. The Eastern District of the US Attorney's Office also presented me with an award for my work on the case and the care of the dogs. Professor Rebecca Huss wrote a letter of commendation to Chief Wright praising Chesapeake Animal Control staff for their cooperation and the excellent care of the 10 dogs in our custody.

Dog Angel took two months off from his work and vacationed in the Outer Banks of North Carolina. John Goodwin made an effort to get him involved in investigating game cock (chicken) fighting. Dog Angel looked into some cases, but his heart was in the pursuit of dog fighters. He joked with me about becoming Chicken Angel. For him it will always be the dogs.

In 2008, the Virginia General Assembly overwhelmingly passed new measures to strengthen Virginia's animal fighting statute. There had been efforts in past years to strengthen the cock fighting law, and these had failed each time. However, the Michael Vick case focused such a light on the grisly sport and Virginia itself that politicians realized 2008 was not the year to vote against an animal fighting bill. The changes that passed included increased penalties for cock fighting, for allowing minors to participate in the fighting of animals, and new bond and custody hearing provisions for seized animals. VACA and the VAFTF were part of the work group that drafted the language. Dog fighting was also added to the Virginia RICO statute.

In the Sussex County, Virginia courthouse on November 24, 2008, Vick pleaded guilty to one charge of dog fighting. He received a three year suspended sentence. At the state hearing, Surry County Commonwealth Attorney Gerald Poindexter appeared to defend Vick, stating he hoped new President Obama, would reform and reign in the Justice Department. Vick's mother, Brenda Boddie, his brother Marcus and his fiancée Kijafa Frink were present in the courtroom. Afterward, Poindexter hugged Vick's mother, telling her, "At least some of this is over." The situation preyed on Dog Angel's mind, and put him back on the Vick trail. He is convinced that there is more about this case that has not come to light.

Purnell Peace was released from federal prison January 6, 2009. Phillips was released in February. Along with Tony Taylor, all three pleaded guilty to state charges. Like Vick, none received any additional time.

The Badd Newz was certainly over for our dogs. Buster was adopted by a San Francisco volunteer from Bad Rap. His name was changed to Johnny Justice and he became a working dog in a program called Paws for Tales. One day each month, Johnny Justice helps young children practice their reading skills. The children are encouraged to read aloud to their non judgmental canine audience.

Little 86 was adopted and underwent surgery on both knees. In early 2009, he was scheduled to begin obedience and agility training. He also has a new name, Audie.

Miss Petey stayed with Nicole for a year. Then she was moved to another foster home in a more urban area, where she might be more easily featured for potential adoption.

Tessa was adopted by a San Francisco family with three young children including an infant, and two other dogs—Crash, and another rescued pit bull named Roller. Tessa is now known as Zippy.

Socks, who went to Animal Rescue of Tidewater (ART), was also renamed when she was adopted. ART has never revealed her new name or her location, as part of their efforts to protect her. They will only say she is an adored pet, has a number of canine friends, and has never shown any aggression.

A scarred dog kept at another Virginia shelter was known as Aretha. She turned out to be extremely smart, eager to please and a great obedience candidate, as Nicole discovered when she worked with her. This dog was sent to the Georgia SPCA. Sadly, Aretha was fostered to a rescue group from whom she escaped. She was hit by a car and killed. Nicole was devastated.

Nicole also still thinks of Sneaky Eyes, the dog that stole all of our hearts, and she regrets that Bad Rap did not have an available foster placement for him. She hopes he will be able to transition at Best Friends from sanctuary to foster, and eventually to a permanent adoptive home.

Sadly, Bonita died from the unexpected effects of anesthesia during a routine dental cleaning on February 19, 2009. The one consolation was that after all she had suffered she had 22 months of kindness at the end of her life.

USDA OIG Special Agent Jim Knorr retired in June of 2009. Surry, the puppy he was given by Bill Brinkman is a happy, healthy member of the Knorr family. Had it not been for this case, Knorr would never have met her.

Many people have come forward to praise the rescue of the Vick dogs, while at the same time condemning shelters for not assuring this type of ending in every dog fighting case. What many do not understand is that Michael Vick was a very poor dog fighter! He had a few winners, Jane, Big Boy and Magic, but overall he had a dismal record for wins, around 33%. Most of his dogs were long bodied, short legged, big headed animals that bore little resemblance to real game dogs. Vick had never been willing to spend the money necessary to acquire good stock bred by real dogmen from game bloodlines. Even when Vick went to a real dogman, he ended up buying inferior less expensive dogs. The argument that if the Vick dogs could be rehabilitated all fighting dogs can is really a comparison of apples to oranges.

There were other reasons the Vick dogs could be placed. First, the federal government appointed a guardian for them, effectively removing the animals from the legal, if not physical custody of the shelters. If rehabilitation did not take, the shelters, unlike in most dog fighting cases, would not face any liability in the event the dogs harmed a person or an animal. It also did not hurt that $928,000 was set aside for the care of the Vick dogs. Vick was not the first dog fighting case, but it was certainly the first time rescue groups had ever jockeyed with one another to rescue the dogs involved.

Now animal control officers and other animal care professionals worry what will be expected of shelters in future dog fighting cases. Few defendants will have the resources to pay such a price for the evaluation, care and rehabilitation of the dogs. Shelters can little afford such an undertaking. On the contrary, many of us struggle to pay basic utilities and veterinary bills. Will the general public clamor for someone to take the dogs in each new case? These may be real game dogs, and vastly different from the Vick dogs. Where will the money come from? Finally, just because people want *someone* to rescue the dogs, will they agree to put their own pets at risk by adopting one themselves? Or even agree to live next door to a real game dog?

Some people will argue that dogmen would not pay big money in stud fees if years of experience had not taught them that careful breeding of the right two game dogs will produce game puppies. Look at other breeds, they argue. As a rule, Chihuahuas don't herd, Border Collies are not couch potatoes, Jack Russells are rarely laid back, Shelties are not police dogs, Labradors are not guard dogs, and Standard Poodles are not fighting dogs. Other people will assert that everything depends on how dogs are raised, and almost every fighting dog can be rehabilitated. So, what is the answer? Does training and upbringing make a fighting dog? What about pit bulls that have been raised by a family as a house pet and upon maturity they "turn on", as dog fighters call it, killing a neighbor's dog or attacking a child? True, many pit bulls never behave like this. They are loving pets. They live with other dogs and cats. They go to dog parks and play with their dog friends. Dog Angel recalls one particular Grand Champion fighting dog who enjoyed playing with other dogs, evidently able to differentiate between inside the pit and outside! So what will shelters do with all the pit bulls that they receive? How will they be able to tell the difference? One thing is clear, the nature versus nurture debate about pit bulls will continue.

A second debate has been settled, and the poor voiceless dogs who suffered horrors at the hands of these cruel men have finally been given a measure of justice. Thanks to the officers, agents and citizens who worked on this case, truth has triumphed. Michael Vick fought dogs. Michael Vick actively worked to build a dog fighting empire in Surry County, Virginia. He created a partnership and a kennel for the sole purpose of breeding, training, and fighting dogs. He provided the cash to bet on the life or death battles they fought. When the dogs did not perform to his satisfaction, Michael Vick killed them—he not only ordered his crew to do it—he actively took part in the killings.

Michael Vick was just one dog fighter. Though some others became so frightened by the Vick case that they sold their dogs and gave up the game, plenty more continue their barbaric sport of torture and abuse every day. It is my hope that this book will inspire law enforcement officers and ACOs to vigorously pursue these criminals to put an end to the suffering inflicted on man's best friend. For all of the dogs that have been saved and the ones still being victimized,

This book speaks for them.

EPILOGUE

Dog Angel and I talked many times as Michael Vick neared the end of his incarceration. We talked of the ongoing debate about whether Vick should be allowed to play professional football again. Dog Angel believes that we are a country where people who have paid for their mistakes are permitted to take up their lives again and to move on.

Reports surfaced near the end of Vick's sentence that he had been speaking with HSUS president Wayne Pacelle about the possibility of making anti-dog fighting public service announcements. Some opposed this plan, doubting Vick's sincerity. Dog Angel is of the opinion that it does not matter. Whether he is sincere or not, if his words stop even one young person from becoming involved in dog fighting it will be worth it. And, who knows? Vick may even come to believe the words he will say. In the end, Dog Angel says we do not forgive people because they deserve forgiveness; we do it because they need forgiveness. After all, Dog Angel was able to redeem himself and turn his life around, so why not Michael Vick?

Vick must be allowed to play again.

ACKNOWLEDGEMENTS

When I finally made it home on that second day of the initial search of the Moonlight Road property, I got a phone call. The caller had a bit of advice for me. I should begin to record my impressions of the case and what transpired at the end of each day. I would be surprised at how much I would forget if I relied simply on memory. I took this advice to heart and began tape recording the events of the day each and every evening. As the case became more complex and took the twists and turns that captivated America while terrifying those of us in its midst, these tapes became a living record of the wild ride that was the Badd Newz Kennels case.

Throughout the case I was constantly amazed at the compassion and gritty determination of seasoned investigators—people from whom I expected a cynical detachment. Instead they put 100% of their hearts, minds and talents into this investigation. At the other end of the spectrum were those who seemed to do everything in their power to ignore, excuse, rationalize, and blame the investigation on everything and everyone except the perpetrators.

But there is no need to dwell on the nay sayers. The outcome of our strange David vs. Goliath battle was vindication enough. This space is put to much better use thanking the many, many people who contributed in so many ways to the successful outcome of the case and to this book.

The real heroes of this case were Mike Gill, Jim Knorr, and Bill Brinkman. Without their determined and dogged pursuit of justice, this case would not have had the successful conclusion that it did.

Mike Gill could have refused the case, leaving it in the hands of the state where many believe it would have been buried. He knew he would be up against a first class team of attorneys determined to protect their famous client at all costs. The media would scrutinize his every step, win or lose, Gill's name would forever be linked with that of Michael Vick. Undaunted, Gill was determined to do what was right and honorable in the pursuit of justice. His commitment, skill and precision meant that all of the defendants found themselves with no choice but to plead guilty. Mike Gill truly spoke for the animals who could not speak for themselves.

USDA Special Agent Jim Knorr is a seasoned investigator who shared with me his amazement about the way the case began to consume him. Dog fighting disgusts him, and he pursued this case with the dogged determination of a pit bull.

Surry County Sheriff's Deputy Bill Brinkman gave more than anyone else to this case. He faced ostracism and persecution because he did his job and investigated criminal activity. The case would have died if not for him, and in the end instead of the thanks he so richly deserved, he lost his livelihood when he was fired from his job in Surry County, Virginia.

The undercover and behind the scenes work by Dog Angel provided information throughout the case. A tenacious bane of dog fighters, his tactics were amazingly resourceful, and imaginative.

And there were many more—National Animal Control Association President Mark Kumpf for intelligence and research, Alison Gianotto of Pet-Abuse.com for her online tracking of Badd Newz Kennels and its players, John Goodwin and Ann Cheynoweth of HSUS for their unfailing support and intelligence gathering, Virginia Animal Fighting Task Force President Richard Samuels, Task Force member Attorney Michelle Welch, Virginia Animal Control Association President Kevin Kilgore, USDA OIG Special Agents Kristin Hamman and Beth Ann Dinkins, Sandy Christiansen of Spartanburg South Carolina Humane Society, guardian for the dogs Dr. Rebecca Huss, ASPCA forensic veterinarian Dr. Melinda Merck, ASPCA Animal Behaviorist Stephen Zawistowski and his team of evaluators who performed the assessment on the dogs, Chesapeake Animal Control Officers Melanie Tobin, Tracy Stevens, Kathleen Perry, Sharon Pesar (Maddox), Chesapeake Office Assistant Deb Zwirlein, Chesapeake Shelter Attendant Billy Cartwright, Dr. Ruth Ann MacQueen, DVM, Chesapeake Chief of Police Kelvin Wright, Lieutenant Randy Farney, Detective Mike Lawton, Officer Lenny Stolecki, and a constant voice of encouragement and support, my mother, Patricia Strouse.

I am eternally grateful to my friends who encouraged me, who read, critiqued and helped to edit the manuscript. Your insights and advice were appreciated more than you will ever know— Ray Willis, John Goodwin, Assistant Commonwealth Attorney for Chesapeake Amy James, Retired Virginia Beach Detective Don Rimer, my attorney Andy Shilling, and of course, Jeannette Rainey. Thank you, Jeannette for being my cheerleader throughout this journey, for your ideas, suggestions and constant support. Author Janine Latus, thank you for your kindness to an aspiring author.

I have to thank Bart Baker, my other half, for holding down the fort, cooking, making me tea, doing housework, taking care of the animals, and understanding when I would get annoyed if he tried to talk to me during those long days and nights of writing and rewriting. You are the kindest man I have ever known, good to the bone, as you Texans would say!

I wanted this book to speak for the victims of dog fighting—the pit bulls so cruelly exploited and killed for the vicious pleasure of men. The very sweetness and forgiveness of the dogs that survived is a lesson for all of us. Like my own dogs Phoebe Lynn and Mickey Mouse, these creatures teach us all so much about love, devotion, courage, and patience. Animals have always provided inspiration and purpose for my life and my chosen career. I continue to dream of a day when every single dog and cat will have a loving, permanent home, and dog fighting will have been eradicated once and for all.

After the conclusion of the Vick case, grants from the Holland M. Ware Foundation and other individual donors allowed HSUS to double its reward program offering up to $5,000 in exchange for information leading to the arrest and conviction of anyone involved in animal fighting. They continue to provide trucks and on the ground personnel to assist in raids against fighters, and they pay real dollars for the care of seized dogs. The American Society for the Prevention of Cruelty to Animals (ASPCA) also provides real assistance in the form of dollars and their highly specialized animal forensics unit and team of experts.

Law enforcement raids on dog fighting operations doubled soon after the Vick case, and the number of arrests increased by 150% the year after his arrest. HSUS has been involved in 114 animal fighting investigations and prosecutions since the Vick case. Some "dogmen" have decided to shut down their yards because they are afraid being arrested. "If they can take down someone like Vick with all his millions, none of us are safe". The officers and investigators who worked on this case are determined to prove the dogmen right.

I want to honor the Virginia animal control officers who have been lost-Susie Caskey, Keegan Merrick, Robert Tune, Sherman Logan, Emmett Edmonds, Chad Carr-and those from across the country, including Bobby Evans of Texas who was murdered at the animal shelter.

Finally, this book is dedicated to my very best and most beloved friend of 46 years. Carolyn, you always believed in me and I in you. Together we could do anything. I love you, and I miss you every day. I hate that you had to leave us so soon and so cruelly. We were supposed to be old ladies together throwing spit balls at the nurses and having wheel chair races up and down the halls of the nursing home. This one's for you, babe!

GLOSSARY OF TERMS

ACO: Animal control officer

American Dog Breeders' Association: (ADBA) A registration organization for American pit bull terriers

American Society for the Prevention of Cruelty to Animals: (ASPCA) Founded in 1865, the oldest animal welfare organization in America

Badd Newz Kennels: Kennel name of Michael Vick and crew members Purnell Peace, Quanis Phillips and Tony Taylor

Bay Area Doglovers Responsible About Pitbulls: (Bad Rap) California based rescue group dedicated to the rehabilitation of pit bulls

Best Friends Animal Sanctuary: Utah based animal rescue organization

Bona Fide Kennel Club: A registry for American pit bull terriers

Box: See pit

Break stick: A stick usually made of wood or polyurethane that is used to pry open the jaws or two fighting dogs in order to separate them

Bump: A fight, usually a practice fight, also known as a roll

Carpet Mill: A device used to condition dogs for dog fighting consisting of a carpeted disc, approximately 6' to 8' in diameter, mounted so as to turn on a stationary shaft. A dog is leashed to an object above the disc. His forward motion causes the disc to turn beneath his feet.

Catmill: Also known as a Jenny, this device resembles a horse walker, and is use to condition dogs for dog fights

Chain Weight: The normal day to day weight of a pit bull prior to any conditioning for a fight

Champion: A pit bull that has won 3 sanctioned dog fights

Courtesy scratch: Usually offered to the loser who is picking up his dog whereby he is allowed to show that his dog would continue to fight on

Cur: Any breed of dog other than a pit bull; a pit bull that quits or stops fighting in the pit

Dead game: Used to describe a pit bull that does not give up and continues to try to fight even in the face of life threatening injuries

Dogman: A dog fighter

Down dog: A dog injured so badly he collapses unable to fight on

Forfeit: An amount of penalty money, usually established by contract, that a fighter will have to pay to his opponent if his dog comes to the fight over the agreed upon fight weight

Game: (n) The illegal sport of dog fighting; (adj) the quality in a fighting dog of tenacity, endurance, and aggression that compels a pit bull to fight on despite its own pain, injuries or even death. This quality is most prized by dog fighters

Game dog: A pit bull used for dog fighting

Grand Champion: A pit bull that has won 5 consecutive dog fights and has never had a loss

Handle: The act of placing hands on a dog in the pit, at the direction of the referee, to separate them and return them to their corners

Humane Society of the United States: (HSUS) Animal welfare organization founded in 1954; responsible for more investigations and convictions for animal fighting then all the other humane organizations combined

Jenny: See catmill

Keep: The period of preparation before a dog fight, usually about 6 weeks in length, during which a dog is conditioned using a program of exercise, nutrition, dietary supplements, and often drugs or steroids

MV Kennels: Early kennel name used by Michael Vick

Man Biter: A pit bull that is aggressive to humans

Match: Usually an official sanctioned dog fight, often based on a written contract

National Animal Control Association: (NACA) Organization representing animal control officers across the United States

Office of the Inspector General: (OIG) Investigative arm under USDA

Off the Chain Match: Also known as an OTC, a dog fight where neither dog has been conditioned or prepared for battle

People for the Ethical Treatment of Animals: (PETA) Animal rights organization often regarded as radical and known for flamboyant campaigns against fur, meat consumption, hunting and more

Pet-Abuse.com: Online data base of animal cruelty and fighting cases administered by Alison Gianotto

Pick up: The act of conceding a fight by picking up one's dog

Pit: (n) The arena where dogs are fought. This may be an actual constructed pit, usually about 14' X 20' with carpet or other material to provide traction for the dogs, and with painted or taped scratch lines across opposite corners. It may also be a simple clearing in the woods, a room, a basement or any other location where dogs are fought; a nickname for a pit bull terrier; (v) the act of placing two dogs together for the purpose of fighting

Racketeer Influenced and Corrupt Organization Act: (RICO) Federal statute that provides for enhanced criminal penalties seizures for crimes performed as part of an ongoing criminal organization

Red shirt: The practice of extending an athlete's college playing eligibility by requiring that a freshman sit out his first year. The red shirt may practice with the team, but may not play.

Register of Merit: Also known as ROM, a designation awarded to a male pit bull that has sired 4 champions or 3 champions and 1 grand champion, or a female pit bull that has whelped 3 champions or 2 champions and 1 grand champion

Roll: A dog fight, usually for practice or testing; also known as a bump

Rub: A caustic substance put on the body of a fighting dog in order to discourage an opponent from biting him

Quit: Stop fighting

Scratch: The act of a pit bull leaving its corner of the pit within a specified amount of time and attacking his opponent

Scratch lines: Lines made by paint, tape or other material across two opposite corners of a pit, from behind which fighting dogs are released to attack their opponents

Scratch to win: Usually offered to the winner of a dog fight in order to show that although the opponent may be conceding, the winner's dog is ready to fight on

Show: An event which usually features more than one dog fight

Sporting Dog Journal: (*SDJ*) Infamous underground magazine dedicated to dog fighting

Too Bad Kennels: Kennel name of Purnell Peace

Treadmill: A device used to condition dogs for dog fighting; may be constructed with a circular belt made of wooden slats fitted over ball bearings which is free rolling and continues to turn due to the forward motion of the dog, or it may be an electric treadmill known as an E mill

Turn: The act of a fighting dog turning its head and shoulders away from its opponent in a dog fight; cause for a handle and a return of both dogs to their corners for 30 seconds before the turning dog is required to scratch (See scratch)

Vick's K-9 Kennels: Michael Vick's allegedly legitimate kennel that offered Rottweilers, Presa Canarios, pit bulls and beagles for sale via its web site. Also alleged to be a cover for the Badd Newz fighting dog kennel.

Virginia Animal Control Association: (VACA) Professional organization representing animal control officers in Virginia committed to training, education and furthering the profession of animal control

Virginia Animal Fighting Task Force: (VAFTF) Group made up of animal control officers, veterinarians, attorneys, HSUS members and law enforcement officers formed to combat animal fighting in Virginia

Yard accident: Euphemism for a dog fight, accidental or otherwise, on a dog fighter's yard

Yard boy: Person responsible for clean up as well as feeding and watering the pit bulls on a dog fighter's yard

BIBLIOGRAPHY

American Game Dog Times
APBT Pedigrees Online
Associated Press
The Atlanta Journal Constitution
CNN.com
The Daily Press
ESPN.com
ESPN "Outside the Lines"
FanHouse-AOL Sports Blog
Fox News
Fox Sports on MSN
Newsday
The Official Michael Vick Website
Pet-Abuse.com
Political Gateway
Portfolio Magazine
Sporting Dog Journal (1999-2004)
The Sporting News
Sports Illustrated
Sports Illustrated.com
Sports Wrap
USA Today
The Virginian Pilot
WAVY TV 10 (NBC Affiliate)
WVEC TV 13 (ABC Affiliate)
Yahoo Sports

United States Department of Agriculture Office of the Inspector General – Investigations – Report of the Investigation of Bad Newz Kennels

Indictment Federal Grand Jury - United States of America vs. Purnell A. Peace a/k/a P Funk and Funk, Quanis Phillips a/k/a Q, Tony Taylor a/k/a T, Michael Vick a/k/a Ookie

Summaries of Facts: Criminal No. 3:07CR 274 - United States District Court for the Eastern District of Virginia

United States of America vs. Oscar Allen a/k/a Virginia O

Plea Agreements: Criminal No. 3:07CR 274 and 389 - United States District Court for the Eastern District of Virginia

United States of America vs. Approximately 53 Pit Bull Dogs: Civil Action No. 3:07CV397

Made in the USA
Middletown, DE
09 June 2015